T0024760

The Selfish Romantic

How to date without
feeling bad about yourself

MICHELLE ELMAN

WELBECK

Published in 2023 by Welbeck
an imprint of Welbeck Non-fiction Limited,
part of the Welbeck Publishing Group
Offices in: **London** – 20 Mortimer Street, London W1T 3JW &
Sydney – 205 Commonwealth Street, Surry Hills 2010
www.welbeckpublishing.com

A CIP catalogue record for this book is available from the British Library

ISBN
Hardback – 978 1 80279 502 8

Typeset by IDSUK (DataConnection) Ltd.
Printed at CPI UK

2 4 6 8 10 9 7 5 3 1

MIX
Paper | Supporting
responsible forestry
FSC® C171272

For every woman whose love life is a mess, and wondered if it is because you are unlovable – you aren't.

AUTHOR'S NOTE

Some of the names and identifying details in this book have been changed to protect the privacy of the people in the examples used. All stories involving clients have been included with their permission. My writing is informed by lived experience and therefore it is also limited by it. Within the book I have used the words men and women intentionally, as there are aspects of the book that directly refer to how the patriarchy affects the gender imbalance in romantic relationships. As a straight woman living in a heteronormative society, a number of the examples will be in relation to that. Despite attempting to be as inclusive as possible, I will have blind spots. I never want my writing to be a source of exclusion. If an example doesn't fit your reality, please apply it to your own situation and orientation.

CONTENTS

CONTENTS

Chapter 1

Introduction

From the earliest age – especially as girls – we are told that we are not good enough unless someone loves us. We are told that if we are not coupled, it is because there is something wrong with us and we are unlovable. This persists into adulthood with innocent comments like "Why are you still single?" – the subtext being that not being paired off is our own personal failing. If we try to "fix the problem" and start dating, we will be bombarded with even more confusing advice that makes no sense: "You will find a relationship when you are least looking for it!", they will hark, and we are forever stuck between not looking too hard (in case we seem desperate) and not looking hard enough (so that we only have ourselves to blame for our singledom). Either way, it is our fault.

The dating advice out there just echoes this message. We are told to change ourselves in order to be more palatable and attractive, particularly to men. We are told to lose weight, remove our body hair and strive to appear as close to the current beauty ideal as possible. It's not just our looks, though. We are supposed to keep our needs small, for fear of being called "needy"; to bury our true emotions, for fear of being called "emotional"; and to make no requests of our own, for fear of being branded "high maintenance". When you speak directly, you will be dubbed "rude" – and if you have opinions, that's "unladylike". All of this makes you undateable. And if you don't make dating your top priority, you are selfish – because what if your parents want grandbabies? We actually haven't come that far from the norm of dismissing any woman over the age of 25 as a spinster and telling women that their mission in life is to get wifed up and procreate.

It's time for a new kind of dating book. Changing yourself in order to achieve an outcome (finding a life partner) is not only short-sighted but it is also manipulation. These books tell you that it's fine when you drop the mask and go back to being yourself, because by then, your partner will be hooked. But what if you don't want to trick someone into liking you and instead want to find someone who is actually compatible? There are people who aren't intimidated by your needs, who will see your emotions as a strength, can meet your requests and are attracted to opinionated women. In order to find these people, though, you actually have to be honest. We get told things – like the "fact" that men hate loud women. They don't. Some men hate loud women, and some men love them. But in order to meet someone who loves a loud woman, you need to keep being loud. If you continue pretending to be quiet when you aren't, then of course you attract someone who confirms this lie. You don't need to change yourself. You need to stop pretending to be who you are not.

If you've followed any of my career, you know that in every area of life, I have found a way to challenge all of society's implicit messaging around the way I should be and how I should live my life. And yet, within my love life, I would readily accept what I was being told. In my last book, *The Joy of Being Selfish*, I took you on the journey of how I found my voice and learned how to set boundaries – and the area I found setting those boundaries the hardest was my love life. I believe we all could do with being a little more selfish. As I say within the pages of that book:

> I believe in order to have self-love, it is necessary to be selfish. It requires you to reorder your priorities to ensure you come at the top of that list. The word 'selfish' holds a stigma in modern society because it is associated with the idea that you have a disregard for other humans. But when you regard others more highly than yourself, the unfortunate consequence is often that you

are completely forgotten. I think one of the most loving things you can do for the people around you is to take care of yourself. When you don't, the people in your life often feel a responsibility to do that for you.

Conversely, when we are selfless, we do things like get married for the wrong reasons to make our parents proud, stay in relationships longer than we should rather than admitting we are unhappy, and put up with more bad behaviour than we deserve. By being selfless, we tell ourselves we are unimportant and everyone else comes first – even some fuckboy who can't make time for you. Men have been acting selfishly for years. It's why they plan a date when it's convenient to them. It's why they will text you at 2 a.m. rather than at a respectful time. If they can get the same result with less effort, why would they make more? It makes sense, and as soon as I got my own boundaries, I actually stopped getting annoyed about it. Of course they are going to organize their life in a way that is most convenient for them with the least effort. So why wasn't I doing the same? Why wasn't I saying no when it didn't work for me?

Boundaries are how we teach the world to treat us. They are the line between who we are and who the world wants us to be. Being selfish doesn't mean I won't do things for other people – it means I no longer do things in exchange for someone's favour or because it made their life more convenient. Boundaries are my way of saying no to doing anything at the expense of myself. If that makes me unlovable, undateable and selfish, so be it. Enter empowered dating: the revolutionary idea that it is possible to date without sacrificing your self-esteem, self-worth or happiness.

Dating is different when you look like me. I am mixed race, plus size, scarred, and I have a complex medical history. This is something that books about finding love seem to avoid talking about. The intersections that individuals – with our various labels and identities – bring to our relationships mean we are all different. Yet most dating books treat us like a conglomerate, with the only divide being the gender binary and, of course, the knee-jerk assumption that you are heteronormative. Whether it's race, sexuality, disability, illness, gender identity or size, conversations around these topics in regards to dating never existed, and that silence confirmed my fear that I would be forever alone. It hurt even more because, at heart, I was a romantic. I wanted the fairy tale. But for me, dating was about navigating body shame, consent conversations due to medical caveats, and confronting partners' racist parents. While most of my friends could turn to a magazine for all the hints and tips they needed, at age 16, I was sitting on Google and looking up "how to tell a boy about my scars". It came up with no results and unintentionally, I had confirmed my worst fear: that I was alone in facing this problem.

Considering this, it will come as no shock to admit that I was a "late bloomer" when it came to love. At a time when fitting in was paramount, I noticeably didn't. I wasn't thin like my friends, I was mixed race unlike most of my friends, and I was marked with surgery scars that resembled an incomplete game of noughts and crosses. My medical issues left me with dilemmas that most kids my age hadn't faced. When all my friends started getting crushes, kissing people for the first time, and wanting to discuss their latest boy drama, I remember thinking there was something wrong with me. I found talking about boys mind-numbingly boring and the idea of actually interacting with a boy even more so. While my friends worried about how much tongue you should use when kissing someone, I was worrying about how the catheter scars on my thigh look like pee droplets. While they were debating whether it's OK to kiss a boy that your friend has already got with, I was contemplating when exactly was the right time to tell someone they can't touch my neck because there is a tube in it that could break. My constant medical problems that resulted in 15 surgeries before the age of 19 were difficult enough to talk about to friends, but the idea of sharing that with a guy terrified me, so it was easier to avoid the situation completely.

It is no wonder, then, that the first relationship I ended up in was an emotionally abusive one. I let society convince me for too many years that because of what I looked like, I should just accept whoever wanted me – and that I didn't have the right to ask for more, let alone have actual standards. I should accept what I was given, and if I was able to delude someone or trick them into being with me, it would only be because my personality was able to compensate for my body. Standards, good treatment and, ultimately, romance were reserved for the people who fit the beauty ideal. Being fat, mixed race, chronically ill and scarred, that was certainly not me. No wonder every time I tried to date it made me feel like crap. I was treated like shit because I believed that was what I deserved. But how could I know what I wanted from a relationship if I didn't even know what I wanted from life?

After my first relationship ended, I began a journey of being single that revolutionized the way I started thinking about dating. Being single is sold as the ultimate punishment for the destitute and unlovable, but I started seeing it as a gold mine for fun and opportunity instead. I realized that I had been using dating as a plaster to stop feeling bad about myself. Its main purpose was to fill the void in me that screamed that I wasn't good enough. So for the first time in my life, I decided to be consciously single – and I was going to stay that way until I sorted myself out. I was a mess in every way, from not knowing what job I wanted to do to my mental health, and the only decision I could make was that I didn't want to add another person to that mess.

It would take three years until I felt the urge to date again. The moment came when I arrived home after completing my TEDx Talk. My life finally felt fulfilling and satisfying, so to notice something was missing took me off guard. I had spent the majority of those last three years working on myself and I had found satisfaction in a life without dating. So returning to an empty house with this pang of wanting another human surprised me. By taking the pressure off dating and learning to fulfil my own needs, I could recognize the true value of dating – not because I needed it or there was an absence in my life, but because I wanted it and it would make a great addition to my life. I now had the confidence, the boundaries, and the self-esteem to be dating from a place of valuing myself. I don't know what I was expecting when I had my first foray into the world of dating, but it wasn't anything like I remembered.

It all started with an innocent question that I was asked one Tuesday: "If you could slide into the DMs of any guy, who would it be?" I was on a photo shoot and two of my friends had booked the same job. As we were chatting in the make-up chairs, I mentioned how I was having this craving to start dating again. They'd asked this question and, long after we had left the photo shoot, it lingered in my mind. I kept thinking about one person whom I had briefly dated a couple of years ago who was, simply put, the best sex I'd ever had. It had ended with him ghosting, but I had always wished there was just one more night. So, with a lot of encouragement and the vague threat of them signing in to my Instagram account and doing it for me, I added him on Instagram and sent him a DM: "Hey stranger! How's things? xx". He added me back two minutes later and within three hours he was at mine, having driven two hours from Windsor, bailing on his own party to come over.

Up until this moment, the world had told me if I ever found anyone to like me, it would be for my personality – that only people who fit the beauty ideal could pull moves like this. But it had all been a lie. Yes, he just wanted sex, but so did I, and I had gone after it with the same energy I would have if it had been a job. When he left, I kissed him goodbye at my door. He pressed the button of the elevator and then turned back with a nod and said, "You are definitely going down as the most confident girl I have ever met." There was something about that statement that awoke something in me. The girl he had known two years before didn't exist anymore. I wasn't that person. Stood in her place was a boundaried woman who had her shit together, was living her dream life, and could bring so much to the table – in general, but also in love. It was an epiphany realizing I had been going after everything in my life with confidence, but never thought to apply it to love. This realization, frankly, pissed me off.

How many people were walking through the world convinced that they had to settle? How many people who were being treated like crap because they thought their looks, their size, their disability, their race or their scars limited their dating pool? How many people who exist outside of the beauty norm have to tolerate their "more conventionally attractive" partner being treated like a saint because, God forbid, they love someone bigger than size 14? I had been lied to for years and I was on a mission to prove that I – as well as anyone else who wanted to – could date as much as the next person, and that what you look like is never a reason to deserve any less. I started acting as hot as I am, and it changed my world. What if you walked into a bar and actually assumed the people who you find attractive would also find you attractive? What would happen if you didn't limit yourself by seeing yourself as a bunch of labels, and instead saw yourself as a person who brought a lot to the table romantically? What would it be like to navigate dating with confidence? How fun would it be to be single without questioning your lovability, to date without taking rejection personally, and to have sex without hating your body?

The more I loved dating, the more it pissed me off that this message about how hard dating should be was everywhere, especially for people who look like me. I had always been a private person when it came to my love life; I never spoke about the people I dated and I never mentioned dates I went on. But after years of being on Instagram, I grew frustrated that any time you ever talked about anyone outside of the beauty norm, the only love stories we heard were negative ones. I started wondering why this was. Then it hit me one day, while I was talking on a panel for Oxford University. The problem wasn't in the answers I was giving – it was in the questions I was being asked. Every question was about being racially fetishized and being body shamed. I couldn't say the same of the queries directed at the thin people or the white people on the panel. It wasn't the fact that I hadn't had positive dating experiences, it was that, as a society, we only make space for the negative dating stories of marginalized people. I had multiple positive stories I could share but, because that question was asked directly of me, it forced me to talk about one story from when I was 18, ignoring over a decade of experiences since. It didn't matter that it was only one example out of years of dating, and it didn't matter that the white people or thin people on the panel probably also had bad dating experiences, because that was never asked of them. Unconsciously, this is part of what builds the narrative that the only things waiting out there for marginalized people are abuse, rejection and hurt.

In a bid to counter this, I started sharing this mentality of confidence in dating and, in turn, coined it "empowered dating". When I first started sharing it, people thought I was crazy, that I had this absurd confidence that wasn't realistic for other people. In fact, some people even compared me to a fuckboy for the mere suggestion that a person who looks like me should keep swiping and not just stop at the first match. It was so shocking to them that I didn't just take the first offer anyone gave me. Over time, the messages I received changed. They went from "This is crazy" to "OMG, it worked": "Wow, I did that thing about changing your mentality before a first date and he just asked me out!"

Most of the dating advice out there is written by people who fit the beauty ideal. But when you walk through the world in a body like mine, dating is different – not worse, just different. We need books that cater to marginalized identities. There is irony in calling us "minorities", as it implies there are few of us; there aren't. In the UK, 20 per cent of people are disabled, roughly 15 per cent are people of colour and approximately 40 per cent of women are plus size – so the chance of you sitting in at least one minority is actually quite high. If you add it together, we are the majority. It is naive to think that our appearances don't alter how we approach dating. So it's important that dating books are written by a range of people with differing life experiences in order to truly encapsulate the intersections that affect our dating lives.

The world of dating has changed and, as much as we can try to resist these changes by scorning dating apps and holding on to "meet-cute" stories of bumping into people at the bus stop, these changes are happening, and they are happening quickly. There is an outdated idea of going to the people who have been in the longest relationship to get your love-life advice, but it doesn't work like that. Love and dating are two distinct skill sets. Relationship advice and dating advice are different. It's like cooking and baking. Some people might put them in the same category, but you can be good at one without being good at the other. It's why every friendship group has a single friend who you *really* get all your love-life advice from. Those childhood sweethearts who have been together since school might know how to make a relationship work, reignite sex once it gets dull, and how to fight without wounding each other too much, but they aren't the people you go to when it comes to how to manage dating apps or ghosting and how exactly to reply to a nude.

Even if you turn to Instagram for much-needed advice, you will be equally disheartened. The love-life information that I see online is largely composed of opinions that are not backed up with any professional qualifications. This kind of advice leads to contradictory and overly simplistic solutions to complex problems. It's a lot easier to say "Dump him!" than it is to say "You need to have a difficult conversation about how your boundaries are being crossed, set a consequence for that boundary, reinforce that boundary and if the behaviour is repeated, then end the relationship." In fact, I actually wrote those words online today and was met with the following comments:

> The world is on fire, ma'am, we don't have time to give men second chances.

> All I am hearing is, "Let's ignore his crossing boundaries the first time." Heal yourself, sister.

> No, because sometimes the answer is to break up.

Our culture has lost the ability to have hard, complex or nuanced conversations. This is exactly the mentality that gave birth to ghosting, and it's not helping any of us. It's all too easy to yell "red flag" and run, without contemplating that this could be a way you are affirming your fear of intimacy. It's simpler to believe that your "strong independent woman" mentality is empowering, rather than questioning whether this is leading to a hyper-independence that means you shame yourself whenever you ask for help. We need to be able to live in the contradictions and the grey. Dating is complicated, and complicated problems deserve nuanced answers, even if they can't be dissected into a pithy and snappy viral Instagram quote. This book will not include absolutes on the right and wrong way to date because I am not a guru who holds all the wisdom. I'm not going to sell you on a lie that there is a formula to falling in love. I am a life coach who has fucked up just as many times as you have and, through navigating my mistakes, has found a way to date without feeling bad about myself.

Throughout the book, I will use the term "relationship" frequently. In our love lives, relationships usually refer to the arbitrary point at which you both put a label on it, but my definition of a relationship is very liberal as I have found no benefit in creating hierarchies depending on the length or seriousness of your encounters. I believe all experiences are legitimate and therefore they will all be treated under one category whether it's a one-night stand or anything longer. If I am discussing being official, I will specify that. At the end of every chapter, I have included a "Take Action Toolkit", because it's important to me as a life coach that my advice is practical. A book can't change your life – it's what you do after reading the book that will do that, and these sections give you the opportunity to do so. Throughout the book, there are also numerous texts. These are real examples from my dating life. They are not designed to be perfect templates, but rather a jumping-off point to create your own. I have spent many hours constructing texts with friends and my own life coach, and my goal is to give you the language to create the change for yourself. It's important that you make it personal to the situation and customize it to your own style of speaking. They are in the format of texts, but that is not to imply that all these conversations are appropriate over text. There are times you should be having these conversations over the phone or in person.

This is not a book that will teach you how to get a relationship, but it will teach you how to enjoy dating. It stops treating dating as a means to an end and recognizes it as a legitimate phase in life. It was not until I stood in my power and reclaimed my right to date that I realized I didn't want to marry the first person I went on a date with. I didn't want a perfect love life – I wanted a full one. I wanted to experience the diverse adventures that love could offer and the range of emotions that life can bring. I didn't just want the positives. I wanted to risk my heart, potentially get hurt along the way and, most of all, not lose myself on the journey. Now, my hope is that I can share that with you. If you are miserable, thinking you are unlovable and that finding the perfect person is the solution to your problems, this book is for you. If you, like me, were a "late bloomer" and the mere idea of going on a date terrifies you, this book is for you. It's for you if being single forever is still the worst threat that could ever exist. It's not about whether being single, dating or in a relationship is the best option, it's about accepting which phase you are in and making peace with it. And if you would like to do something about creating that peace, then you are in the right place.

Chapter 2

Single Is Not a Problem to Be Fixed

How to Be Empowered in the Single Period

The Myths of Being Single

When I first had the idea for this book, I started asking my friends about their first relationships. With most of my friends, I didn't know them back then and they were talking about people I never knew. But the more I started asking, the more I realized that nearly every friend's first relationship was emotionally abusive in some way. Back in the 2010s, we didn't have the vocabulary for this type of abuse, but upon hearing my friends' stories, I can't help but think that the fearmongering around being single is at least significantly to blame. People say that the only reason someone stays in an abusive situation is because "the alternative is worse". Except the alternative isn't worse. Being single is better than being in a bad relationship. I wish I had known that when my ex-boyfriend was screaming "You want to make me fat just like you are!" because I fried his egg instead of boiling it the way he liked it. If we lived in a world where being single was the default, I wonder if I would have settled for that.

Here's the thing: single is the default. We are born single. And if we are repeatedly sold that single is this nightmare, it will be. It took me until I was 21 years old to realize that most people, if they want to be, spend the majority of their lives in a relationship. If that was the inevitability of my life, I wanted to treasure this precious and sacred time where I could enjoy my life not being beholden to anyone, make myself a priority and not have to think about anyone else. I wanted to enjoy the time when I had no responsibilities or dependents so I could fully be selfish. Here are just some of the lies we have been told:

"Every person that is single wants a relationship."
Single is not the consolation prize for not landing a relationship. It is not a holding station for people who are waiting to be coupled off. Society tells you that one of your main goals should be to be in a relationship and that if you aren't in one, it should be your highest priority. Is it so unthinkable that your sole purpose in life isn't to be paired up? There are many people in the world who consciously choose to be single.

"Being single means no one wants to date you."
Being single is not confirmation of your unlovability. It's not a punishment for bad karma and it's not an illness that says there is something wrong with you. The reality is that if you wanted *any* relationship, you'd be able to find one. Being single means you are secure enough to wait for what you deserve. They say "no one wants to date you", but what if you don't want to date them?

"No one would be single if they had a choice."
Being single is not a burden that gets inflicted upon you when the latest person dumps you; it can be an active conscious decision. After all, for every person that is dumped, there was a person who was doing the dumping, which is proof positive that there are people choosing being single over their current available relationship. What they mean when they say this is that *they* would never choose it. It's important we stop treating being single as a layover until your next relationship and actually see it as a valid choice.

"If you've been single too long, it's because of what you look like."
We can thank the beauty and diet industries for this myth. Society creates a fear of being single by convincing us there

is a small window of time in which we are attractive. These industries see an opportunity to make money, so they give you a solution to that problem: lose weight, wear more make-up, have plastic surgery. They believe our self-worth should be tied up in whether or not other people find us attractive. Even if we find ourselves attractive but other people disagree, we are still told to change what we look like in order to fit their definition of beauty. Madness, frankly.

"If you are beautiful and single, you are too picky."
The idea that lowering your boundaries and settling is the solution to your problems is flawed. What's wrong with being picky? If I am supposed to spend my whole life with that person, you'd bloody hope I was picky. I have no interest in choosing misery. If I have to spend time with you, then you need to meet the standard of the people who are already in my life. That standard is high because, after years of having no boundaries, I now refuse to tolerate bad treatment.

People ask why you are single for the same reason they tell you that you need to lose weight: because *they* wouldn't be that way. *They* were unable to enjoy their single period and therefore they have assumed you are having the same experience as they did. It is impossible for them to fathom another reality where being single could actually be fun, because it would put their own single period into question. It would challenge the idea that all single people hate being single and therefore put doubt in their mind that maybe the problem is them. This is an uncomfortable thought – rather than experience that cognitive dissonance, they find it easier to shut down the possibility entirely. It doesn't fit in with their reality of the world being a better place when you are in a relationship – therefore, being single and being happy must not exist.

So if being single is not a burden, an illness or a punishment, what is it instead? It's whatever you want it to be. It can be a time where you focus on your personal development, or put time and energy into your career. You can take advantage of the fact you aren't moored to another human, giving you the flexibility to relocate or travel. You can use that time to date or be consciously single. For me, I decided to be consciously single for three years and I spent four years having the most fun I could dating. Ultimately, what being single actually means is nothing. We think being single is this monolithic experience of boredom, loneliness and sadness – and it's just not. Being single is just as varied an experience as being in a relationship is. Much like each relationship can feel vastly different from the next, your single periods can too. I know for me, being single at 18 felt different to when I was single at 25. Not better or worse, just different. Once you liberate yourself from everything you were taught about being single, you are no longer limited. You are able to embrace the positives of the single life. Once you lose the fear of being alone, you realize the luxury of being alone. You do not have to love being single as a prerequisite for being happy in a future relationship. But as long as being alone is your worst fear, you may not know if you have actively chosen your relationship or simply fear the alternative.

Forget Me Nots

- Being single is better than a bad relationship
- Being single is not the consolation prize for not landing a relationship
- Being single is not confirmation of your unlovability
- How people react to your singledom is a reflection of their own hatred of being alone

Take Action Toolkit: If you are anything like me, you are sick of the word "self-care". I blame the fact that every brand under the sun has used this word to sell everything from bath bombs to diet pills to gold-leaf face masks. My version of self-care is a little different. I define it as being a parent to yourself. Remember when you were a child and your parents wouldn't let you hang out with your friends because you had too much homework? Well, as an adult, self-care is when you force yourself to stay home to do your taxes rather than going out. A parent would turn the TV off and tell you to go outside and get some fresh air – so self-care is taking yourself on a walk even if you don't want to. If you were a parent and your child was hungry, you would get up and make them a meal; when you are lying on the sofa and can't be bothered to make yourself food, that's when self-care matters. A parent would never schedule a child's week without any rest time, and you should have the same considerations for yourself. Sometimes being a parent means staying home to do the laundry because they would never let a child go to school wearing dirty clothes, so why are you treating yourself with any less care? In the past, when I used to date people, my self-care would be neglected. So when I decided to be single, I wanted to establish a solid core of self-care that wouldn't waver when my love life did. Start paying attention to the small voice in your head that goes, "I really should go to sleep." Hear that as the parent inside you and listen to what they say.

Do I Need a Dating Detox?

For the first three years of my seven-year single period, I was consciously single. This decision came a year after university. I had just been qualified as a life coach, I had hired my own life coach (who is still my life coach today!) and another guy I had dated had ended in disaster. Actually, it didn't end so much as he ghosted, only to reappear three weeks later saying, "Hey! Sorry I didn't reply, my dishwasher broke and my mates moved in next door so understandably, it's been rather hectic xx". Thankfully, I had the sanity to not reply, but it was one of those moments where you stop and go "What is my life?", and I realized something needed to change. He was the last one in a slew of awful guys. Every time I dated one of those guys, I actively found myself regressing. I was making so much progress in my personal development and yet, any time I would walk into a session with "I'm dating someone new", my life coach would have to visibly restrain herself from sighing. All my life-coaching sessions would stop being about me and become about how to reduce the damage and aftershock of the latest guy – and I hated that. It started feeling like every new person I was dating was halting my growth. So I made an extreme decision: I was going to stop dating, cold turkey. I deleted whatever numbers I had on my phone and dedicated my time to me.

My dating detox, while initially hard, ended up being so liberating. I got off the rollercoaster that was my dating life. Men dictated so many of my emotions – or, I should say, I let them. I never decided on a time frame for my detox, I didn't declare a year of being single and I didn't tell anyone. Not even my life coach. All I knew was that my life was a mess. I would get back to dating when, and only when, I had figured out how to exchange the rollercoaster for one of those calm river rides that are quite peaceful. The extreme highs were great but, of course, they would come with extreme lows. While life will always come with peaks and troughs, I wanted to exchange the bounce of a bungee jump for the bounce of a bouncy castle. I was finally sorting myself out and addressing the leftovers of my PTSD. In many ways, I swapped the validation that I was used to getting from men for the validation that came from working on my negative patterns and doing something different.

Over those three years, I never deleted the dating apps. I'd exchange a few flirty messages, and even potentially kissed a random person in a club that I couldn't name, but that was it. There's such a cliché around the idea that being single and not actively pursuing a love life is a waste of time, but I've never learned more about myself and about dating than I did in those three years. I'm certain I wouldn't be the person I am today without this period in my life, and I can guarantee I wouldn't be writing this book without it.

For me, the signs that a dating detox was overdue was that my mood would rise and fall with each man. The ambitious and driven woman I have always been would suddenly stop caring about my career and instead would swap all kinds of work for texting a guy. I would tell everyone how special the guy was, but the reality was that he was no different to the last. Every date I went on was just an avenue for me to gain self-esteem and feel a little less unlovable that day. I needed to learn I was more than my relationship status.

The key to taking a dating detox is that it needs to be intentional. Dating detoxes don't have to be as intense as three years. Sometimes it can just be a few months when your life gets busy. I often get messages from people saying "I am too busy to date" – then don't, but also don't complain. Make it a conscious decision and respect your choice. There is no point deciding not to date and then berating yourself for your lack of dates. When you make a decision, own it. For example, I would take a break from dating every December. Towards the end of December, I always go to Hong Kong to see my family for Christmas, and I had got into this weird pattern of starting to date someone just before I was about to fly across the world. Cue the whole Christmas period, texting every day for a month with a person who I had only been on one, two or three dates with. And every time I would get back to London, we never went on another date. It led to so much being built up in my mind and such great disappointment. I am a stickler for "If you want different results, you need to do something different", so I stopped swiping a month before I left to avoid this situation.

Make it work for you. You decide the rules. You decide the length. Or do as I did and keep it flexible, but explore what it would feel like to consciously choose being single. If you don't know who you would be without a love life, it's your duty to find out. Below is a quiz to find out whether you would benefit from a dating detox – the more questions that are true for you, the more it might be the right time to take a pause from dating.

Do You Need A Dating Detox?

> – Does your love life dictate most of your conversations with friends? **Y/N**
> – Do you find yourself checking their last seen/read receipts when texting? **Y/N**

- Do you get attached as early as the first date? **Y/N**
- Is your love life the butt of the joke in your friendship group? **Y/N**
- Do you think being single is a reflection of your worth? **Y/N**
- Does your mood rise and fall with the matches you get? **Y/N**
- Are you more pessimistic about dating than you were in the past? **Y/N**
- When you go on a date, do you compare the person to an ex? **Y/N**
- Do you feel deflated about dating when even just opening the app? **Y/N**
- Do you struggle to be yourself on dates? **Y/N**
- Do you find yourself visualizing long-term commitment (marriage, kids, them meeting your parents) after only a few dates? **Y/N**
- Do you see being single as a worst-case scenario? **Y/N**
- Does your productivity decline at work when you are dating someone? **Y/N**
- Do you feel drained after most of your first dates? **Y/N**

Forget Me Nots

- Extreme highs come with extreme lows
- If you want different results, you have to do something different
- If you choose not to date, then you can't complain about your lack of dates
- Your dating detox doesn't have to be a predetermined length of time

Take Action Toolkit: Throughout the book, I ask you to trust your instinct. There are many words that are used interchangeably, so use whichever resonates with you, but we are going to locate your intuition, gut, inner voice, inner knowing, higher self. I want you to go back to a time where, in hindsight, you should have listened to your intuition. Float into your body at the time so that you can hear what you were hearing, see what you were seeing and feel what you were feeling. Close your eyes so you can visualize what you were experiencing and breathe like you were breathing in the moment. Now hear that inner voice telling you to make the decision you didn't make. Where is the voice coming from? Is it inside your head or coming from outside? Is it coming from the left or the right? Is it a loud voice or a quiet voice? Is it high-pitched or a deep, low voice? Is it talking quickly or slowly? Notice as many distinguishing features of that voice.

Repeat this with another situation where you should have listened to your instinct, or even a situation where you did listen to your instinct and it worked out well. Check that it's the same voice in the same location with the same sound. Then I want you to get up, shake yourself around and think about what you had for breakfast. Sit back down. This time, I want you to go back to a memory where you listened to your fear and you wish you hadn't. Maybe it was a time you were overthinking and then got overwhelmed. Notice all the details of this voice. Do you notice how the two voices sit in two physically different locations? Do you notice how one speaks faster than the other? Maybe one is a feeling and one is a voice? Notice all the differences so that next time, you know whether you are listening to your gut or your inner critic.

What if I Feel Lonely?

It's normal to feel lonely from time to time. Single or in a relationship, loneliness is an emotion that occurs in every human and it is not an indication of your self-worth. Get out of the mindset of blaming everything on being single. Yes, there were days when I was lonely, sad and frustrated. And there are days now when I feel all those things in a relationship. It's not your relationship status, it's life. It's being a human with emotions. The social media narrative that we are able to slather ourselves in so much self-love that we will never feel lonely again is just as illogical as saying if you drank a gallon of water, you'd never be thirsty again. The importance of being alone lies in something much more specific: being able to spend time with yourself. Once you spend time with yourself, you get to know all facets of your identity. It's easy to love the strongest part of you, but do you love the version of you that can't seem to drink something without spilling it down your top? How about the version of you that snorts every time you laugh? Or the version of you that cries too much? I might be clumsy, ungraceful and emotional, but through spending time with myself, I got to know myself and, as a result, no one can tell me who I am because I know myself better.

As a society, we are going through a loneliness crisis and I believe it stems from our lack of community. Robert Putnam describes it as a loss of social capital in his book *Bowling Alone*. In the past, people had religion and, failing that, you had smaller neighbourhoods. You actually knew the person next door and had strangers asking about you at church on Sunday. These are important ways people feel seen, heard, and cared about. Without that, it can seem like you are all alone on a big planet without anyone caring. It has meant we have come to rely on our primary partners for more. We want them to be our best friend, our therapist and our travel buddy. All of this puts excessive pressure on our romantic relationships because we cannot be everything for one person. It's also why so many people gravitate to diet culture, because things like weight loss clubs feel like community, even if what you are bonding over is self-hatred. It's why we are so invested in sports – for that same sense of camaraderie. By having a strong feeling of "us versus them", you get the feeling of belonging. Additionally, it's more acceptable in these groups to express emotions than in other social interactions. Think about it: if you saw someone crying in a diet meeting, at a football match or in church, you wouldn't bat an eyelid. You'd assume one hadn't lost weight, one was so happy their team was winning (or frustrated they weren't), or someone was having a quiet moment with God. Experience this level of emotion in any other group setting and it would induce awkwardness.

Without this level of community, it is understandable that we have become more reliant on our romantic relationships and without one, we can feel quite unmoored. The way we combat it is by keeping our support network strong by investing in our other relationships just as much. Loneliness is a pivotal part of empowered dating because until you accept loneliness as a part of the process (and life!), you will use your feelings of loneliness as validation to return to unhealthy relationships.

Loneliness versus being alone

Lonely and alone are not the same thing. The loneliest I have felt is not when I am alone but when I'm in a room full of people who don't understand me. Loneliness has redefined itself to feel like self-abandonment. It arises because I have chosen what others want me to be, rather than being authentic to who I am. Alone time, however, has now become associated with peace, tranquillity and rest. The thought of returning home to an empty house conjures up the word "freedom". My home is my safe space and there is nothing that brings me more joy than being able to enjoy it alone. Stop using your loneliness as confirmation you need a relationship. After all, people in relationships get lonely too. Being alone isn't a last resort, but a necessary life skill. As Elizabeth Gilbert puts it: "We all have to learn how to walk into a party or a restaurant alone. Otherwise, we will be willing to walk in with *anybody* (or worse, walk out with anybody)." Until we see being alone as a valid choice, we remain vulnerable to choosing a bad relationship over being single. Loneliness, like all emotions, is a signpost to show you a need that is being unmet – so look underneath it in order to get more specific. The unmet need could be community, connection or intimacy. These all can be fulfilled outside of a romantic relationship and should be a part of your life regardless of your relationship status. The brutal irony is loneliness can make us want to isolate further. Avoid doing this. Instead of pushing others away when you feel that pang of loneliness, reach out to someone. It is so easy to ignore the people who already love you, so send a "thinking of you" text and let the responses remind you that people care.

Sitting in the loneliness

When you don't like yourself, you don't like spending time with yourself. It gives you time to hear your thoughts and when those thoughts are hateful, it can feel like your mind is a torture chamber. To actually be OK alone, you need to stop being scared of your own thoughts. They can't do anything if you don't believe them. You were taught those words, and you were told that was how you should speak to yourself. Wrap yourself in cosy blankets, make yourself comfy, and sit there and do nothing about it. Remind yourself these thoughts aren't true, and let them exist without fighting them. The more you argue back, the louder they will get. You don't have to do anything other than just breathe and keep your mind as clear as possible. Let the thoughts drift in and out like clouds. Let the feelings rise in waves and settle again. When you first sit in the loneliness, you might only be able to tolerate listening to that voice for a few minutes before putting the TV on or plugging your headphones in. But, over time, by tolerating that voice, you teach your unconscious that speaking negatively to yourself doesn't result in action. When your brain tells you that everyone hates you, reach for your compassionate side and be kind to the part of yourself that believes that to be true. Empathize with yourself by saying "That must be so lonely for you", and validate yourself by saying "I know it feels that way, but I love you and I am always here. I will be here for as long as you need and I am not going anywhere."

You are retraining yourself to talk to yourself compassionately, and if you grew up in a household where you weren't allowed to have your emotions or people spoke to each other harshly, this will be a new skill for you. It will be the first time your inner child is actually listened to, so if tears start to surface, that's completely normal. This is the practical side of the cliché quote "Talk to yourself like you would a best friend". This is what it means to sit in the loneliness and not be afraid of it. The reason we run from loneliness is because that pain is what we are avoiding. Showing ourselves we can not only sit in it, but also truly and deeply feel it, liberates us from the fear and allows us to no longer carry it around.

Having romantic friendships

We live in a world that prioritizes romantic love. As a result, we often forget about the love that already exists in our lives, whether that's family or friends. For the last 17 years of my life, my friends served as both the love of my life and my family. As I lived half a world away from my actual family, they made the perfect surrogates – but they didn't become so by accident. I invested in them and recognized that as much as romantic love and familial love is wonderful, friendship love was just as important to make my life feel full. I find it ironic when people moan to their friends about how unlovable they are, completely oblivious to the fact that the people they are moaning to are people who love them. It's the same mentality as the person who is out for brunch with their friends, but secretly checking their phone for a text. You want the attention of a certain person, but as a result, you're ignoring the people whose attention you have at that moment: your friends. If you ignore the love that already exists in your life, when more love shows up in the form of romantic love, what makes you think you'll notice it this time? I started injecting more romanticism in my friendships. I buy my best friends Valentine's Day presents, I hold hands with my friends when we walk down the street and I have become known for my "koala bear" hugs. I stopped treating friendship as a second-tier version of love and made a vow to never be the person who automatically invites their partner without asking, cancels on their friends for a date or disappears when they get into a relationship – only to reappear again when it's gone tits up. If you treat your friendships like they're disposable, they will be. There's an effort you make when you are single that I promised myself I would never stop making, no matter what my relationship status was.

Creating a life you love

A few years ago, I was dating a guy whose favourite hobby was bouldering and for our third date, he promised to take me rock climbing. When he ghosted, I found myself moaning that I was actually more gutted about the rock climbing than the third date. So the next day, I made a plan to go. I was sick of putting off things just because I didn't have a date, so I started a "Dates men have promised to take me on and haven't" list. I started filling it with things like minigolf, inspired by the professional golfer who promised to take me. Then I retitled my list: "Dates I am going to take myself on". At the bottom, I scrawled the words "We don't wait for men", and it broadened my horizons. I tried things like puppy yoga, taking a hot-tub boat down the Thames, going axe-throwing or doing an aerial meditation class. The problem wasn't that I was single, it was that I put my life on hold to wait for someone to give me permission to have fun. I'd walk past my favourite restaurant and think "I wish I was with someone". Now I force myself to go in and get a table for one. The ironic thing about becoming this kind of person who goes out and does the fun thing is you become the first person people ask. Gaining a reputation for being up for spontaneous fun has landed me adventures like kayaking down the Thames, going to a white-collar boxing match and roller skiing. We spend so much time searching to be with someone we love, we forget to be someone we love. If you make your life one that you love, you don't let just anyone walk into it and disrupt that. It's the greatest dating hack of them all. When you love your life, you consider it an honour to let anyone else join you on the ride called life. When you are capable of loving your life, adding a romantic relationship just becomes a bonus.

Forget Me Nots

- Loneliness is a normal human emotion that occurs in everyone, regardless of relationship status
- Until we see being alone as a valid choice, we remain vulnerable to choosing a bad relationship over being single
- If you ignore the love that already exists in your life, when romantic love shows up, you won't notice it
- If you make your life one that you love, you don't let just anyone walk into it and disrupt that

---

Take Action Toolkit: One of the hardest parts about being single during the pandemic was the touch deprivation I experienced, so I was grateful I knew some self-soothing techniques that would work in the absence of another human. These techniques have their roots in the therapy technique of Havening, but are said to work because they imitate the way a child is soothed when young.

Put both hands on top of your opposite shoulder so your arms cross. Stroke down the length of the arm until you reach your elbow, making one stroke per second. Another exercise is to tap on your heart with your hand or to rest it there firmly, which you might find more soothing. It's a great one to use in public because it is subtle. I even use it when I am public speaking. Another way to self-soothe is to brush your right palm across your forehead from left to right starting with the bottom to the top of your palm and then your fingers. Repeat with the left palm. In public, you can touch the bottom of your palms together and then brush one palm up and down until your fingers brush. If you would like a video of these demonstrated, there is a Story highlight on my Instagram page called "Self-soothing".

What if I Have Never Dated?

Let's be honest: the world is set up for coupled people. And when you haven't had the romantic experiences you are expected to have by a certain age, it's really easy to feel left out. Out of all the queries, insecurities and concerns I receive around dating, the most common take the form of "I am *enter age you believe is too old* and I've never been kissed/had sex/been in a relationship." This will be accompanied by people asking if there is something wrong with them, if that is normal and does that mean they are unlovable. There is nothing wrong with you – you are normal and you are lovable just as you are. Just because you have never been in love doesn't mean you aren't loved. Whatever age you believe is "too late", I can guarantee that there is someone else who has asked me the same question who is older than you. It's not about when you start, it's about how quickly you learn. If you keep making the same mistakes and expecting change, you can do that for decades and you still won't have the love life you want.

I understand the insecurity that comes with what society terms a "late bloomer". I was one myself. I was the last in my friendship group to have romantic experiences and I was deeply insecure about it. At 15 years old, I was already worrying about the fact I hadn't been kissed. When I went to university, I guarded this fact with so much secrecy because I believed no one would be friends with me if they found out. It's no surprise, then, that I kissed the first guy I could find on the second day of university, and four days later, I would lose my virginity in a rush, overly concerned with the worry that my brand-new friends would find out how inexperienced I was. Even hitting those milestones were not the relief I thought they would be, because I still used the delay to confirm the worst beliefs around my appearance. Once all my friends started being in a relationship, I felt pressure to do the same and, at 20 years old, ended up in a relationship with the first guy I had ever been on a date with, because I was insecure about the fact that I had never been in one.

Remembering that time now, at 29 years old, it makes me laugh. Why was I in such a rush? Twenty is so young. The problem is that, at the time, you don't feel young. Instead, you feel a pressure to have ticked boxes by a certain age because society only gives a voice to one narrative. Remember that the only expectation is the societal one. It's not that there are fewer people having sex for the first time in their thirties and forties, it's the fact that it isn't discussed. It's not that everyone has their first kiss in school or university, it's the fact that those are the stories that see daylight. I felt judged at that age because I was judging myself. In reality, no one cares as much as you do! I was too busy playing catch-up with my friends and not wanting to be left behind that being in any relationship was better than staying single. How wrong I was! Getting into a relationship for the sake of getting into one will never land you in a good relationship. Unless you want the specific person in front of you, it won't work. And what's worse is that you prevent yourself from finding someone who actually interests you by attaching yourself to the first person who will have you.

I had all my "firsts" in a hurry, and rushing through these milestones made me settle for behaviour that I should have never tolerated. If only I had just had enough confidence to believe that I could have taken my time, I could've gone at my own pace and let it happen when it was meant to. It was only once I hit all those milestones of first kiss, first sexual experience and first relationship that I understood how unimportant they are. Just as you only realize how irrelevant school exams are once you are an adult with a complete CV and no one has ever asked you what you did for school exams to gauge your competency in your job, no one is going to ask you when your first kiss was to decide if they want to date you in your twenties.

The morning after I had sex for the first time, I felt duped that everyone had convinced me it was such a big deal. To wake up and not feel like a brand-new woman was underwhelming and a let-down. The sad thing is, you only see that there was truly no need to rush only after you've rushed. I genuinely believed sex would revolutionize my life in that it would give me knowledge that could not be garnered in any other way; I never stopped to think that my first was simply the beginning of the journey. Once you've had that sexual debut, there is even more to learn, grow and develop. That's why your first experience will rarely be your best, and in years to come, it's not even very memorable . . . well, unless it was memorable for all the wrong reasons.

Stop trying to find meaning behind why your love life has happened at a later age than some others. We need to remove the idea that "everything happens for a reason" and understand that sometimes there is no reason why your first relationship happened at 25 or why you didn't have sex until you were 35. Even if you do have a reason, it's not always an indication of you and your self-worth or level of confidence. From a practical standpoint, I went to an all-girls boarding school and, since I'm straight, the opportunities to meet people I could potentially kiss were lowered. On top of that, I had a wealth of medical trauma to sort through, which was a top priority. Whether it's because you are a carer for your parent, you grew up in a culture where teenage dating was frowned upon or you were busy working extra jobs to help your parents with money, there are countless reasons why your love life might not have been your highest priority. Not all teenagers are love-obsessed, and while my interest in having a love life came later in life, for some people, it might not come at all. If you fall on the asexual or aromantic spectrum and want to opt out of these milestones that society tells you are so crucial, then opt out. If your reason for waiting is because of insecurity or not feeling safe or ready yet, that's perfectly valid, and rushing yourself is not going to make that journey easier. Putting love or sex on a pedestal and turning them into pivotal life moments will add unnecessary pressure. Instead, remind yourself that there is no rush and all of it is waiting for you if you are ready. How exciting that you have all of that fun ahead of you!

We need to eradicate this idea that you can "fall behind". Everyone believes they are doing life wrong at some point. Different is not wrong. Life is not a race. You can envy your friend who has been in a relationship with her childhood sweetheart and got married at 25, but there is nothing to promise you that they won't be divorced within a year. As much as this book is written in chronological order, do not be fooled. Love lives do not come in the linear trajectory that we have been sold: dating, relationship, engagement, marriage and kids. It just requires one match, one conversation, one date or even one moment talking to a stranger in a club that can change your entire love life – in the same way that it takes one break-up, one divorce, one argument and one too many mean words to end a relationship. When you look at all of this together, you realize there is no "behind" or "ahead". Where you are in your love life can change in an instant, and we need to re-evaluate what we constitute as stages.

The solution to it all is to focus more on your path. Comparing your love life to those of others is like going on the road and looking at other drivers. You will crash! You aren't going to learn anything from other drivers; you need to experience it yourself. Staring out your window will only distract you from where you are going. We are all on our own journey. When we get lost admiring someone else's, we forget how far we have come. Remind yourself how much you have improved over the years and the wins you may not have noticed. Accept that your path is the right way for you and remove this idea that taking a break from dating is a roadblock. It's not a delay, it's preparation.

Comparison, to some extent, is inevitable. It is inbuilt in humans, so to say "stop comparing" is like asking us to go against our hardwiring. When we compare, we do so either up or down. We compare ourselves up to the person who just got a divorce after being cheated on after 25 years of marriage and go, "Phew! Thank God that isn't me." Then we compare ourselves down to the newlywed who just announced their pregnancy, and we use their marital bliss as confirmation that we will forever be alone. So instead of making the goal to stop comparison completely, just make sure you are comparing yourself in context. Maybe your love life isn't where you want it to be – but you've never had to worry about your health or experienced the loss of a sibling. You don't compare yourself in those contexts because you don't even think about them. When we look at our life with a big-picture lens, we see the things we should be grateful for, usually things that we have overlooked. There is no point comparing if you know that you've been putting your time and energy elsewhere. For example, I spent the first three years of my single life focused on my career. If I compared my love life to those of my peers at the end of the three years, I would have gotten sad. But if I compared my career, I was far ahead of a lot of my peers. Once

I switched my focus and wanted more of a work/life balance, many of them caught up career-wise.

When we rip it out of context, we only see the accomplishment and not the work to get to that point. We see someone get a book deal and feel jealous, but we forget (or never know about!) the years of rejections that person endured. The same works for our love lives. We are jealous of the wedding day, but forget the fights, vulnerability and improvement in communication the couple had to work through to create a relationship with a person they wanted to marry. It's really easy to look perfect from the outside, but what you are envying is often an illusion. Everyone is happy on their wedding day, but you have to live with that person all the other days, too.

The feelings that you have when you envy someone for the love life you don't have are providing you with valuable information about what you want more of. You can begrudge someone else their happiness – or you can channel that into motivation to go on a date this week, or getting specific about what you are looking for. The difference between comparison and inspiration is "That will never happen for me" and "That will be me one day". When you label something differently, you feel differently about it too. Use the opportunity of seeing something that you want up close to more vividly imagine what you hope for in your own future. Ask yourself how you would want your friends and loved ones to feel about your happiness, and make an active effort to feel the same way about this person.

If you are reading this and are yet to tick off a few milestones, you deserve to take your time. The best thing you can do for yourself is remove the word "normal". There is no normal, only average. And for an average to exist, there need to be people above and below the average. You can write your own story; it's your life, so the order, the rules and the timing are all yours too. If someone tells you that you are running out of time, what they are actually telling you is that if they were in your position, they would feel pressured. Thankfully, we are not on the same clock. Your clock can work to your advantage and you can decide when it stops and starts. And as Jane Fonda says, "It's OK to be a late bloomer, as long as you don't miss the flower show."

Forget Me Nots

- You don't need to rush and you are allowed to take your time
- Focus on your own path – looking at someone else's journey is just a distraction
- If you must compare, compare in context
- It takes one conversation to change the trajectory of your love life

Take Action Toolkit
In order to change the way you utilize comparison, you need to start asking different questions. When you find yourself admiring someone's love life, use those feelings as a signpost to what you want in your own future.

- What story am I telling myself about why they are so happy and in love?
....
....
....
....
....
....

- What story am I telling myself about why I do not have the same?

....
....
....
....

- What specifically about their life do I desire for myself?

....
....
....
....

- What am I ignoring about their story in order to romanticize it?

....
....
....
....

Reflect on how much you have grown over the years by answering the following questions about the past you at several junctures: five years ago, one year ago and six months ago.

- What do I know now about myself that I didn't know?

....
....
....
....

- What do I want from my love life now that is different from the past?

  ....

  ....

  ....

  ....

- What would I have tolerated in the past that I no longer accept?

  ....

  ....

  ....

  ....

- Where have I grown in my communication and vulnerability?

  ....

  ....

  ....

  ....

- How have I developed sexually over the years?

  ....

  ....

  ....

  ....

- What specifically am I currently looking for?

  ....

  ....

  ....

  ....

Chapter 3

You Can't Know What You Don't Know

How to Be Empowered in Your Dating Knowledge

How Do I Stay Away From Toxic Narcissists?

A quick scroll on Instagram and it would be easy to be convinced that the world is full of toxic narcissists who will gaslight and love bomb you. It's hard to believe that even five years ago, these are words that most of us had never heard of, let alone used. But as therapy has become destigmatized, the psychology jargon that used to be confined to a therapist's office has become a part of our everyday vernacular. As these words become more mainstream, people have learned them from second- and third-hand sources. Therefore, the meanings have become distorted and the understanding of when to use these words appropriately has been limited. Especially when used in the manner of clickbait, presented without context and nuance, these labels can easily be reductionist.

As a disclaimer, I am a life coach and am not qualified to make diagnoses. Because of this, I stay away from using diagnostic terms like "narcissists" within my work altogether. Instead, I work with the symptoms you are facing and how they are impacting your life. For example, calling your ex a narcissist doesn't give me the information I need to help you. If you tell me that he repeatedly invalidated how you felt, that gives me more information. I am then able to ascertain that your difficulty is that this experience has broken your ability to trust yourself, and that is a problem we work to address together. We focus on you, and what diagnosis does or doesn't fit your ex is irrelevant.

When it comes to traditional psychology, these labels are useful, but they are applied by professionals who are qualified to do so. In order to meet the criteria for them in a psychology setting, you will often need to pass a threshold of symptoms. You can't diagnose someone without this criteria. When we medicalize imperfect behaviour within romantic relationships, we are in danger of prematurely diagnosing others. It's crucial we stop using these words as insults for every ex that hurts us and reserve it for people who need the assistance that the label warrants. When we use these official diagnoses as casual terms, the people we end up hurting are the ones that need help the most.

Every label is inherently a generalization formed from symptoms. When misused, the labels become harmful. I believe a lot of this stems from cancel culture trickling down to the individual level. Cancel culture has made us want to put people in boxes of "bad" and "good", and that's just not how the world works. Putting exes in a box labelled "toxic" implies the same permanence as when you attempt to cancel a public figure. In both cases, we are so quick to write someone off at the first sign of imperfection that we no longer give people a chance to change or evolve. The way we undermine each other romantically is often with the phrase "bare minimum". I once said online that it's important to notice the small things that someone does, like making you a cup of tea, only to be met with jokes that the bar for men is so low. Yes, men have been held to lower expectations than women – but there is a very fine line between not settling for the bare minimum and taking someone for granted. One of the comments read: "It's a cup of tea, he doesn't deserve a fucking medal for it." Not a medal, but how about just a basic thank you? You can enter relationships with a "Why should I have to thank him for the basics?" mentality, but it becomes a slippery slope to only notice the bad. Take a moment to notice the good.

We have to be careful not to use terms like "red flag" and "bare minimum" as an avoidant strategy to keep people at arm's length. You can't write off the whole world when you aren't perfect either. By putting them into a box so early on in dating, you don't give them permission to climb out of that box. The thought pattern is that if you can put someone in the "bad" box early enough, then you can bubble wrap yourself from getting hurt. That's an illusion. If you interact with humans, accept hurt is a likely side effect. The issue with wanting to sanitize our love lives from human errors, baggage and flaws is that, as a consequence, we judge ourselves more harshly when we are not perfect. When you cancel others so readily, how do you think you will feel about yourself when you make a mistake? You rob yourself of the opportunity for growth when you define yourself by your worst mistakes and others by theirs. This is why boundaries are important. You set the boundaries, you communicate your needs and you give the other person the opportunity to alter their behaviour. If the problem persists, then you communicate the ending of the relationship. But to do otherwise is not setting a boundary, it's putting up a wall. It's a defence mechanism because you are scared.

Ultimately, the reason words like "narcissist" are becoming overused is because people do not feel validated in their experiences. They have been ignored and dismissed when they talk about their horrible ex, so the next time, they call them "toxic". When that is ignored, they escalate to calling them a "narcissist", in the same way that people who have been repeatedly dismissed when they talk about having "a bad day" start to say they had "the worst day ever". The problem with this is that our language shapes our experience, so when we repeat exaggerated words, we are reinforcing the reality we are trying to move away from. The solution is to validate people when they say they are angry, so they don't need to yell. We need to listen when someone says they are sad, so they don't need to sob to get the attention, love and care that they deserve. People shouldn't have to exaggerate their situation to feel like their pain is important enough. It starts with hearing them out.

Forget Me Nots

- Our language shapes our experience, so when we repeat exaggerated words, we are reinforcing the reality we are trying to move away from
- The issue with wanting to sanitize our love lives from human errors, baggage and flaws is that, as a consequence, we judge ourselves more harshly when we are not perfect
- You rob yourself of the opportunity for growth when you define yourself by your worst mistakes and others by theirs
- When people feel unheard, they will feel the need to exaggerate. The solution instead is to validate the emotions they feel and hear them out even if it's not an extreme.

Take Action Toolkit: Inner child work has been essential to both my personal and professional life. Nowadays, it's become more widely known, but back when I learned it, people would give me strange looks when I would mention how we all have an inner child that lives within us. There are many schools of thought, but one is that our unconscious mind stops growing after the age of seven. Another is that childhood wounds that are unhealed become integral to who we are and when new issues arise, they touch upon old wounds because the two are related. The first way I started working with my inner child was through meditations – you can find many audiobooks on Audible, or on YouTube for free – and these forced me to carve out time to sit down and have a

---

conversation with a younger version of myself. Sometimes, as an adult, you might be feeling many emotions that don't really make sense to you. Having these conversations with your inner child helps explain why you feel the way you do. This practice is my space to give my inner child what she needed when she was younger and was never provided.

How Do You Know if Someone Is Emotionally Unavailable?

Emotional availability is something that is made a lot more complicated than it needs to be. Simply put, someone who is emotionally available to date has the time and energy to put effort into dating. You are literally available: you make time for a person, you make plans for the next date, you reply to texts and, ultimately, you don't play games. Emotionally unavailable people are the exact opposite: they are physically unavailable and, even when they are physically available, they create distance. I once dated a guy who said he had a policy against phone calls. I asked for a reason for this, but was never given one. In hindsight, it was just a way to keep me at arm's length. It was his way of avoiding any in-depth conversations – because no matter how much you try to make texting simulate phone conversations, you can't. Another way you can create distance is by not being present on the date. One of my clients went on a date where he had pushed the timing back twice. When he eventually turned up, he spent the entire date checking his emails every 10 minutes. If you actually need to check emails that much, you are not available to date – you are only available to your workplace. If you didn't and were using your phone as a barrier to intimacy, you are also unavailable – emotionally. For years, I had a tendency to attract long-distance situations, no matter how close I put my settings on dating apps. Physical distance makes it easier to create emotional distance.

The hard truth that people don't want to hear is that if you date emotionally unavailable people, it means you are emotionally unavailable too. If you were emotionally available, you would not entertain a possibility with someone who didn't have that capacity too. Whenever someone tells me they have a crush on someone who is married or that they are interested in someone who is not interested in them, they are saying they are chasing emotionally unavailable people often because it feels safer that they are not available. Emotionally unavailable people convince themselves that they can change the other person, and they entertain that illusion because the idea of letting go of that possibility – and instead searching for someone available – terrifies them. People will send me questions like "What do you do when your crush is still in love with his ex?" or "Is it wrong to tell someone in a relationship that you fancy them?" and in the same breath ask what emotional unavailability means. Stop entertaining thoughts about unavailable people. An example of this is if your partner is hiding you. My question is: why are you staying? Being someone's secret is humiliating; if they don't want to acknowledge you in public, then they don't get to know you in private.

What emotional unavailability comes down to is self-esteem. Dating emotionally unavailable people is self-sabotage. It's how you confirm your fear. What better way to convince yourself that you are undesirable than to attract a person who will hurt you to prove it? Unconsciously, you think the only way someone could like you is if something is wrong with them, so you pick people who are obsessed with someone else to prove to yourself how unlovable you are. An emotionally unavailable person can never fulfil your needs; you keep pursuing them because every time you get rejected, you believe you deserve it, and you give yourself more evidence that you are not good enough. Do you find that every person you like doesn't like you back and every person who does like you, you aren't attracted to? This is a key sign of emotional unavailability. We have to remember that when you are attracted to someone, that attraction is subjective and can change or disappear. Two things are likely happening if this is the case: you are attracting emotionally unavailable people because their lack of availability actually makes them more attractive to you, or you are losing your attraction to the people who like you because you don't like yourself. Therefore, you deduce there is something wrong with them that you just don't know about yet.

Whether you call it being a commitment-phobe, a fear of intimacy or trust issues, they are all different ways of saying you're unavailable. It's ultimately a protection mechanism that enforces the belief that if you don't let anyone get too close, they can't hurt you. With some people, this manifests by them leaving first so no one can leave them. With others, it's by never getting attached in the first place. Some of this can relate to their past, either childhood or previous relationships. If they felt like everyone depended on them too much, they might experience the dependence within a relationship as constricting. And for some, it's because they felt like whatever they did, it was never good enough, so commitment has become equated with letting people down.

The truth is everyone is scared of intimacy and commitment and has a hard time trusting. As Sigmund Freud said, "We are never so vulnerable as when we love." Intimacy is scary if it's with someone you can't trust. No one wants to be committed to the wrong person, and trust can take time to build, especially if your trust has been broken in the past. If you are reading this and realizing that you are emotionally unavailable, that's a good thing. You can go from being emotionally unavailable to being emotionally available. I would know – I did it. I used to shut down, push people away and run when I felt vulnerable. I used to also throw myself on the first person who would give me attention because if you can't be loved, you settle for being needed. The way we learn to change this is understanding our patterns, getting better at noticing when we do them in specific moments and choosing to do something different. It's noticing the temptation of the silent treatment and wading through the resistance when communicating. It's avoiding the satisfaction of running away and taking a breath to get vulnerable and admitting, "This is quite difficult for me. Can you be patient while I work on this?" It's leaning into doing the harder option and accepting that taking the risk and getting hurt is better than not trying at all.

Forget Me Nots

- An emotionally available person has the time and energy to put effort into dating
- Only emotionally unavailable people date emotionally unavailable people
- Dating emotionally unavailable people is a protection mechanism that enforces the belief that if you don't let anyone get too close, they can't hurt you
- You can go from being emotionally unavailable to being emotionally available

Take Action Toolkit: When you lack self-awareness, you can project on to others and that can make interactions more complicated. One way to notice your projections is to name three people you hate. These can be people you actually know, celebrities or even fictional characters. If you don't hate anyone, then ask yourself who are the three people who you dislike, annoy you most or simply get under your skin. Then ask yourself to describe each person with three characteristics. Notice the common themes. You might find that words reoccur. I believe everyone is a mirror and if you have such an emotional reaction to a certain trait, the likelihood is it's a reflection of your own wounds. For example, if people are selfish, it doesn't bother me. I know I can be selfish and when someone else is selfish, my reaction is often "Of course, they are going to do what's most convenient for them. My job is to do what's most convenient for me." However, if you find it hard to take time for yourself, set boundaries, or put yourself first, selfish people will annoy you. Similarly, if the common theme among all the three people is that they're lazy, it begs the question, do you connect your self-worth to your productivity? Do you find their ability to rest jarring because you never give yourself the same permission? As Carl Jung states, "Everything that irritates us about others can lead us to an understanding of ourselves."

....
....
....
....
....
....
....
....
....
....
....
....
....
....
....
....

Why Does All Love-life Advice Contradict Itself?

Who knew dating would come with a vernacular all of its own? These new words and phrases have dripped into the mainstream, losing not only their meanings but also their origins along the way. Unfortunately, even the psychology world is not immune to trends, and a lot of these words have risen in their usage as the latest and greatest way to resolve all romantic heartbreak. If you are going to use these words, I want to make sure you are using them accurately. I love that these words are growing in popularity, but I am passionate about keeping their educational foundations intact.

My intention with this chapter is not to dismiss any of these models of thinking, but instead to provide the full picture so that you can make your own decision. The majority of these concepts are useful in better understanding ourselves and our behaviours. Where I draw the line is when they are misused and then incorporated as pieces of our identity based on misinformation. This section seeks to inform you of the origin of these words or phrases and empower you through education. Within life coaching, I don't spend much time analyzing whether something is right or wrong. Right or wrong is a judgement. Instead, I look at if something is helpful or not. When I use a technique and it works on a client, the client does not care why it works, just that it does. I want you to look at the following entries in the same way. If it serves you, keep it. If it doesn't, disregard it.

Attachment styles

What does it mean?
The terms "avoidant", "anxious" and "secure" stemmed from a 1970s experiment, known as The Strange Situation, which explored how children attach to their caregivers. The children were left in a room just with their mother or with their mother and strangers. Secure children explored the room freely and engaged with the stranger when the mother was present, but were distressed and explored less when she left, and were comforted by her when she returned. Avoidant children took little notice of their caregiver, and didn't explore much even with them there. Anxious children also didn't explore much on their own, even in the presence of the mother, and were likely to be distressed before the mother left. They were then clingy and difficult to comfort on their mother's return. How this experiment became more popular was the suggestion that it might affect adult romantic relationships.

What is the criticism?

- It has been suggested that the correlation between childhood attachment and later relationships is only a probability and not a certainty (Clarke and Clarke, 1998)
- The experiment only looked at the main caregiver relationship and not other aspects like the temperament of the child, the role of the father or the child's wider support system
- More recent research suggests that we may have different attachment styles for different relationships (Caron et al., 2012)
- Popular books like *Attached* (Amir Levine and Rachel Heller, 2010) put securely attached people on a pedestal, portraying

them as rare unicorns while writing off those with an avoidant attachment style; this feeds into the harmful idea that humans can be neatly sorted into healthy and unhealthy

What can be learned from it?
Attachment theory has allowed people to understand their behaviours better, show themselves more compassion, and stop shaming themselves and dismissing their needs as crazy. It also argues against this pop-psychology idea that you are weak for wanting to depend on others, and does a great job of putting the beliefs of co-dependency in context, which I discuss next.

<u>Co-dependency</u>

What does it mean?
It was originally used in Al-Anon, an organization that runs meetings for friends and family of those in Alcoholics Anonymous (AA). Both alcohol and drug addiction were referred to as a "chemical dependency" in the 1980s, and family members were referred to as being "co-chemically dependent". This was eventually shortened to "co-dependency". Its initial association to addiction got lost completely as more self-help books reshaped its meaning, such as *Codependent No More* (Melody Beattie, 1986), where it is defined as "one who has let another person's behaviour affect [them] and who is obsessed with controlling that person's behaviour".

What is the criticism?

- The co-dependent characteristics are so broad that it would be harder to not fit the criteria than to fit them

- There is no research to support the idea that friends and family of addicted people have a disease like the addict because they put up with the illness and often enable their loved one
- The co-dependency movement has encouraged a culture of hyper-independence where we shame ourselves for depending on anyone for anything – we are sociable creatures and some level of dependency is required in order to be in healthy relationships
- Associating any dependency with weakness is destructive, as allowing others to help you and care for you requires emotional vulnerability and, ultimately, is a strength

What can be learned from it?
If you struggle with a lack of boundaries, it highlights areas you can work on and gives you ways to detach if you get attached too quickly or easily. Taken as a tool to understand ourselves better, it can provide valuable insight and helps the person focus on what's within their power. Relationships are never going to be a perfect balance of dependence. There will be times when you rely more on each other as well as times when you need more independence.

Father and mother wounds

What does it mean?
The origin of the term goes back to Freud, who used the term "father complex" in relation to the study of the father–son relationship. The mother wound is seen as the generational baggage that gets passed down from grandmother to mother to yourself. Parental wounds are thought to be created out of loss, unmet need, absenteeism or even death. They are your

childhood self seeking to heal the approval, validation and affection that was missing in childhood. Some physicians, like Gabor Maté, believe it is even wired in our nervous system, as our "future relationships will have as their templates nerve circuits laid down in our relationships with our earliest caregivers". As he states in *When the Body Says No: Exploring the Stress–Disease Connection* (2003), "The disruption of attachment relationships in infancy and childhood may have long-term consequences for the brain's stress-response apparatus and for the immune system."

What is the criticism?

- These generalizations can be harmful – not all people with father wounds are scared of commitment and not all those with mother wounds are clingy
- We should not pathologize all childhoods; most are imperfect because it is impossible to parent perfectly, especially without the support we had with communal parenting
- The colloquial terms "daddy issues" and "mommy issues" carry with them blame and shame that imply that the child is responsible for their parent's missteps
- It is sexist and problematic that we only talk about mommy issues in relation to men and daddy issues in relation to women

What can be learned from it?
Instead of asking "What's wrong with me?", father and mother wounds allow us to ask "What happened to me?" The concept asks you to look at your behaviours in the context of your life and upbringing. In this way, it can be used to reduce the self-blame and understand your behaviour in a way that allows

you to give yourself compassion for your past and not see yourself as the problem.

Gaslighting

What does it mean?
Gaslighting is the action of manipulating someone by psychological means into accepting a false depiction of reality or doubting their own sanity. The word comes from the 1938 play *Gas Light* by Patrick Hamilton – made famous by the subsequent Oscar-winning 1944 film of a similar title, *Gaslight* – in which a man manipulates his wife into believing that she is going insane. The title, from which the concept takes its name, is a reference to the husband's insistence that the woman is imagining the gas lights brightening and dimming, when in reality this is part of his machinations.

What is the criticism?

- People use gaslighting too broadly, for example to describe someone disagreeing with your version of events. True gaslighting must come with the intention to undermine and confuse you to lose self-trust – there is a difference between a manipulation tactic and people dismissing your feelings and not understanding you
- It is a loaded, accusatory word and therefore a natural response to it is defensiveness, which can obstruct productive conversation, derail the conflict and prevent resolution

What can be learned from it?
Gaslighting is an important term in being able to spot abusive tactics, but it loses its power when it is watered down.

When it applies to every form of conflict, we both downplay how harmful persistent gaslighting can be to the individuals in those situations and we are not able, as a society, to distinguish the people in abusive relationships who really need protection.

Love addiction

What does it mean?

"Love addiction" is a term that was coined by Pia Mellody in *Facing Love Addiction* (2003). She defines a love addict as someone who is dependent on, enmeshed with and compulsively focused on taking care of another person. There are three major behavioural symptoms: assigning a disproportionate amount of time, attention and "value above themselves" to the person to whom they are addicted; unrealistic expectations for unconditional positive regard for the other person; and neglect to care or value themselves. The other term she uses is "love avoidant", which is largely defined in relation to the love addict. Their behaviours include avoiding both intensity and intimate contact via distancing techniques.

What is the criticism?

- Love has not been classified as a chemical or behaviour addiction (Fisher et al., 2016)
- This model has been criticized for pathologizing traditionally female traits and behaviours
- The lack of diagnostic criteria makes the idea of love addiction complicated
- Some believe "addiction" should only denote physical changes to the brain

What can be learned from it?

The cycles that Pia Mellody outlines have been useful to explain behaviour, as well as the fact that she recognizes that both anger and seduction can be used to increase intensity. She refers to these as "anger bombs" and "seduction bombs", the intentions of which are to get your partner to engage and connect with you, either through a fight or sexual acts. She talks about the importance of detaching when an unhealthy dynamic arises, and this can be beneficial to those who also relate to the co-dependency model.

Love bombing

What does it mean?

"Love bombing" is a term that describes a manipulation technique often used at the beginning of dating when one person overwhelms the other with love, luxuries and flattery. This can be in the form of gifts, compliments, attention, or commitment, and is often used by abusers and con artists. By giving you a lot early on, whether it be gifts or affection, the love bomber creates pressure to reciprocate the feelings, and so they are able to garner trust more rapidly and use that to control you – especially as moving at a fast pace can be overwhelming. The term was originally used in discussions about famous cults like the Unification Church of the United States (more commonly known as the Moonies). Cult leaders, like Jim Jones of the Peoples Temple, were known to use these tactics to manipulate new recruits into signing up – after which, they would isolate them from family and friends. Once you are "hooked", they stop love bombing and use your self-esteem for their own personal gain, wanting things in return and becoming abusive and manipulative.

What is the criticism?

- There is little research on the term, leaving a lot of room for speculation
- This is an extreme behaviour that is associated with manipulation and is part of the narcissistic abuse cycle, so shouldn't be used casually in respect to any grand gesture
- We have to look at all the behaviour in context; people behave badly without it being abusive and people change their minds without some manipulation tactic underpinning it

What can be learned from it?

The easiest way to avoid love bombing is to see intensity as a warning sign. If it feels too fast, it is too fast. It's great that there is more discussion of manipulation tactics and emotional abuse, as it means the signs will be easier to spot if there is awareness around them. But this strength becomes a weakness if they are applied to every slight wrongdoing instead of being reserved for situations where they are warranted.

Love languages

What does it mean?

Love languages are a concept created by Gary Chapman in his book *The 5 Love Languages* (1992). He believes that we all have different ways of communicating and expressing love, and that we often have primary and secondary ways that are more important to us than the rest. The five languages are: words of affirmation, acts of service, receiving gifts, quality time and physical touch. He makes the comparison to language differences in his book: "Your emotional love language and the language of your spouse may be as different as Chinese from

English. No matter how hard you try to express love in English, if your spouse understands only Chinese, you will never understand how to love each other."

What is the criticism?

- Love language compatibility was a poor predictor of relationship longevity (Bunt and Hazelwood, 2017)
- "Love languages" makes it sound like these are optional bonuses as opposed to compulsory components of a healthy relationship, e.g. you would struggle to have a healthy relationship without quality time of some sort
- The love languages are five broad generalizations that don't encapsulate every way of demonstrating love, and there are other, more specific ones that don't fit in any category
- The model is meant to be used to understand other people's love languages, and not to force your partner to fulfil your own
- We need some of all the love languages, so even though you likely have one or two that stand out or rank higher, that doesn't mean the others are unnecessary

What can be learned from it?

The important principle that I gathered from Chapman's book is that you shouldn't assume people think the same way you do. Not all humans are comforted in the same way, express joy in the same way and, indeed, show love in the same way. Before assuming, always ask. The conversation of love languages also allows us to see when a partner is unwilling to make us feel loved. If you ask for more of a certain love language and that is dismissed or ignored, notice that they are not making an effort to meet your needs.

Red flags

What does it mean?

Red flags are warning signs. They are there, like in other contexts, to denote potential danger, not definite danger. Red flags are not the same as deal-breakers. A deal-breaker would be if someone slaps you. A red flag is someone turning up late to a date. So clock it, make a mental note of it and then see if others arise. Red flags are also not universal – they are specific to the individual and based on what your criteria are for a relationship, and can differ depending on the type of relationship you are looking for. A red flag in a friendship might not be a red flag in a potential partner.

What is the criticism?

- If you go through the world seeing every human as a walking red flag, then dating will be very difficult; if you are constantly searching for a problem, you will find one
- We all have red flags, occasionally behave badly, and are imperfect, so if you have a one-strike policy with everyone, you will have a one-strike policy with yourself
- Sometimes the discussion of red flags can be used as a tool to punish ourselves, but you will make mistakes and have regrets and sometimes you need to learn the hard way

What can be learned from it?

Red flags have made people be more conscious and pay attention. If you are able to notice them earlier on, you might be able to save yourself a bunch of heartache in the long run. The majority of things that end a relationship were there in the beginning, and the idea of red flags is a mani-festation of that – but we can't delude ourselves into think-ing we can have the benefit of hindsight while still living in the present. Forgive yourself – you are not a fortune teller. If it's useful, then see the idea of red flags through a self-compassionate lens.

Narcissists and narcissistic abuse

What does it mean?
Narcissistic personality disorder is one of 10 personality dis-orders recognized by the *Diagnostic and Statistical Manual of Mental Disorders, 5th Edition* (2013), known as *DSM-5.* The disorder can be summarized as an inflated sense of self, lack of empathy for others and need for constant attention. To fit the diagnosis, individuals must meet 55 per cent of the criteria listed and the disorder must impact their life to the extent it becomes difficult to form relationships and creates a disturbance socially or in their work life.

What is the criticism?

- The term "narcissistic personality disorder" has been con-tested as a personality disorder and was almost removed from the *DSM-5*
- The shortened version ("narcissist") should not be used as a casual insult, in the way that "psychopath" was used in the past, as this diminishes the intent of the word
- Someone can just be an arsehole, vain and conceited without being a narcissist
- Narcissism is a spectrum disorder – you can meet some criteria without having the personality disorder

- Everyone is capable of narcissistic tendencies, and a small dose of narcissism can even be healthy and helpful in terms of survival

What can be learned from it?
When it comes to the personality disorder, narcissistic abuse can create a huge amount of harm on the whole family system. The behaviours of those with the disorder are extremely destructive for the people who surround them, and that should not be trivialized by being overused. Doing so means it becomes harder for people to get. Use these words carefully, without exaggeration and deliberately.

<u>Toxic</u>

What does it mean?
It has been used to denote any negative relationship or even non-positive behaviour or experience. In 2018, the same year that "gaslighting" was named one of the most popular words of the year, Oxford Dictionaries gave the top spot to "toxic" and since then, it has not gotten less popular. Although we can thank Britney Spears for making 'Toxic' a catchy song, it is believed the rise in popularity came with the rise in use of "toxic masculinity". It has remained hard to define, yet that hasn't diminished its use.

What is the criticism?

- Dismiss someone as "toxic" and in a word, you have painted yourself as the good character in the situation, garnered sympathy and removed all nuance and complexity
- "Toxic" implies permanence – if we don't believe people can change, it leads to less effective conflict resolu-

tion, and failure to listen or set boundaries (Dweck and Ehrlinger, 2006)
- People are not toxic, but dynamics can be: you can be toxic with one person and not with another, even in the same context, so accept that the toxicity you have in one relationship doesn't apply to all relationships

What can be learned from it?
People who love you sometimes do shitty things. They can fuck up. If they care for you, they will mend and repair the relationship, apologize and change their behaviour. When we label them as "toxic", we write them off before we give them a chance. We have all been toxic at one point. We need to remove this idea that if you decide someone is toxic, then they are. They can be a good person and you can still end a relationship for how they treated you.

Trauma and trauma bonding

What does it mean?
"Trauma" is defined by the *DSM-5* as requiring "actual or threatened death, serious injury or sexual violence". Stressful events not involving an immediate threat to life or physical injury, such as psychosocial stressors, are not considered trauma. Within life coaching, the definition is broader and includes any stressful and emotional event where you have the inability to escape. "Trauma bond" is a term that defines the attachment an abused person feels for their abuser. The bond is created through a cycle whereby, after the abuser commits abuse, they become extremely apologetic and remorseful about their behaviour, only for the cycle to repeat. This destabilizing effect and the power imbalance

explains why a trauma bond means people stay in abusive situations and are unable to seek help.

What is the criticism?

- Trauma-related language has been shown to have expanded both in terms of quantity and severity, and the worry is that we make ourselves victims when we pathologize everyday behaviour (Haslam, 2016)
- There seems to be a commercialization of trauma, with social media content involving trauma receiving higher engagement, making it difficult for the creator, and the consumer, to realize they are more than their trauma and aren't defined by it
- If we see ourselves through the lens of our trauma first and foremost, it can be hard to imagine a healthy romantic relationship for ourselves
- People interpret "trauma bond" literally and this creates confusion – bonding over a shared trauma is not a trauma bond

What can be learned from it?

The increased awareness around trauma has led to people being able to seek help, especially around post-traumatic stress disorder. We are living longer and have the best medical technology we have ever had. As a result, people are surviving events and accidents that they previously wouldn't have. The more of us that survive, the more trauma we have to process, so the need for trauma-informed therapy has increased. We need to maintain the integrity of these words by only using them intentionally. When you understand the danger that comes with trauma bonding, it is clear that support is essential in order for a person in an abusive situation to break that bond, and we can only be alerted to the severity of it if the word holds true to its original definition.

Twin flames

What does it mean?

The phrase "twin flames" was largely born in spiritual circles to describe the belief that one soul can be split into two people, or that two people become mirror images of each other. When these two people meet, it is meant to feel like an instant connection and, much like a mirror, your twin flame is supposed to reflect back your worst insecurities and deepest fears. Twin flames are not necessarily romantic and not everyone will get one. They are considered rare, as not every soul gets divided, and they differ from the concept of soulmates because twin flames are meant to be two halves of a whole. It is thought that "twin flames" originated from Greek mythology, when Zeus divided an androgynous human into two. It is also mentioned in Vedic texts, which note that everything is manifested in both feminine and masculine energy and therefore every soul has both parts. The goal is to find each other in order to be free at the end of the soul cycle. The majority of the origin stories around twin flames imply that the unification will lead to a completeness.

What is the criticism?

- The concept of twin flames becomes problematic when it embeds this idea of destiny – when we think we are "meant to be", we tend to overlook the incompatible parts to try to force it to work

- Believing someone is your perfect match can set you up for unhealthy patterns (Lee and Schwartz, 2014)
- One of the twin flames is seen as the "runner", and the other the "chaser", and this can be easily confused with pursuing someone who is either emotionally unavailable or completely uninterested (for example, in 2014, Ryan Gosling got a restraining order against a stalker who claimed to be his twin flame)
- The "chaser" is meant to help the "runner", who is the spiritually unawakened one, but trying to change or fix someone is manipulative and controlling and should not be romanticized

What can be learned from it?
It is important to note that the concept of twin flames does not imply that a relationship of this nature will be effortless and require no work. Even in a twin-flame relationship, you won't just click and slot into each other's emotional and physical lives easily with no hiccups along the way. If you find using this term empowering spiritually, be cautious of the assumptions you are making and how you might prematurely fast-forward your relationship due to the belief that you are of the same soul.

Forget Me Nots

- Take what resonates and leave the rest
- Question what you see online and think about it critically before accepting it
- If something works, it doesn't matter why it works
- Overusing extreme language will diminish its true definition for those who need help

Take Action Toolkit: Regardless of which model of thinking resonated most with you, it is undeniable that your childhood will have an impact on your relationships. These models are theories on how it does that, but I believe how your childhood resonates in your life is much more individual than that. Two people may not react to the same event with the same feelings. When a caregiver behaves a certain way, you either unconsciously do the same or do a pendulum swing and decide to be the opposite of what they were (and they become an example of what you don't want). The prompts in this exercise help you explore your personal feelings around your childhood. I have used the term "caregiver" below to describe any formative figure in your life, but I suggest you do this exercise with every person who had an impact on your childhood, rewriting the prompt with the exact name you would have used for that person. For example, if the name you used for your father was "Papa", then use Papa instead of Father, as it will evoke more connections. This is your opportunity to look after that child who asked for love and may never have got it.

- My caregiver was

  ....
  ....
  ....
  ....

- When I was younger, I wanted to be like my caregiver in how they

  ....
  ....
  ....
  ....

- When I was around my caregiver then, I felt

....
....
....
....
....
....

- I sought my caregiver's approval most in

....
....
....
....
....
....

- In the eyes of my caregiver, I was never good enough when it came to

....
....
....
....
....
....

- I could never tell my caregiver that

....
....
....
....
....
....

- I wish I could hear my caregiver say

....
....
....
....
....
....

- In order to receive my caregiver's love, I had to

....
....
....
....
....
....

- I received my caregiver's attention the most when

....
....
....
....
....
....

- I have to accept that my caregiver was unable to give me

....
....
....
....
....
....

Chapter 4

Would You Date You?

How to Be Empowered in Your Dating Mindset

The Myths of Dating

I remember the first time someone asked me the question "Would you date you?" It felt like a kick in the teeth. My answer was clear and unsurprising: no. What shocked me, though, were the reasons that jumped to mind had nothing to do with the way I looked. We live in a society that emphasizes appearance first. So when our love life isn't working out, we decide we are undateable, and commit to an endless uphill climb of trying to fight against our own genetics. We dedicate time to improving our looks rather than improving how we interact with the people we date. We blame it on our thighs, instead of considering it could be because we shut down any time someone gets too close to us, we use the silent treatment when we are annoyed or we make passive-aggressive digs instead of communicating how we really feel. These are things we can actually work on. But before we learn how, we have some unlearning to do.

There are two particular veins of advice that I despise the most. The first camp of advice is the outdated rulebook that says "Never let a woman pay", "Play hard to get", "Let them make the first move". That school of dating reeks of patriarchy, assumes every relationship is a straight one and, in doing so, places the woman in the helpless position of sitting, waiting and letting life happen to her. This is the same school of thought that tells women to stop being picky, that they are too needy and that men are completely different creatures who communicate in a foreign language that we need to translate. All the reasons for despising this way of thinking are pretty self-explanatory, but when we rebel against an old way of thinking, we usually do a pendulum swing to the opposite extreme, and the other extreme can be equally harmful.

It is the "Never settle", "Love yourself first", "You don't need a man" school of thinking that was largely born out of the female empowerment and self-love corner of social media. When it first started, it was much-needed messaging to combat the ever-present idea that you can't be complete without a relationship. It liberated single people and helped them get rid of the shame. As a result, fewer people were staying in relationships just for the sake of it, but as this ethos has evolved, it has lost its nuance and brought with it this encouragement of hyper-independence. Hyper-independence is the mentality that you can't rely on anyone around you. It's often born out of trauma and the fact that when you have relied on people in the past, you've been burnt. Therefore, many take the "If you want something done, you have to do it yourself" approach to life. But this is unrealistic and, as a result, people now feel shame when they depend on others. They feel that they are weak if they are unable to achieve this mentality of never needing anyone, and it's connected to this approach of diagnosing everyone as avoidants or narcissists in a bid to overprotect yourself.

The independent person is OK to admit that they need people at times, whereas the hyper-independent person is unable to ask for help, because when they did so in the past, they were shut down, ignored, or the help they asked for was weaponized or used as currency against them at a later date. Over time, their trust was shattered by people claiming to care about them and then not following through – so they learned to do everything on their own. What originally started as an empowering message telling largely women to raise their standards now brings limitations. Humans are not meant to be islands; we are designed for human interaction and connection, and wanting these things does not mean you don't love yourself enough. Much like how, in my previous book *The Joy of Being Selfish*, I discuss how there is a difference between boundaries and walls, there is also a difference between high standards and unrealistic standards. Boundaries keep the wrong people away, whereas walls keep everyone away, and overdiagnosing people as "toxic" is the equivalent to building a wall around you. Your expectations become so large that they actually are unattainable. You can't expect what isn't in you. As a general rule of thumb, if you are asking for something you are unable to provide to them, then your ask is too big.

As much as quotes like "Turn your red flags into deal-breakers and watch your love life change!" sound great on social media, they fail to remember that humans are complex, and our interactions will be too. If you cut and run at the first sign of a red flag, you fail to learn how to communicate. You avoid hard conversations and you actually never learn how to set boundaries. It's a defensive approach that means you will never learn how to communicate your needs and give people the opportunity to change. Both points of view hold a grain of truth, but we need to find a middle ground. There is a balance between giving too many chances and not giving someone any at all, so let's take a look at these overused phrases and apply some critical thinking.

Dating myths
"All the good ones are taken"
This idea is flawed because it presupposes that everyone is looking for the same boxes to tick in a dating situation. Everyone has different interests, tastes, senses of humour – and also different deal-breakers, red flags and turn-offs. You don't have to look any further for evidence of this than the fact that most

people who are in happy, successful relationships have had a break-up before that; it is less about the perfect individual and more about the compatibility between two people that makes a relationship last. I understand there is a frustration when you feel like your dating life keeps resulting in dead ends, but this phrase creates a scarcity mindset. If you behave as if "good ones" are a finite resource that are soon to go extinct, that is what you are going to notice. People get divorced and break up every day, and the amount of available people is not stagnant.

"Men are trash"
This tongue-in-cheek phrase, while a generalization, has captured the justified anger at the patriarchy and therefore, by extension, at men. Logically, we know that the patriarchy affects men too, but after one too many encounters with the double standard, it's understandable that we have resentment. It's not all men, but it's usually men. According to Women's Aid, in a study carried out in 2019, 96 per cent of domestic homicide victims are women, 98 per cent of the suspects are men and 92 per cent of defendants in prosecutions related to domestic abuse are men. Knowing these statistics, it leaves those who date men in a difficult position. How are you meant to date without a legitimate fear that your life and safety are at risk? Society's solution seems to be to put the onus on women – changing how we dress, when and where we walk late at night and even suggesting curfews to keep us safe. We are not the problem, and I refuse to put that responsibility on women. The truth is that until we dismantle the patriarchy and increase accountability for men, our society will not change. We are not going to change the system overnight, and for the more sceptical of us, potentially not even in one lifetime. So what can we do instead?

We remember that our frustration is valid. I've felt it myself – particularly when organizing a date – how useless some men are. I've felt it when men feel an entitlement to my body. I've felt it when I've been judged for having sex while my male counterpart is praised. Loving dating does not make you immune to these feelings. The issue with the phrase "men are trash" is that the more you repeat it, the more you are likely to attract the thing you want to avoid. Our brains have something called the reticular activating system that filters out unimportant information and decides what is necessary. In the same way, if I asked you to look around the room and notice everything that was pink, your brain would do that. But if I closed your eyes and asked what was blue in the room, you would struggle to name the blue items. This is what is happening with your beliefs. We can't change our sexuality and we can't change the system overnight, so we must focus on what's within our control: who we let into our lives. Of course, trash men exist, but that doesn't concern you, because those are not the ones you are going to be dating.

"Opposites attract"
Differences between partners can be amazing. But this phrase falls short when it is used in order to justify a dynamic where one person gives a lot and the other takes a lot. When you are selfless, you spend your time and energy carrying other people's burdens and fixing other people's problems. You pride yourself on being a giver because you lack self-esteem and giving makes you feel good enough. Being different is great if they are quiet and you are talkative and that creates balance. It is something else entirely if you are the person who plans all the dates, organizes all the schedules and does all the emotional labour and they . . . don't. Don't use differences as a way to explain away lack of reciprocity.

"It'll happen when you least expect it"
Can you imagine if this rule was applied to our careers? "You will find your dream job when you least expect it." If being on a dating app makes you desperate, then I guess sending in your CV for a job makes you desperate as well. I've always been a proactive person, so this expectation that you should just let your dating life happen to you never sat quite right with me. You are an active participant in your love life! This phrase is one that coupled people say, alongside a story of how they had an unexpected meet-cute that is the exception to the rule. The only reason the exceptional stories travel so far is *because* it's so rare. But for every fascinating story, there are tons of boring ones too.

"You'll know when they are the one"
We need to lose the idea of "the one" completely. Throw it in the bin alongside the idea of soulmates. The maths just doesn't work out on this one; the probability of you meeting one person out of eight billion is just too low that I can't even entertain it. Also, what happens if your "one" dies – is that you done with your love life for eternity? That doesn't seem fair. It also further perpetuates this idea of effortlessness and that a healthy, successful relationship doesn't require work. It becomes impossible to date when you continue to be told that you should know from the outset whether something is going to last. Sitting on a first date, trying to decide if this is the one you are going to end up with, is a really quick way to ruin a first date. Some people know early on, while others need some time to warm up and get to know a person.

"Love conquers all"
Love can improve your life, it can make your day brighter and your world fuller, but it cannot fix things that are broken. The

problem is that everyone has a different definition of love. Some people can yell, scream and throw abuse at a person and call it love. Others can body shame you while telling you that they love you. If that's your version of love, I don't want it. I have been in too many situations where abuse has been sugar-coated with the word "love", and too often "But I love them" becomes an excuse to stay with a person who is unravelling your self-esteem piece by piece. So no, love does not conquer all. Apart from love from a parent to a child (not even the other way around), love should not be unconditional. We should have conditions on our love and if they are not getting met, they should be noticed, not brushed over with romanticized notions that encourage complacency.

"Who you attract is a reflection of you"
There is something so shameful about this statement that makes you believe that you are responsible for any bad treatment you receive. Shame has never helped anyone make an empowering decision, and the more we shame people for their choices, the more they stay stuck in abusive situations. The shame that this statement embeds results in people thinking they will never find any better, and that's simply not true. Everyone attracts dickheads. The only difference is that people with good self-esteem get rid of them faster. If I take their bad behaviour as a reflection of me, then they win. People don't gaslight and abuse you because you deserve it, they do so because of their own wounds and insecurities that they are unwilling to face. They are projecting, not reflecting. Their bad behaviour belongs to them. I refuse to be responsible for someone else treating me badly. However, I will be responsible for ensuring that any person who enters my life maintains the same level of respect and trust that I ask of anyone else in

my life. You don't attract the wrong people, you accept them. Therefore, who you attract is not a reflection of you, but who you keep *is* a reflection of you.

"You just need to love yourself more"
Of course self-love is important, but it's human that you want relational love as well, whether that is in romantic relationships or platonic ones. What strikes me as most ironic is that the people caught saying this are often the people in relationships in which they are co-dependent and inseparable. Self-love and relational love are not mutually exclusive; you don't need one over the other and one can't replace another, either. There is a Maya Angelou quote that says "I don't trust people who don't love themselves and tell me, 'I love you'." She references an African saying: "Be careful when a naked person offers you a shirt." But this comparison is not accurate. Unlike a shirt, which is a physical object, loving yourself is not a stagnant state that you reach and stay at. There will be moments when even the most practised at self-love will waver and, in those moments, relational love can be a beautiful reminder. I wouldn't be who I am today without being assisted by people who loved me more than I could love myself. Once, when I was really insecure about my scars, a guy kissed them and told me they were beautiful, and that helped me see them in another light. We need to remove this idea that romantic love and self-love are at war in any way. You can work on your self-love while also seeking to increase the amount of relational love in your life. You deserve both.

"You're just too picky"
According to the Office for National Statistics, couples spend, on average, two to two and half hours a day together. If I am

going to spend that much time with a person, you would hope that I wouldn't just pick anyone. Think about the number of meals you share, the number of conversations you have and the number of nights you share a bed. You better be selective! The more criteria you have – especially if you don't see being single as the greatest threat – the harder you will have to look. It's basic maths. You are trying to find the chocolate chip cookie in a plate of oatmeal and raisin. If you don't know what you are looking for, the raisin is perfectly fine. But if you know you are looking for chocolate and take a bite, the raisin will suddenly taste awful in comparison.

This phrase presupposes there is a length of time where you cross over from just being single to being single for "too long", reinforcing this idea that single is only a waiting room to be paired up. Of course, with each myth there is a grain of truth, and this one is that there is a difference between being picky and nitpicking. We are seeing it on TikTok as people discuss their latest ridiculous "icks", anything from wearing a cycling helmet to when they walk backwards after their turn in bowling. Forget the harmful notion that a person has to be attractive every moment of the day – this is less about being picky and more about using any excuse to end it due to a fear of intimacy and connection. You feel vulnerable, so you nitpick over the tiniest thing and inflate it large enough that it becomes a reason to end the relationship. However, unless you are behaving like Chandler Bing in *Friends* and dumping people because their nostrils are too big, then chances are you are not too picky.

"Do not raise him, he is not your son"
This is a newer, more modern myth that seeks to combat women who do too much for the men in their lives. It addresses co-dependency and lack of boundaries, and is a helpful phrase

if you do for a partner what they should be doing for themselves. It isn't helpful for those who overprotect themselves and find it hard to show they care. I will hear this phrase in contexts like "I shouldn't have to teach a grown man how to apologize" – and it is said as if teaching him how to apologize wouldn't directly benefit you, when it would. It is said as if there is one default way of apologizing. Different components of an apology will matter to different people, and part of dating is learning what's important to each other. Teach him how to apologize properly and if he still doesn't do it, then judge him based on that, but do not judge based on the fact that they don't know something you do. Some people are more evolved emotionally, others are more practised at communication and some were raised with less opportunity to have hard conversations. Should he have learned it from his parents? Maybe. But we weren't all given the good fortune of communicative parents. Is there a greater expectation on women to grow up faster and learn how to be self-sufficient? Absolutely. And as a result, there are men in this world who can't do basic tasks for themselves. But shaming the individual for something they don't know doesn't solve the problem.

We do not walk into romantic relationships as fully formed humans. There will be times when you will have to teach another what you want and need, and there will also be things that you will learn from them. "You are not his mother" has become the feminine equivalent of calling a man "whipped" for doing kind, caring things for the person he loves. So where is the line? The line is boundaries. If you are able to distinguish what is your responsibility and what is not, then you won't fall prey to someone else taking up your time and energy on things that they should be doing for themselves. There is a difference between care and caretaking. It's the difference between showing them how to book a plane ticket and doing it for them. You can explain something with care without doing it for them.

"If he wanted to, he would"

Stop listening to jaded people. This way of thinking sometimes works when assessing whether they are making enough effort in the early stages of dating. When it stops working is when it becomes paired with "I shouldn't have to ask" and "If they knew me, they would know". How many times have you wanted to do something but didn't? This is what is known as the single cause fallacy. It's when there is more than one potential cause but we choose to focus on just one. X caused Y, so therefore X was the only cause of Y. There are a million reasons why someone who is interested wouldn't ask you out, from nervousness to fear of rejection to the fact that you look uninterested. It's too much of a generalization to work. It presupposes that we all have the same needs, the same way we like to be comforted and the same expectations. Even you won't want the same thing in every context. There are times you will want to talk about it, and there are times when you will want a hug. Humans are not predictable. If you want something that you are not getting, tell them. Stop running tests in your relationship and communicate instead. When you tell them what you want, their response and whether they change their behaviour will tell you more than how much they can read your mind.

Forget Me Nots

- If you cut and run at the first sign of a red flag, you avoid hard conversations and you fail to learn how to communicate
- There is a difference between high standards and unrealistic standards

- We are designed for connection, and wanting these things does not mean you don't love yourself enough
- Romantic love should be conditional

Take Action Toolkit: One of my most hated phrases is "That's just the way I am". I specifically hate it when it is used mid-argument, as if who you are is some unchangeable inanimate object. You get to decide who you are! Whenever I find myself wishing to be something I'm not, I tell myself to go be that person. I envied those who loved dating so I told myself to stop waiting to become that person and to just be it. Embody it and behave like it.

Today, you are going to decide who you are by writing a list starting with the phrase "I am the type of person who . . .". There is something about this word prompt that helps me visualize the person I want to become more clearly. It is a generalization that benefits us, because when we categorize ourselves in a group of people we like, we like ourselves more too. Get as specific as you like. As with all my Take Action Toolkit prompts, they come from exercises I have done myself, so I've shown you a few of my examples to get you started.

I am the type of person who . . . laughs at themselves when they trip over their feet in the street
I am the type of person who . . . gets out of bed excited for the day and wakes up smiling
I am the type of person who . . . makes you feel welcome when you don't know anyone at a party

I am the type of person who ....
I am the type of person who ....
I am the type of person who ....

Is a Healthy Relationship Possible for Everyone?

Regardless of how long a relationship lasts, you deserve a healthy dynamic from the start. If you do not have this belief, you will not date people who are good for you. It's not that you won't attract them, it's that you won't notice them when they are standing right in front of you – and if you happen to somehow end up on a date with an emotionally available person, you will find them boring because there will be no intensity and no drama. It's so easy to say "Great, that's what I want! I want consistency and reliability." But if you've never had it before, this will be unfamiliar to you; humans hate the unfamiliar because it puts us outside of our comfort zone. Because of this, you will either convince yourself that there is no spark or you will self-sabotage in a bid to push them away, restore your safety and return to what you know.

We need to unpick the "All girls love a bad boy" and "Nice guys finish last" messaging. We put both of these phrases on the same spectrum and see bad and nice as polar opposites, when actually they are on different scales. When a woman describes a guy as "nice" in a dating context, they aren't actually saying that their kindness was a problem. We use the word "nice" to describe someone when there is nothing else to say. You can't say they are smart, funny or even interesting, so they were just *nice*. Nice means neutral. Nice means no strong feelings either way. There was nothing wrong with them, but there was also no attraction. It does *not* mean if only they had treated me like shit, I would have been more interested. It is coming home to your housemates and them asking how your date was: Fine. What were they like? Nice.

What if you are described as "too nice"? This is something different. This doesn't mean neutral, it means a pushover with no boundaries, who agrees with everything I say because they are a people-pleaser and have no actual opinions themselves. In these contexts, "too nice" describes a person who is so desperate to be liked that they lose themselves and, in the process, any defining characteristics that make them unique. The polar opposite of nice is not mean, it is interesting. That's why the messaging that "Nice guys finish last" is so flawed. It's not because of their niceness, it's due to their blandness. If you are dull, whether you are nice or mean, no one will want to spend time with you.

I also think it's important to add that there is a subsection of self-proclaimed "nice guys" who are neither nice nor neutral but will also proclaim that nice guys finish last. These are not nice guys at all – these are entitled guys. These are the ones that feel entitled to having whoever they are interested in just because they are decent for a moment. They believe being "nice" for a second means they are owed something, whether that be a kiss, a date or sex. If you are only being nice for something in return, that's manipulation. They will endlessly moan about the friendzone when actually, they just can't accept they were rejected. Can you imagine if women walked around offended because we smiled at you and you didn't suddenly go weak at the knees? These are the type of guys who don't believe women are owed respect unless they find you attractive – and they're also the type of person who, when you turn down their offer, will retort "Well, you're fat, anyway." Funny that, I was fat when you hit on me two seconds ago as well. Entitlement defines every aspect of their interactions with you: they feel entitled to your attention, entitled to get whatever they want in exchange for basic human decency and also entitled enough to think they know what you want better than you do.

The polar opposite of a bad guy, therefore, is not a nice guy but a kind guy. They don't believe they are owed anything in return for kindness. Bad guys treat you badly and a kind guy will treat you well, communicate how they are feeling, be clear when they are uninterested and respect you enough to end it properly. When people date "bad boys", it is because they are replicating the love they had from their caregiver – the relationship they know, are familiar with and also have come to expect. They think the inconsistency and unreliability is normal and so they seek it out. As Gabor Maté states, "We will understand ourselves as we have felt understood, love ourselves as we perceived being loved at the deepest unconscious levels, care for ourselves with as much compassion as, at our core, we perceived as young children." For example, let's say you had a caregiver who would only give you attention when you did something for them, like cleaning the kitchen, but they ignored you the rest of the time. In an oversimplified way, this could mean you think it's normal for people to only show you affection when they want something from you. You believe that's love, so you seek it out in romantic partners because that's familiar, that's what you know.

The "bad boy" messaging starts the moment we tell little girls on the playground that boys are mean to them, pull their hair or push them because they like them. So what do you think happens when those girls turn into women and play-fighting turns into actual fighting? More than that, this notion teaches that we must forgive men who can't articulate themselves, and that whatever behaviour results from their bad communication is understandable. Surely it would make more sense if we just taught boys how to communicate and told girls that they like them, and that it's OK to be vulnerable and admit that? The reason it is so hard to stop being attracted to the "bad boy" trope is because the story you are telling yourself in your head convinces you to stay. You over-romanticize them because dating a "bad boy" makes you seem like you are flirting with danger, and it sounds cooler than saying your type is "men who treat me like crap". The term sugar-coats the reality. The truth is, if you date someone who treats you like shit, you will feel like shit. And if he was good enough, you wouldn't have to romanticize him.

Ultimately, there are gaps in your self-esteem that mean you don't believe you deserve better, and this is where we build that self-esteem back up. If you have been starved of love from others, no wonder you will exchange anything to be loved. I used to be like that too. I would have given everything to be wanted. I would give up my music taste, my friends, my career or any personality trait that made me *me*, just to be loved and secure that label of "girlfriend". I am reminded of this whenever I put my phone on shuffle and an hour-long house music track starts to play. For a year, I changed my music taste for a man because I wasn't confident enough to say I just really wanted to listen to 'Call Me Maybe' on repeat. It's so easy to think that if we are with someone who can remind us that we are good enough or lovable, that wound will heal, but it won't because that person didn't create the wound. Someone else did. You need to recognize the impact that person had on you in order to realize that they were wrong. People are not medicine. They are not cures for your childhood wounds, nor for your insecurity or loneliness. Whatever problems you have when you are single you will bring into a relationship, whether it's just one night or longer-term.

Once the change started happening though, there is a broken-heartedness that occurs when you start dating emotionally available people after a string of "bad boys". To this day, I'm sometimes taken off guard when someone is a decent human, and it's often in the small things – like when they FaceTime you when they say they will, or when you end it and it doesn't end in abuse. Your heart breaks that you didn't know what was out there, that you didn't know you deserved better. Your heart breaks for your younger self who wanted love so badly that they would turn themselves into a pretzel to appease the other person. And you will want to grieve for all the times you put your heart in the hands of someone who shouldn't have been trusted, and you put your body in harm's way because someone who didn't deserve to raise you taught you the wrong definition of love.

When we date "bad boys", they make it easy to never look at our own behaviour. They are always behaving worse than we are, so we never see how we are playing a part in the dance. We spend so much time analyzing and blaming the other person in our relationships, but it's important we look in the mirror. It's time for you to take accountability for your side of the street. You are your greatest asset and it's time you started acting like it. You need to know what you bring to the table. Until you do that, you will continue to look to others to deem you worthy enough. We focus on who we want to be *with* in a relationship, but instead I want you to ask yourself who you want to *be* in a relationship.

Forget Me Nots

- A consistent, reliable and emotionally available person will feel unfamiliar, so it's easy to convince yourself they are boring or push them away

WOULD YOU DATE YOU?

- If you date someone who treats you like shit, you will feel like shit
- If he was good enough, you wouldn't have to romanticize him
- If you have been starved of love, no wonder you will exchange anything to be loved

---

Take Action Toolkit: Would you date you? Truly and honestly ask yourself this question. I urge you to stay away from anything about your physical appearance, as we always place too much emphasis on that area. Instead, I want you to put yourself into a hypothetical partner's shoes and see if you would choose yourself. Here are some prompts to help:

- What would you find most difficult about dating yourself?
- In which moments can you be the most challenging?
- How do you make it hard to communicate with you?

It's OK if, at this point, you wouldn't date you. When I first did this exercise, I didn't want to date me either. The first thing I realized when I asked myself this question is as soon as any conflict arises, I get defensive, and that makes it impossible to get resolution from the conflict. But doing this exercise made me aware of this. Today, I can say I don't do this anymore because I worked on it. This exercise highlights all your blind spots and gives you a list to work on to make you someone who you would actually want to date, and if you want to date you, you can go on dates with the energy of knowing you are someone who is great to date.

How Do I Stop Getting So Attached?

For a feeling to exist, there is a thought that precedes it. If you've ever been totally besotted with someone on a first date, pay attention to what you are saying to yourself. Have you ever been guilty of foreseeing the future, imagining them meeting your friends or even visualizing your next date and playing in your mind all your future conversations, complete with how you would reply? You are getting feelings from this fantasy in your head because your brain doesn't know the difference between real and imagined. The same way that writing on this page about you biting into a lemon will make your mouth salivate. Your body has reacted to you simply imagining biting the lemon. So when you are imagining your wedding, your body is creating appropriate feelings for the wedding stage of a relationship, yet the reality is you have only just gone on the first date. This is why we have to be so careful with what our mind is doing. You are suffering more in your imagination. Falling in love with a fantasy is painful, and it prevents you from enjoying the reality in front of you. If you are unable to see the reality, then you are unable to spot the warning signs you should be noticing in the early stages of dating.

I was such a culprit of fantasizing about people. Three days after my break-up from my first boyfriend, I attended a twenty-first birthday party held at a massive estate. It was there I met a mutual friend who I ended up stargazing with while we told each other the most personal and intimate details of our life. He told me he had depression and I told him I had PTSD. At the time, I thought it was romantic. It's not. It's intense and oversharing. The next morning, after we all slept in tents, we said goodbye. Unsure if I would ever hear from him again, and given my fragile state post-break-up, I was happy for it to be just one magical night. He got a later train, ending up next to my bully from my old school, who spent the entire train journey from Durham to London telling him all the worst stories about me aged 11 to 17, only for him to get off the train, add me on Facebook and tell me about their conversation. He reassured me that he didn't believe a word and that even if the stories are true, for every awful teenage story of me, he had 10 that were much worse and could trump any embarrassment I was feeling.

The next few months, we had nine-hour-long Skype sessions. I would come back from work, log on to Skype and talk to him until the sun rose, only to go back to work with no sleep. Our late nights would be filled with us dissecting every single song on Taylor Swift's *1989* (the album had just come out and he was a fan) and him filling our conversations with compliments like "You are forever fascinating." He even peppered in some comments that allowed my fantasies to truly run wild. When telling him about how I had failed my driving test seven times on automatic, he joked, "Remind me never to let you drive my car."

"When would I get a chance to drive your car?"

"When you come up and visit me in Durham and meet my parents."

"When would that be?"

"I don't know, at some point. Michelle, I'am pretty sure I'm going to marry you and therefore, you will meet my parents eventually."

Swooonnnnn. Oh, wait – did I forget to mention that in all these months, we hadn't met up in person? I could excuse him because he lived in Durham and I lived in London, but that would be conveniently forgetting that in the three months we were chatting, he had come down to London twice and failed to mention it, only for me to see it on his Snapchat. You are breaking your own heart every time you exaggerate your importance in their life.

Eventually, I called him out on it.

> Hey gorgeous! I'm so sorry, I was actually going to say that I'm coming down to London and I've actually planned the most incredible date for us. It's a three-parter but you are only allowed to know the first part. The rest is a surprise xx

Cue him forgetting to tell me that he couldn't make it down to London because he needed his wisdom teeth removed. It would take nine months to eventually go on our first proper date and the only thing that sustained the whole nine months was holding on to the idea that this guy had so much potential. I tell you this story to show you that I am not coming from a place of superiority. I come from a place of "I've been there" – and don't worry, I have done worse, so please learn from me. Fantasies can be a lot more insidious than this, though. I once went on a date at Gordon's Wine Bar (like everyone else in London), and every time I walk past there, I have to stop myself from playing a story in my head of bumping into that guy again and what I would say. It would often start with recalling memories from the date, then it would evolve to how I would have handled things differently, namely him crying on the first date and then eventually imagining a future conversation. I didn't even like him – I was the one who ended it – but my brain will still try to play out that "what if?" if I don't stay conscious.

In many ways, the art of staying out of fantasy is about improving your skill in mindfulness. I know the word "mindfulness" can elicit dread, especially with how it's been capitalized on, but all mindfulness means is staying present in the moment. In order to create a fantasy, you either have to go into the future or go into the past. The way to stop this is by disrupting the pattern. First, you have to get conscious of when you are doing it and the more you catch yourself doing this, the faster you notice. Then do something different in your mind. Allow yourself to fantasize positively about something else in your life. For me, I fantasize about a goal I want to achieve, like wanting my own talk show one day, and I will let my mind run wild and imagine every little detail of it. This is a helpful way to use your imagination because by being able to feel how you would feel when you achieve your goal, you can create motivation to work towards it. Another technique to prevent you from fantasizing is one from my own life coach, Michelle Zelli. She suggests allocating one hour a day where you are allowed to let your mind go. The trick with this is that at least you are doing it intentionally, and it boundaries the time-wasting that often comes with endless fantasies. Whichever technique works for you, the goal is not to get ahead of where the relationship is, stay out of your head and, if on a date, focus on the person in front of you.

If you have ever found that there are some people who you fantasize about more, and some you fantasize about less, this is not a coincidence. For example, with the date mentioned above, I remember responding compassionately when he started crying, yet when I ended things he had such an intense level of anger that I never understood. When your mind is given a question that doesn't have an answer, it will fill the gap. Our brains are meaning-making machines. That's why when you show your brain an inkblot, it will see a rabbit that isn't there. If you start a story and don't give your mind an ending, it will finish it for you. The problem is the ending it has created is an illusion. The only reason you fantasize about a person is that the reality of them is not good enough. As the wonderful author Abigail Mann once told me, it's like you've gilded them. You've covered them in gold, but the reality underneath is just an old wooden chair. It looks fancy from the outside, but it's just for show. The book *He's Just Not That Into You* (Greg Behrendt and Liz Tuccillo, 2004) states "When it comes to men, deal with them as they are, not how you'd like them to be." Stop focusing on who they have the potential of being, and focus on the person they actually are. It's this idea of potential that also keeps you hanging on to hope that you can change another person.

The easiest fantasies to tell are about the past and entertaining the idea of "what if?" The media have even created phrases to help you:

"The one who got away"
High on the list of what I look for in the people I want to date is "actually wants to date me"; therefore, if they got away, it's a clear no.

"Right guy, wrong time"
It's a fallacy. If it's the right person, then time would not be an issue.

"Unrequited love"
When you continue pursuing someone when they have told you no, it's called harassment. There is nothing romantic about ignoring their no.

"Hopeless romantic"
Seeing the good in everyone means you ignore the reality.

"Mixed signals"
This is a misnomer, because it implies that there are both positive and negative signals, when actually the whole signal is just inconsistency and unreliability.

It's not just the narratives we tell ourselves about our love lives, but also what we tell ourselves about how lovable we are and even the role we play within our friendship group. For years, I was the person in my friendship group with a messy love life. I was the one who entertained the group with all my first-date stories. The problem was, the more I laughed along about my chaotic love life, the more I bought the narrative that I was the fuck-up in the romance department and my love life was never going to improve. It was a self-fulfilling prophecy. My friends outlined how badly they expected my love life to go and, being the people-pleaser I was, I lived up to that expectation. Be wary of what you say about yourself – your unconscious mind is listening. Everything we tell ourselves is a story. Once, at university, my housemates and I sat around the kitchen table having one of those random hungover conversations about what we would want written on our tombstones. I responded so quickly they were shocked, but what they didn't know is I had already spent months thinking about it the previous year when I was bedridden in hospital for six weeks. My answer: "She was loved."
My friend laughed.
"What's so funny?"
"Why would you write something so obvious? Of course you are loved. That's like a minimum requirement of life."
What I didn't realize at the time is I wanted that on my tombstone because for years I never felt lovable. The pieces of information that I had from my life had helped me build a story that I was "hard to love". Surrounding yourself with people who

treat you like you are something to be tolerated will do that. How you describe yourself is very telling and, as I upgraded my friendships, I started saying I was "good in small doses" and then eventually made it to "You have to get to know me to love me." Most recently, I found the words "I'll win them over. I'm easy to love when I want to be" coming out of my mouth. Sometimes personal development will kick you in the teeth and you won't know how much you've changed until you have.

The fact is that all of these phrases are stories, positive or negative, and they build your perception of yourself and your self-image. I was never hard to love and neither are you. We were just surrounded by people who didn't know how to love. I was reminded of this the last time I introduced someone I was dating to family friends. They turned to him and said, "I don't know how you date her, she's so difficult." When you were younger, you couldn't leave. But in adulthood, you can, and you get to choose who to surround yourself with. He responded, "If she was difficult to date, I wouldn't date her", and put his arm around me. We get to choose people who remind us how lovable we are each and every day. You get to write your own story, one that is based on reality and one that empowers you and gets you excited to date.

Forget Me Nots

- For a feeling to exist, there is a thought that precedes it
- In order to create a fantasy, you either have to go into the future or go into the past, and to stop fantasies you need to stay in the present
- The only reason you fantasize about him is that the reality of him is not good enough
- Unconsciously, we think it's the safer option when we settle, but a person you settled for can still dump you

Take Action Toolkit: In order to ask for your needs to be met in dating, you need to be aware of what they are. The Center for Nonviolent Communication (USA) has created a Needs Inventory to help you. They state clearly: "The following list of needs is neither exhaustive nor definitive. It is meant as a starting place to support anyone who wishes to engage in a process of deepening self-discovery and to facilitate greater understanding and connection between people."

Connection: acceptance, affection, appreciation, belonging, cooperation, communication, closeness, community, companionship, compassion, consideration, consistency, empathy, inclusion, intimacy, love, mutuality, nurturing, respect/self-respect, safety, security, stability, support, to know and be known, to see and be seen, to understand and be understood, trust, warmth

Physical well-being: air, food, movement/exercise, rest/sleep, sexual expression, safety, shelter, touch, water

Honesty: authenticity, integrity, presence

Play: joy, humour

Peace: beauty, communion, ease, equality, harmony, inspiration, order

Autonomy: choice, freedom, independence, space, spontaneity

Meaning: awareness, celebration of life, challenge, clarity, competence, consciousness, contribution, creativity, discovery, efficacy, effectiveness, growth, hope, learning, mourning, participation, purpose, self-expression, stimulation, to matter, understanding

What if I Am Too Ugly to Date?

I spent most of my teenage years believing that I was too ugly to date. This belief might have originated from the first time I wore a bikini and my scar-covered stomach was stared at with shock, pity and horror, or it could have been the time a family friend told me that no boy would like me at my size. It might even have been when my best friend in university set me up with a guy who had a heart surgery because "He has a scar too." Whatever incident created this mindset, or perhaps the accumulation of those events, it was a formidable belief and one that dictated most of my early experiences of dating. It's why, when we had the opportunity to socialize with boys in school, I opted out. Until, one day, I accepted that I was ugly and I was going to stop trying to change it. I was 15, so excuse the bluntness of this thought, but it occurred to me that ugly people live fulfilled lives all the time. Ugly people can be successful and ugly people even fall in love – far from a body-positive thought, but genuinely where my body confidence began. I accepted I was ugly and decided the bigger problem was the time and energy I was wasting on trying to change that, whether it be entertaining the idea of plastic surgery to remove my surgery scars or hatching a plan to lose weight. I decided beauty was not on the cards for me but realized that even if I wasn't in the beauty elite, I still could enjoy my life and that being ugly did not cross off anything I wanted, not even marriage.

Since I am not 15 anymore, I would alter the above statements, but the sentiment rings true. First of all, I truly believe no human is ugly and that whatever I thought "ugly" was at 15 was simply outside of the beauty ideal. When I stopped trying to improve my looks, I realized there were parts of me that I loved that had nothing to do with my appearance. After all, we are so much more than our bodies. Within the dating world, there is too much emphasis on aesthetics. They are blamed if you can't get a date, a date doesn't work out or even if you've been in a decade-long marriage and it ends. When we face rejection, because of our pre-existing insecurities about our appearance, we deduce "It's because I'm ugly", with no reason or evidence for this belief.

One of my clients demonstrated this in one of our sessions when, after a third date, the woman she was dating ghosted. She had decided it was because she was fat and Black. I asked her how her appearance had changed between the second and third date. She said it hadn't and so I asked why she had deduced that the reason was her appearance. She stayed silent. Her beliefs have validity, they aren't founded on nothing but in this instance, they didn't apply. If someone is fatphobic and racist, they wouldn't ghost you after a third date, they wouldn't even go on the first date. Of course, we live in a society that has told her time and time again that being fat and Black equates to a rubbish love life, so it's understandable that it is her go-to assumption – but the fact is, it is an assumption. You don't know how they feel, so you project how you feel. Since you don't know the reason they ended it, you fill in the gap with why you would have done so. Inherent in ghosting is the fact that you won't know their reason; whatever conclusion you draw and reason you give for their disappearance is pure fiction. The reason you choose to settle on is often the loudest message that society has passed on to you. Since we live in a world where racism, ableism, homophobia, fatphobia and discrimination exist, the reason you choose is likely down to your differences to the beauty ideal. It's important we find a balance between listening to people's lived experience and not affirming the lies that society wants us to believe about desirability. This paragraph is a summary of an hour-long conversation but essentially, if we take their opinion as fact, then they win!

These stories you tell yourself mean that you see failure where failure doesn't exist. If you go on a date and decide someone isn't for you, that's a success because it means you didn't waste your time entertaining something that wasn't for you. If you go on three first dates in a row and none amount to a second date, then you are honing your skill of figuring out what you are looking for. Stop trapping yourself in a story that serves no purpose. When we are hurt, the story we make up will likely be the one that will hurt us the most. Since we live in a society that profits from our insecurities, particularly in terms of our looks, it becomes the easy default. Romcoms don't help. They teach you that in order to bag that man, you need to undergo the classic physical transformation. Think *The Princess Diaries*, *Grease*, *My Big Fat Greek Wedding*, *She's All That* or *Pretty Woman*. Not a single one emphasizes that you can change your dating life by improving the way you think and your mentality around dating.

By blaming your lack of success in your dating life on your body – whether that be your size, race, disability or anything else that is a factor that you cannot change – you are putting your love life out of your own control. This is why it is important to fact-check ourselves when something ends and we deduce it's because of the way we look. A relationship can't exist on aesthetics alone. If it does, it's not a quality one. Choose a person merely on looks and a few years in, you'll be craving good conversation. Regardless of how you feel about your appearance, looks will only get you past the first date. After that, what makes a first date turn into a second date is a lot more complex than aesthetics. It's a lot scarier to consider it could be something about your personality or the way you acted on a date.

This is demonstrated most in the discussion of "types". Are they into blondes or tall, dark and handsome? Let's be honest, no one is going to say their type is fat, mixed race, and covered in scars, are they? All a type really means is who you have dated in the past, and that isn't necessarily correlated to who we date in the future. When we think it does, we find ourselves asking questions like "Have you ever dated a plus-size person before?" as a way to invalidate their attraction to us. We can't believe their interest and therefore we undermine it. Can you imagine if we did the same with personalities? If I'm not going to check if they've dated an ambitious person before, why would I check if they've dated a mixed-race person before?

You believing you are ugly is not your fault. It has been drilled into you since you were born. It was an intentional plan of the diet, fashion and beauty industries. Look at most diet adverts that end with ". . . and then I found the love of my life". Adverts perform better when they trigger emotions; not only does it sell more products, but it also keeps your attention on the advert. By adding this at the end, it will tap into your fear around being single. It sells you the promise of a solution to your problems, so if you don't act on it and buy the product, it's your own fault. Once you realize that people are profiting off your insecurity, it awakens a real sense of anger. If you don't have insecurities, don't worry, they will create one. They create terms like "hip dips" so they can sell you a product. Cellulite only became a problematic part of our body when Nicole Ronsard wrote an article in an issue of *Vogue* in 1973. Before that, it was just a normal part of our thigh. But the most successful businesses create a solution to a problem, so Nicole created a problem. Oh, and by the way, she was an owner of a beauty salon that, no surprise here, sold cellulite treatments. They can't profit off people thinking they are beautiful or loving their body so they capitalize on your fear of being alone by selling you the message that your body is the problem.

Everywhere you look, people are buying this message! We are seeing it at the moment when it comes to Pete Davidson. Everyone's jaws are dropping on the floor at how he can date such attractive women, and no one even pauses to consider how offensive it is to be writing articles that it would be so unthinkable for a person to find him attractive. It's been happening to plus-size women for years too. Why do you think people were so flabbergasted when Lizzo had the apparent gall to hit on someone like Chris Evans? We bought the "thin equals beauty" lie. Even if you go on TikTok and you see a muscly man with a plus-size woman, all it takes is a quick scroll through the comments section to hear about how he's a saint and she's punching. The reason we stare at couples like this in shock is because society has taught us like should date like, especially in regards to weight. It's nonsense. Short people don't only date short people. Asians don't only date Asians. It becomes even more insidious if you consider stories like Pierce Brosnan's marriage to Keely Shaye Smith. They have been together for 20 years. Yet the narrative in the media is how amazing Pierce – who played James Bond and was once voted Sexiest Man Alive – is for staying with his wife through ageing and weight gain. These are full, complex humans we are talking about, and it is so dehumanizing that all that is stripped away and all they can focus on is their outer meat sack. Keely's appearance might have changed, but she was beautiful then and is beautiful now. If we didn't live in a society that put certain criteria in a hierarchy, we would be able to see the beauty in both.

More than that, the underlying message is that we should only be with someone for their outsides and if that changes, we

are entitled to end the relationship because that's not the con-
tract we signed. Except it is. You signed up to marry a human
being not a body. You don't want someone who only likes you
for your appearance. There is no part of a marriage agreement
that commits to maintaining the same appearance. The other
underlying message in all the articles about this couple is that
Brosnan is a hero for continuing to love his wife. This is such
a gross message. You do not get applause for loving someone
bigger than yourself. You are not a better person for dating
someone outside the conventional beauty norm.

We use phrases like "letting yourself go" as if the norm is to
look the same as we did two decades ago. Unless you are able
to maintain the same appearance as when you were in your
teens and defy the ageing process, you have "let yourself go". It
is another marketing scheme in order to market "anti-ageing"
products. As I say in my TEDx Talk, "The alternative to ageing
is literally dying. Ageing is a privilege." Once you start looking
at all of this as a big moneymaking scheme, it suddenly makes
sense. It's why the beauty ideal has to be constantly changing.
Take, for example, bushy eyebrows. When I was growing up,
I was made fun of for my bushy Jewish eyebrows. They were
called "caterpillars". I even had an older girl pin me down
and try to pluck them, and was constantly teased for having
a monobrow. Now, bushy eyebrows are in. Why? Because if
they are always changing the trend, then no one can ever truly
fit the beauty ideal and that means everyone becomes a potential customer. Money will always explain it! My insecurity was
transformed into the most coveted thing – and my eyebrows
didn't change at all.

Even the people who fit the beauty ideal are constrained by
the fact they have the continuous fear of falling outside it. This
is amplified by how we segment women into categories even

further. It's not just a standard of beauty you are trying to attain, it's different types of beauty. So yes, you might be cute, but are you sexy? Within my school, there was a differentiator between whether you were "girl hot" or "guy hot", which made it damn near impossible to fulfil both. I was 15 years old when that became a thing in my school, which highlights the broadest message: no matter how hard you try, you will never be good enough.

We have all heard that beauty is in the eye of the beholder, but it truly is. Want proof? Ever looked back at old photos of yourself with your ex and wondered how you ever found them attractive? Or have you ever looked back at old photos of yourself and realized how drop-dead gorgeous you were, but you could never see it at the time? Beauty is subjective and it is affected by our moods, our past, the beauty ideal, our media, our exes and our social circle – it is impossible for us to all have the same version of beauty. If you aren't angry yet, then let's take a look at how those beliefs have penetrated our society so deeply that the impact of them has no bounds. On the further end of the scale, it leads to cases like a 17-year-old in Canada who was sexually assaulted by 49-year-old Carlo Figaro. Judge Jean-Paul Braun, however, thought this was unfathomable because she was a "little overweight but has a pretty face" and that she may have been a "bit flattered" by the attention because "maybe it was the first time he showed interest in her". Forgetting the fact that sexual assault is not about attractiveness but about power and control, it demonstrates how deep those beliefs run. Once we connect all of these things as being related, we start to see it is not really about beauty at all. On an individual level, we can't fall for the lies that are fed to us as we then perpetuate a system that has gone on for far too long.

Part of the trap these industries have created is telling us that if we see our own beauty, we are self-obsessed and vain.

It's why women in particular are conditioned to shoot down compliments for fear of looking arrogant if they respond with "thank you". It strikes fear in people that they might actually see their beauty too. Because if you don't see your beauty, you are still vulnerable to be capitalized on. When we respond to compliments about our face with "No, my face looks so tired" or, when it's our outfit, "This dress? Oh, it's an old, tatty thing", we are honoured with feeling like we are humble. Fuck humility! Stop playing small and insulting yourself so as not to bruise people's egos. Do you think it's cute to not know how beautiful you are? Because it's not. We shame women for not being confident and then people have the nerve to call us self-righteous if we agree with their positive assessment. They will say "Oh, she's so into herself", and I always think "As she should be!" If you aren't into yourself, why should anyone else be?

The biggest turning point in my love life came when a friend of mine described the scars on my stomach as a "dickhead filter". As my friend George said in my first book, *Am I Ugly?*, "Your scars are just a filtering process for all the douchebags in the world. You're lucky. Most girls don't have that and they have to find out the hard way, months down the line." We are fed the illusion that having an appearance that makes us different in any way will limit our dating pool, but I want to challenge this. Even if I was completely white, I would still find racist comments a turn-off. Even if I was thin, I wouldn't want to date someone who body shames fat women. Even if I had no scars of my own, I would not go on another date with someone who stares at a person with visible differences – therefore, it actually doesn't limit my dating pool. The only difference is a white person would find out on date 10 that they were dating a racist, not date one. If I fit the beauty ideal, yes, I would get more matches on a dating app and get hit on in the street more.

More people would ask for my number, but I'd likely have just as many third dates.

You attract more people when you fit the beauty ideal and so you have more junk to sort through. It's like your email inbox: if you are getting 100 emails a day, it takes more time and effort to sort through them to figure out what's actually important than if you got two emails a day. But isn't it better to have more choice? No. If you are only replying to two emails, the 98 others are just time-wasters. We tell ourselves that if you fit the beauty ideal, you would attract higher-quality people, and this is false. People who fit the beauty ideal don't just attract kind, compassionate people, they attract everyone. Yes, the higher level of attention is nice, but unless you have an accurate filtering system, you will keep the dickheads longer than you should, which leaves you with the same problem that people outside of the beauty ideal have.

And George was right. Unfortunately, if you do not have a body like mine, it means people find out later down the road when they gain weight and get dumped years into a relationship or their health circumstances change and their partner bails rather than holding their hand through it. If you can't cope with the scars from my past, how the hell would you manage if I actually ended up in hospital again? As Gary Younge says in Natasha Lunn's book *Conversations on Love*, "if you're going to crumble at the first sign of gunfire, keep walking." Life doesn't owe you easy. If someone can't handle something as insignificant as weight gain, what makes you think they are going to be any support through parental loss, miscarriage, financial issues or mental health difficulties?

I let the world convince me that my dating pool was small and the most harmful consequence of that is I stayed with people who treated me like crap. I stayed because I thought I was lucky to have *any* relationship. Beggars can't be choosers and I should just accept what I was given. I thought I had no right to have standards, let alone a choice in who I wanted to date, because if I was chosen, I should just be grateful. I bought the lie that if anyone could tolerate my body, it was because my personality compensated for it because, well . . . look at me. Yes, damn right! Look at me! I bring a lot to the table, so come meet me there or be gone. When I'm told I'm punching now, I let it fuel my inner rebel. Let them look at your relationship and question why your partner would be interested in you. Let them underestimate you. Let them stare. The day I woke up and started acting as hot as I am was the day I realized everything society had taught me was a lie. You need to find a person who makes you feel that way – and run as fast as you can from people who make you feel ugly. I had to go out in the dating world to see that for myself. My dating life became the evidence that I needed. Any time I actually dated my standard, it made me question why I ever did anything else. Being different to the beauty ideal does not make you hard to love. You never have to change what you look like in order to be worthy or deserving of a great love life.

Forget Me Nots

- When we make up stories, particularly when we are feeling rejection and hurting, we will make up the story that will hurt us most
- A relationship can't exist on aesthetics alone and if it does, it's not a quality one
- If you don't see your beauty, you are still vulnerable to being capitalized on
- You never have to change what you look like in order to be worthy or deserving of a great love life

Take Action Toolkit: What story have you built in your head about your love life and your ability to love and be loved? What role do you play in your friendship group when it comes to love life? Have you been pigeonholed as the one with a successful career but no love life? For you to create your own story, you need to identify your old story. Answer these questions unconsciously and let it flow freely out of you. Set a timer for 15 minutes and write as much as you can.

- How would you describe your love life?
- What is the story you tell yourself about your past love life?
- What is the story you tell yourself about your love life right now?
- When is the story you tell yourself about your future love life?
- Do you think you are lovable?

Look at what you've written and circle anything that stands out. In particular, notice phrases that you have used repeatedly. For example, if the phrase "waste of time" is written a lot, circle it. This identifies a limiting belief and it begs the question: who taught you that you are not worth someone's time, and time spent with you was a waste? It's not always going to be overt in the exact same phrasing, but it could be in behaviour. For example, when you bother them when they're busy, you feel apologetic. We are going to unlearn this and fact-check it.

- Who taught you this limiting belief?
- How did they teach you this belief?
- What other events happened in your life that confirmed this to be true?
- How has that affected how you act in your love life?

Now it is time to create your own story! If you find it difficult to answer the following questions, then imagine yourself as someone who loves you and answer it through their eyes. If you struggle to find someone in your life who you could pick, you can pick a god, a pet, an angel or even a hypothetical future partner who loves you. What would they say? We need to distinguish fact from fiction.

Fact: My caregiver was unable to spend time with me.
Fiction: I am a waste of time.
Alternative meaning: They were unable to spend time with me because they were working multiple jobs.

Look beneath the meaning you have given it and create alternative meanings. When the word "evidence" is used, as it will be in the next set of questions, that means you have an opportunity to fact-check it. Examples include "People say yes to going on a date with me", "They have chosen to allocate their time to getting to know me", "If they didn't want to go, they wouldn't". Look at reality and take your subjective opinion out of it.

- What is the truth behind the limiting belief?
- What evidence do you have that the previous limiting belief is untrue?
- What would you like to believe instead?
- If you were to look back at your past through a compassionate lens, what would you tell your younger self?
- In the best-case scenario, when you imagine your future love life, what do you see?
- Who is the person you need to be in order for this to become a reality?

Am I Ready to Date?

Whether you've never been on a date or coming off a dating detox, dipping your toe back in the dating pool can be scary and overwhelming. It is tempting to convince ourselves that we aren't ready, and potentially never will be. What does it actually mean to be ready to date? This speaks to a broader issue around the concept of being "ready". A differential between successful people and people who live with regrets is that one wastes too much time waiting to be ready. Successful people know that readiness is a state that will never come and so they do something anyway. I remember when I was first asked to give a TEDx Talk, I thought I wasn't ready and that I needed more time to get better at public speaking. I was so tempted to say no, but I said yes anyway and told myself I would figure it out later. You can read all the books on public speaking, but at some point, you have to get on the stage. The same goes with dating.

In a culture that continually emphasizes that you need to love yourself before you love anyone else, it's tempting to convince ourselves we have not achieved enough self-love. We are in a perpetual state of growth and we cannot let the thought of us being better in the future be a reason we stand still. The danger is that if we are constantly aspiring to be better, we can get a form of perfectionism where we never take action because we feel we are not our best version of ourselves yet. Self-help books are guilty of perpetuating this. You are not just a self-improvement project, you are a living, breathing human who is going to make mistakes. In fact, sometimes I will decide to make what I call "consciously irresponsible" decisions. We are all human, and life is no fun when we are always doing the right thing. So once in a while, I will date a guy who I know is not good for me – and my only rule is I have to stay conscious. The last time I did this in my dating life, I told my life coach, "I know this is going to end disastrously, but I want to have a bit of fun. I'm curious to see how this is going to play out and I'm prepared for the fallout if this ends painfully." Try, experiment, fail. It's all part of the process. Believing dating should always be easy is a fantasy of the uninitiated.

When we say "ready", we often mean an absence of fear or any uncomfortable emotions. That is unrealistic. If you are waiting for certainty in life, you are going to be waiting a long time. If you are only willing to date if you only get good outcomes, that's delusional. No book will protect you from the hurt, pain, rejection and potential loss that occurs in our love lives. If you return to your love life with the expectation that your improved self-esteem, stronger boundaries and higher standards are going to immunize you from any painful emotions, then you need to lower your expectations. Even the best relationships will experience hurt. Choosing to date or engage with any human, romantically or platonically, involves the risk of getting hurt, and within romantic relationships, it is almost inevitable. Realizing that life will never provide you certainty will liberate you. Instead, build your certainty in the fact that no matter what happens in your love life, you will be OK.

There is only so much you can learn without actually going on a date. Dating puts a mirror up and shows you all the old programming that you still have left inside you. It has a way of showing you the things you thought you had processed, but which aren't completely gone. Within that, there is the opportunity to heal even further. Self-love and romantic love do not oppose each other, and you do not need one before the other.

They actually strengthen each other. Any time I was rejected within my dating life, I was faced with a decision to be who they wanted me to be or stand behind who I already was. It forced me to always have my own back and love the current version of myself. There is no such thing as "perfectly healed", but even if there were, and I entered the dating world as the most healed version of myself, I still believe dating would have thrown things in my face that I was not expecting. Dating is tough – but so are you. It healed me in many ways, whether it was teaching myself how to be vulnerable or how to feel good enough to allow myself to receive the love I was given. Dating will trigger you by bringing up old stuff you thought you had left behind. But when you realize that you are going to survive that too, you move forward with even more confidence.

As a culture, we have a very all-or-nothing style of dating: swiping intensely and then wanting to delete the app because you have not achieved the result you want. Instead of a cycle of deleting apps and reinstalling them, find a middle ground. For me, it shifted on a weekly, sometimes even daily, basis. If my mental health is rubbish, I won't swipe on apps. If I am going through a particularly busy period, then again, dating apps are not top of my priority list. There have even been longer periods: I didn't date for three months in the pandemic, because I was seeing my parents regularly and dating would mean exposing them to more health risk. If I am craving attention, then I give it to myself first and turn to people who I know I can trust and am safe with. Then I will return to dating when my self-esteem won't get immediately hooked to another person. If the ending of a relationship or someone I was dating hurt more than I expected, I also take time away to process that so that I don't transfer it on to the next person. If I'm talking to someone on an app and an inconvenient period comes up, I communicate that.

Hey! Sorry for the late reply. To be honest, I've been struggling to cope with the world opening back up and I'm juggling a lot of work at the moment, so I really need to focus on me and what I have on my plate right now xx

Ah, OK, that's fine. Maybe we can talk again when you feel more yourself and are used to things being open :)

Thanks for understanding xx

Make dating work for you. Dating selfishly means you don't need to be beholden to it and you can fit it into your schedule at your own convenience – as long as you communicate. You don't need to dedicate a whole evening to it; instead, find the gaps in time, whether during your commute or during the ad breaks of your favourite TV show. You don't need to see it as a job. You are allowed to swipe for a minute a day and respond to messages in your own time. You are allowed to pause without feeling like you are quitting or halting your progress. The most progress I made in my dating life was often in my pauses, both the short ones and the longer dating detox.

There is no finite moment that will determine that you are ready to date. It doesn't work like that. When you are "ready to date" will be different for everyone. For me, it's always felt like curiosity. For you, it could be a feeling of missing something in your life or a craving for more connection and intimacy. It could even be that you want sex for an evening and fulfilling that urge is what encourages you to get on a dating app. There is no wrong way to jump back into the dating pool, and it's OK if you want to just dip a toe in first and see whether you like it. There is no better way of knowing if you are ready than trying it.

Forget Me Nots

- Choosing to date or engage with any human, romantically or platonically, involves the risk of getting hurt, and within romantic relationships, there is almost a certainty of it
- Make dating work for you – you don't need to be beholden to it or see it as a job; you are allowed to swipe for a minute a day and respond to messages in your own time
- You are allowed to pause without halting your progress
- There is no wrong way to jump back into the dating pool, and it's OK if you want to just dip a toe in first and see whether you like it

Take Action Toolkit: It is your job to know why someone should date you. Let's make sure you know what you bring to the table. This exercise is one of my favourites and was first suggested by my own life coach, Michelle Zelli. For this exercise, you need to write down 100 reasons why someone would want to date you. Sit there for as long as it takes to get to 100. If it takes three hours, it takes three hours. You are worth investing three hours in your self-development. If you give up before you get to 100, what are you telling yourself about your dating life? That you are worth giving up on? Absolutely not! You must be the most committed to the fact that you are dateable. Only put in as much energy as you want others to put into you!

WOULD YOU DATE YOU?

....
....
....
....
....
....
....
....
....
....
....
....
....
....
....
....
....
....
....
....
....
....
....
....
....
....
....
....
....
....
....
....
....
....

Chapter 5

Show the Everyday You, Not the Best You

How to Be Empowered on Dating Apps

Where Is the Best Place to Meet People?

This first time I heard about dating apps was, oddly enough, from my dad. He was flicking through a newspaper that had an article on Tinder (and the dangers of it) when he asked me if I had ever heard of it. I told him no and he responded, "Good, because it sounds dangerous", and nothing more was said. I was just about to go back to university for my final year. Upon my return, one of my friends announced that over the summer she had gotten into a relationship. Confused that I hadn't heard a word about this guy, I asked how they met and she told me he was an exchange student from New York but living in London, who she had matched with on a dating app called Tinder. I recalled my previous conversation with my dad and laughed. "Why do you need a dating app? You are gorgeous." Turns out this phrase would bite me in the arse as all my dates over the next eight years (except for four!) would come from a dating app. She told me to download the app and if I deleted it in a week, I could laugh at her as much as I wanted. If I didn't delete it, I should respectfully shut up. She was right. The app was never deleted and, though I did migrate from Tinder to Happn to Bumble and Hinge, meeting guys off dating apps became my preferred method of dating. My first official date was off a dating app, my first relationship started on a dating app and my latest one did too.

I find there is a clarity to dating-app dates that I never found when meeting people in person. Prior to Tinder, you would hang out with guys, meet them in clubs and even go around to their houses, but you would never use the word "date" for fear of scaring them off, seeming too intense or locking them into a commitment too soon. I remember on one of the four occasions I met a guy in person, we had met at 3 p.m. and it wasn't until 9 p.m., when he reached his hand across the table to hold mine, did I get confirmation that we were on a date. With dating apps, the word "date" loses its intensity. Of course it's a date – it's called a "dating app". I prefer the certainty of knowing that the other person is not only interested romantically but finds me attractive. Your intentions are clear because the line between friendly and romantic is distinct. However, on this date, I was unsure because a friend of mine had asked me to show his friend from America around London while he was busy at work. Was I being his tour guide or was this my friend's plan to set me up? Turns out it was the latter, but it took me six hours to figure it out.

Dating apps work. They do what they say on the tin and if they didn't work, people wouldn't use them. As much as I made my own judgemental comments upon hearing about them for the first time, now, many years on and countless positive experiences on apps later, when I see remarks on dating apps saying, "We should lie about where we met", I internally groan. Even worse, I've seen "Change my mind about ... how shit this app is" on profiles. If you are so ashamed of being on a dating app, then get off it! Why would I waste my time and energy convincing you otherwise? When people say they hate dating apps, it strikes me as peculiar. It's like a business owner saying they hate sending invoices. I have never met anyone who loves sending invoices, but you want money, right? So send the invoice. Want a date? Get on the app. People have bad experiences on dating apps for the same reason that they have bad experiences dating in general. There is nothing to be embarrassed about and considering two years of my twenties was spent in a pandemic, I am beyond grateful for them existing. Yes, we can moan, gripe and complain about all the downsides of dating apps, but meeting people in person wasn't exactly a walk in the park either.

I love that dating apps give us more options. Of course, more choices often mean more complications. But it's better than when people felt they had to stick with the person they were with because if they broke up, there would be no way of meeting someone new. It has helped people who live in rural areas, and those who hate going to bars and clubs have more opportunities. Especially now that there are dating apps for all kinds of niches, people with different sexual orientations often feel safer on apps, and they can change their settings to choose preferences that align. So even if dating apps aren't your cup of tea, it's important we stop belittling them for those who prefer them. If dating apps are trash, then they are a reflection of society. The same people on those apps exist in real life, so it's time we end the stigma around dating apps. Dating apps have had a bad reputation for being a lesser form of dating. We feel we need a cute romcom-style story for our relationship to feel legitimate but, at the end of the day, it doesn't matter how you meet. Where you met goes out the window once you've gone on a second date. It doesn't dictate the longevity, happiness or success of your relationship.

There are positives and negatives to both app and in-person methods of meeting people. Obviously, the main difference is that you don't know each other on an app. You can't ask a friend about them, you have no context about them and there-fore it would be wise, especially from a safety perspective, to take it slower than with someone in your friendship circle who you've known for years. However, that's where the distinction ends, and I see that as a positive. I always hated in university that everyone knew my business. Dating apps avoid that. If it ends, you never have to see them again because you have no mutuals. The downside of that is there is often less accountability for bad behaviour, although I would argue this is debatable. When I was in university, two of my friends slept together, only for him to sleep with another one of our friends two nights later, to then return back to the first one in the course of a week. Of course, this wrecked our friendship group, but knowing we would all find out didn't make him behave any better. If people want to behave badly, they will, regardless of mutual friends. If you met in a club, there is no increased accountability anyway. In fact, the last person I met at a bar was actually the first person to ever stand me up – and yet you never hear people warding off the idea of meeting people in a bar.

If you are adamantly against dating apps and still would like to date, then you need to be willing to be more proactive face-to-face. There is no point moaning about getting no dates, refusing to get an app and then not approaching anyone in person. Even if you are using apps, it doesn't rule out the possibility of meeting someone offline. Why choose either, when you can do both? I remember once being at a bar in the City and walking past a bunch of guys that were all on their phones, swiping on dating apps. It blew my mind that it hadn't occurred to them that they could just turn around and meet people that way, too. It's in those moments that I can't help but agree that dating apps have changed the culture. Dating apps are amazing for increasing convenience, but we can't allow them to make us lazy about interacting with other humans outside of our phones. Even if they didn't talk to other people next to them, at least talk to the people you came with!

When I was single, I made it a point to frequently ask my friends if they had someone to set me up with. I even once asked my followers to set me up with any single guys they knew. There is something liberating about removing the shame around actively pursuing dates, and we shouldn't just ignore the people already in our lives. I often get asked whether dating a friend is a bad idea and whether to risk ruining the friendship. I believe it's always worth that risk. Remove any expectation about the result, but the only way you will know is if you ask. Of course, it's scary but if your friend isn't interested, it's also in their interest to communicate it in the most caring way they can. If your friendship is strong enough, it will withstand rejection. Rejection is always better than regret!

The most important rule about meeting someone in person, and flirting in general, is: "People don't say hi, but everyone says hi back". In fact, this rule also works well in all social contexts, networking included. As much as British people hate talking to strangers and will avoid it at all costs, there is something about the politeness embedded in our society that means people will always respond to you. In a dating context, whether that is a club or even starting a conversation with someone you see at a bus stop, what's great about just saying hi is that you aren't setting yourself up for failure. If they reject you or look at you weirdly, you've got the fall-back of them being the rude one – because, after all, you were just saying hi. Being flirty and being friendly are not too dissimilar. I'm quite an outgoing, talkative person. Without doing anything intentionally, I often make friends quickly because I will talk to anyone, smile at new people and start a conversation with people I walk past regularly, like the cleaner in the building I work in. It's the art of interacting with the people around you. If you wouldn't smile at a cute person walking past you in the street, you are putting too much weight on it. It's the meaning you are assigning to it that's the problem. Remember, it's just a smile!

My go-to place to meet people has always been a club. Before the advent of dating apps, my friends would often joke that it was so obvious when I was "on the pull", because I had a certain move that you could spot across the room. Every time I was teased for this, I would deny it. But since I pride myself on honesty now, I won't lie: I knew what I was doing and it works. I would start by hanging out by the bar. Due to the nature of a university bar, it was easy to start a conversation. You can open a conversation with "What are you drinking?" or "How is your night going?" – it doesn't need to be anything fancy, but the key is to not take how they respond personally. The way I see it is, if they are interested, they will continue the conversation. If they aren't, they will reply in a short way, and if they are a rude person who I wouldn't be interested in anyway, they will respond with a jerk comment. There are certain guys who only treat women with respect when they are attracted to them and it's really helpful when they put themselves in that category early on. If we are both interested and a conversation takes off from there and we are actually getting on, I will touch their arm for a split second. This is why my friends say you can spot it from across the room. It's not some grand move. Anticlimactic? Maybe. Obvious? Absolutely. And there is nothing wrong with that. There is a certain confidence when you make it obvious that you are interested in a person, and it's not the fact that I thought I was the most attractive girl in the room, it was the fact I made myself the most approachable.

The most recent time I met someone in a club, I was with my literary agent. A few of us had just gone to see *Magic Mike Live*, which had led to a spontaneous decision to go for a drink at a club nearby. As the five of us became four, then three and eventually two, I turned to my agent and said, "I want to get with someone." She asked me who I had my eye on and I pointed to a guy in the middle of the dance floor, dancing with his mate and loving life, not caring who was around. If you thought I was unsubtle in my uni days, I've only got worse with age, as he noticed me pointing. My literary agent grabbed my hand and dragged us to dance near them. If you are wondering how I can be so confident to act as if I have the pick of the room, to look around the room and go "I want that one", I don't see it that way. Why would I go after the guy I find second-most attractive in the room if the most attractive guy in the room was there? Rejection still feels like rejection, so might as well get rejected by someone you actually want, not someone you kinda-sorta want. Another way to put it is, as my friend Jenny says: "Act like a VIP, get treated like a VIP."

So as much as I'm human and I was scared, it was already too late. I had pointed, he had seen. We danced next to them and just like the small act of saying hi, I took my glass and cheersed the beer bottle that was in his hand. That graduated into us dancing together and me eventually leaning in to say "What's your name?", and that led to a date a few days later. There really is nothing revolutionary about how you meet someone. You don't need some special pick-up line or charming move that sets you apart from the rest. You just need to break that barrier between strangers who aren't allowed to acknowledge each other. After I clinked his glass, we probably danced alongside them for another half an hour before we started dancing together, and it was another half an hour later, with a few moments of him twirling me around, before I asked his name. I then used another one of my once-secret moves, and looked at his lips while he was talking, stopped talking and let the pause happen. A kiss led to our numbers being swapped and an hour after I left the bar, I had a text asking me out for brunch on Saturday. And while this makes me sound superhuman, I assure you I'm not. About 45 minutes into this, I said to my agent, "I don't think he's interested", but she assured me he was – and it didn't matter anyway, because my agent and I were having a great night and enjoying dancing. We were loving our lives and having it was a fun evening regardless. If I had got a number, it would have just been a bonus!

Forget Me Nots

- People don't say hi, but they always say hi back
- If someone is rude when you put yourself out there, you don't want to date them anyway
- You don't need to be the most attractive, you just need to be the most approachable
- If you are going to be rejected, be rejected going after what you actually want, not second best

---

Take Action Toolkit: Since I don't believe it's a decision between one or the other, there is no harm in increasing the likelihood of you meeting someone in person. Your challenge today is to talk to one new person in real life. The trick to meeting people in person is to practise. I don't believe fun and flirty people are born with it – that side of themselves is just more accessible because they use it more frequently. If you want to get good at meeting people in a bar, then get good at initiating conversations in general. Being a good conversationalist will serve you in more than just your love life. If you want to meet someone in person, you need to talk to people in person. It could be giving a compliment to a stranger walking past you or actually stopping to help the person asking for directions. Take any new interaction as a win!

What Should I Put on My Dating Profile?

Your dating profile is your first impression, and it's worth taking time on. Often, we measure the benchmark of a good dating profile inaccurately. We think the more matches, the better. In fact, doing that will mean you are wasting a lot of time talking to people who were never a match to begin with. We need to focus less on the quantity of matches and more on the quality of them.

Let's get the obvious stuff out of the way. No group photos; this is not *Where's Wally?* We can keep bitching about the fact that people swipe too quickly nowadays, or with one eye on the TV, or we can just accept it for what it is. People swipe as quickly as they tap through Instagram Stories, so if you want them to swipe on you, at least make sure they have seen you. The maximum number of people in a photo should be three. Also, avoid including any siblings or even friends that look similar to you. Remember that this person hasn't met you and some people are awful at facial recognition (I'm one of them!), so remove any confusion. If you can't see your face, it is pointless to include the photo. Keep selfies to a minimum (at most, I include one). I dislike selfies because they rarely show any personality – you are taking a picture for the sake of taking one. You want each photo to demonstrate more of who you are. Selfies rarely do that, but including one in clear lighting is often useful so they can see your face up close. In terms of bikini pictures and topless photos, I am not a fan. I think you should only show as much as you would see if you met someone at a party and, at this stage, it's too soon. If you are looking for a friends-with-benefits situation or a no-strings-attached, one-night-only person, then put as many as you like. It states your intention without having to say it. Photos where you are wearing sunglasses or your face is turned to the side can be the odd photo, but don't include more than one. Try to use recent photos as much as possible, and a real smile is always better than one that was plastered on for the photo.

When we talk about first impressions, the idea is to make a good first impression on as many people as possible. Give up on that and instead aim for accurate impressions! Do not present your best self, present your everyday self. Remember that you want to present an image that you will be able to keep up with. For example, I rarely wear make-up. The most you will see me wearing make-up is twice a week, and I will go to meetings, on dates and give talks make-up free. Therefore, I make sure at least half the pictures on my dating profile are make-up-free. If I was following the advice of presenting your best self, I could easily put up pictures from photo shoots where I have sat in a make-up chair for hours, but that would be pointless. I can't recreate that make-up myself, that's me once a month at most and it's not the me they will be dating. That's me doing my job. Not only that, if I put an image like that on my profile, I would attract the kind of person who wants someone who gets glammed up. If I use my crystal ball and predict the future of this mismatch, it would involve fights where I want to leave the house make-up-free and in my trackies and they go, "Are you really leaving the house like that?", at which point I will hit the roof and be annoyed that I'm dating someone who thinks they have the nerve to dictate how I dress, when all of this would have been avoidable if I had just presented the person I actually am. The person I actually am doesn't want to be waiting for you to get ready and would outright refuse to go to any place that would force me to wear heels. This was demonstrated last week when I had just come out of the shower when

I was told we were leaving for breakfast in 10 minutes. This meant I left the house with wet hair and in an oversized shirt. There are people who would be horrified that I am leaving the house with wet hair. There would also be people who would be happy to wait an extra hour to let me make myself "present-able". One is not wrong and one is not right, it's about being suited, and you can save yourself a lot of hassle if you present that image from the outset.

Presenting the everyday you also means putting realistic photos of you and not the most flattering pictures. I hate the word "flattering" because if we were being honest, flattering means thinner. Your profile is meant to filter out people who don't find you attractive. Your body should not be a reveal; it is not something to hide, and you don't want a profile that misleads the consumer. You are just asking for additional hurt if you do. So that means no Photoshop, no editing, no filters, no airbrushing and no weird angles unless you plan to stay in one angle on the date. Show who you actually are. If they don't like your body, then it's better you find out earlier on so you can get rid of them and find someone who does. There are people who will want to date you at your size. But if you struggle to believe that, what ends up happening is your brain will lie to you and dissuade you from meeting up because "What if I look bigger than my photos?" Avoid this by putting full-body photos of you. If you are really worried about it, it's better to put some photos where you look bigger than you actually are, rather than constantly feeding those worries. This way, you are only dating people who would still be attracted to you if you were 10 pounds heavier or if you gained weight. You want a profile where you can be certain that when people swipe right, they are actually attracted to you, so full-body photos are a must.

I understand the temptation to want to sell your best self on your profile and hide anything you are insecure about, but please let this story convince you otherwise. Here is what it's like to be on the receiving end of it. I once went on a date where he didn't look like his photos. They were clearly him, but him from 10 years ago. He looked so different now that I was standing in front of his table and I hadn't recognized him until he waved at me. He had gained a lot of weight and had gone grey. The sad thing is that I was actually attracted to the guy who I saw in front of me. I find grey hair attractive and I was bigger than he was, but arriving on the date, all I could feel was deceived. If I am standing in front of you and can't recognize you, that's not just a case of him putting his best foot forward, that's catfishing. The deception I felt inside of me was so distracting that I kept losing my train of thought because all I kept thinking was that it was a shame he didn't say who he really was. His appearance wasn't the problem – his insecurity was.

Everyone has insecurities, but because I spent so many years working on my own body image, I find it really hard to date others with bad body image, because it affects my own. I've dated a few guys in the past who have hated what they look like and as a result, there are endless conversations about diet culture and I am unable to provide the constant reassurance of telling them they do actually look good. I know this from experience, so when he asked me on a second date, I declined. The way he asked confirmed what I had suspected: "I don't suppose you want to see me again?" If you are going to ask someone on a second date, do it with confidence. Entering into that conversation with the assumption that they are going to say no is a turn-off. What's frustrating is the fact that I didn't want a second date will likely build his evidence that people aren't attracted to what he actually looks like, when actually it was never about his appearance. There were a number of things about his personality and our senses of humour that weren't a match, but when you are insecure about the way you look, you make everything about that.

The second key to making a successful dating profile is that you want to make it distinguishable. You want to make it so unique that if a friend read your profile and couldn't see any of the pictures, they would know it is you. Again, it will reduce the number of matches, but this isn't Pokémon – you aren't trying to catch them all. You aren't even trying to collect the supposedly "best" ones. You are trying to attract the ones who are suited to you. No one has ever stopped dating someone because they like pineapple on their pizza. There are more profiles with "I'll fall for you ... if you trip me" and "I'm overly competitive about ... everything" than not. These are cliché, bland and boring profile statements that tell me nothing about you. There is only so much space on a dating profile and you don't want to waste it with comments about how you love travelling. Everyone loves travelling. These kinds of comments make you interchangeable with any other person and that isn't the point of a profile. While it can't show everything about you, it should show enough about you that it gives someone the sense of who you are. This doesn't have to just be in what you say, it can also be in photos. I swipe no on gym selfies. I love the gym – I go to the gym three times a week – but if it's in your profile, it makes me think it's a core part of your personality. As much as I love the gym, I don't want to date someone who would choose the gym over me. Instead, I have a picture of me paddleboarding.

To create a good profile, you want a profile that actually turns some people off. In order to attract the right people, you want to repel the wrong ones. Here are my prompts and how I demonstrate my personality with the limited space you get.

> Dating me is like . . . being on *Love Island*, except everyone is fatter, conversation is funnier and we'll actually stay together. I'll probably still be wearing a bikini, though.

This conveys a number of things without actually saying them outright. It says I'm confident in the way I look, I am looking for something more long-term and it shows my sense of humour.

> The key to my heart is . . . ambition, emotional intelligence and passion in whatever you do. Someone who can handle a little sass, a lot of deep chats with cuddles in between.

Writing emotional intelligence ended up being an amazing way to weed out the wrong people. The number of responses I would get asking "What's emotional intelligence?" or "Is that like IQ?" would get rid of people who wouldn't be a great match. This also tells you I'm an affectionate person and that I know what I'm looking for and I know who I am. It's also clear surface-level conversation is not welcome here:

> We'll get along if . . . you can handle someone who's opinionated, ruins a joke by laughing too hard in the middle and is always coming up with ridiculous plans.

This gets rid of all the guys who are looking for easy-going people. I have needs, I have standards and I have opinions. The last line also means I attract people who are up for doing interesting things, so if you are a person who wants to sit at home and binge-watch a TV show together, that's not the dating life I want. I love binge-watching shows, but I want to do that alone.

By actually filling out my dating profile properly, it already sends the message that I'm not just on this app to swipe and I rarely match with someone whose profile is incomplete. The times when I have matched with someone with an incomplete profile, I actually ask them to fill out their profile properly before continuing the conversation. When they have, there is quite a conversion rate to a date. By asking them to fill out their profile, you are inadvertently asking for investment, and that increases the chance of follow-through, but that's not why I do it. I do it because it's about effort. I believe if you are on a dating app, the least you can do is fill out your profile properly. If you can't be bothered, then neither can I.

Notice in all of these prompts I am stating what I do want and not what I don't want. This is one of the crucial mistakes I see on people's dating apps. If you write "no cheaters", you are telling me exactly where your wound is and, more importantly, that you have not worked to heal it. Even if you write something like "no smokers", it doesn't present how you think it does. The mind is unable to hold a negative. This is known as ironic process theory. It's why when you tell someone not to think of a white bear, they think of a white bear; in order to not think about it, you have to think about it first. If you can't state in the positive what you are looking for, then don't state it at all.

If you are feeling overwhelmed right now, don't overthink it too much. The best way to fix your dating profile is to get a bunch of your best friends over and ask them for help. Sometimes the things we dissect and focus on, especially when it comes to our photos, are things that people don't notice at all. Getting an outside perspective is helpful. One friend was complaining that every woman he seems to match with only wants sex. His first picture was him topless doing a handstand. You couldn't see his face, and his bio said "someone who can watch

TV and chill". I asked him if he knew what "Netflix and chill" was code for, and he didn't. It's a lesson in what you project is not always what people perceive. It's a generalization, but men do not spend as much time on their profiles, they usually have fewer photos of themselves and, because of this, often put up bad photos of themselves. They do not think about how their profile comes across. So as much as I do believe a profile is important, it is not everything.

The way I interact on dating apps is I have low standards for who I swipe on and high standards for who I actually go on a date with. And it's a good thing, too. There are countless guys who I have been on a date with who looked so much better in person than in their photos, and the convincing factor wasn't the profile but the conversation we had after matching. If the conversation was good and the photos are iffy, I will always go on the date. For example, my boyfriend's profile really under-sold himself. His profile included his passport photo when he was 15, a sunglasses picture where you couldn't see his face, a skiing picture where he was looking off into the distance and a selfie where he was pulling a funny face. Not only that, once we started talking, he sent me a photo of himself doing Movember (when guys grow moustaches for the month of November to raise money for charity) and it looked so different to the guy in his profile that I showed my friends because I really wasn't sure it was the same guy. When we became official, I showed his family that Movember photo and even they couldn't recognize him in the picture. Meanwhile, he thought it was funny and had no clue that it genuinely gave me so much cause for concern that I called the restaurant and asked for the surname of the reservation so I could Google and check he was actually who he said he was. His explanation for the photos: he genuinely didn't have many photos of himself. So while spending time on your profile will never be wasted, I always swipe with quite a lot of leniency and the expectation that they have spent next to no time on their profile. The camera can't capture energy, how someone acts, their tone of voice or body language and 93 per cent of communication is nonverbal. Even the best profiles can't account for everything.

There are, however, certain words that, with enough experience, set off alarm bells. I follow the principle of when someone tells you who they are, listen. I learned this lesson the hard way when my first boyfriend asked me to be his girlfriend and, when I said yes, he responded with "I should warn you, I'm an arsehole." He was right. Instead, I laughed it off with a "I already know that" and proceeded to learn that lesson firsthand. Could have saved myself a lot of grief if I had just listened when he told me. I can guarantee if I went back to his dating profile, the signs were there. You can't always foresee your own future mistakes, but you can learn from mine. Of course, there are the obvious ones when someone has written "Gold diggers need not apply", or filled their profile out with one-word answers, and that word is the same answer: "pizza".

Here are some other real-life examples and what I have learned they mean:

"I don't know what I'm looking for"
I will mess you around.

"I recently discovered that . . . the drinks emoticon followed by the question mark works pretty well for dates"
I make minimal effort. I don't want someone who communicates in emotions.

"One thing I'll never do again . . . falling in love"
I want to attract the "fixers" of the world.

"I like doing a lot of things but am too lazy and horrible at planning"
You will have to do all the work in this relationship.

"I want someone who . . . can show me real love"
My ex hurt me and I'm not over it.

* * *

Women get all the stick for being indirect communicators, but men can be just as indirect. These are the most common phrases I see on dating apps and here's what they really mean when they write this on their profile:

"No drama"
I will see you as dramatic anytime you bring up a legitimate issue.

"Spontaneous"
I will make plans at the last minute, give you little notice and expect you to say yes with no hesitation.

"Doesn't play games"
If you change your mind, I will accuse you of leading me on.

"Easy-going"
I expect you to never ask for anything and agree to everything I want to do. You must go along with the plan, otherwise I will call you difficult for voicing your opinion.

"Doesn't take herself too seriously"
I will make passive-aggressive jokes at your expense and when you call me out on it, I will tell you that you are being too sensitive.

"Has a sense of humour"
My sense of humour is mean, and when you call me out on making digs at you, I will tell you that you don't know how to take a joke. (This is the same as the profiles that state they will "rip the piss out of you every chance they get" or that they will "mock you mercilessly".)

Be proud of the fact that you don't fit the mould of what these dating profiles are looking for. Instead of changing yourself to become more amenable, embrace the fact that you have needs and are selfish enough to want them met. As I say in *The Joy of Being Selfish*, "Stop comparing yourself to other people and seeing it as a competition as to who can be the most low-maintenance. You are allowed to ask for more; you are allowed to expect more." Stop trying to fit the above criteria. I used to spend a lot of my teenage years trying to play into the "cool girl" narrative of being easy-going, chilled and low-maintenance. I was guilty of seeing the fact that I was "one of the guys" as a compliment, and when I was told I wasn't like other girls, I would beam with pride. The TikTok generation would have described me as a "pick me" girl, which is defined as someone who has so much internalized misogyny that they seek to separate themselves from other women. As the authors of the book *He's Just Not That Into You* put it, "The thing about that cool girl is that she still gets her feelings hurt. She still has reactions to how she's being treated."

Now, I am aware of how toxic this messaging is and how it largely stemmed from my people-pleasing tendencies.

They don't want you to be selfish because they want you to put them first, even higher than yourself. I thought if I kept my needs small, I would be liked more. Instead, I just ended up resentful and would make sarcastic comments to release that resentment. It's why I became so passionate about boundaries and redefining the word "selfish", because you should be allowed to ask for your needs to be met without being called high maintenance. Now, when someone calls me difficult, I take it as a compliment. Difficult means difficult to take advantage of. I no longer aspire to be easy-going, nor should you. I am not easy to be in a relationship with. I am not easy to work with. I am not easy to be friends with. I know what I want and I will communicate that and, at times, my needs, thoughts and opinions will not be convenient to you – it will not make your life easy. No, I am not easy. What I am is simple: I say what I mean and I mean what I say. You will know when I have an issue because I will tell you. So many men say they want a confident woman, but they don't like when that confidence comes with boundaries and standards on how they deserve to be treated. You are allowed to have expectations. Having none doesn't make you chilled, it makes you a pushover.

Forget Me Nots

- Do not present your best self, present your everyday self
- Make your profile so distinguishable that your friends would know it's you without any pictures
- State what you do want, not what you don't want
- Swipe leniently and let the conversation show you whether you are actually interested

Take Action Toolkit: Sometimes it's really hard to see the things in ourselves that we have never noticed. It's impossible to put it on your dating app if you don't know it's one of your best attributes. This is where the people who know us best can help us out. Only ask these of a person you trust, who will answer kindly:

- What is a positive characteristic that I don't know I have within me?
- What are the first three words you would use to describe me?
- If you were to date me, what would be your biggest reason to do so?

Now use this information to fill out your profile. Instead of writing the exact characteristic, describe something that demonstrates that behaviour. For example, if one of the best things about you is that you are outgoing, it's better to say "Let's go on a date if . . . a house party is your comfort zone" than "I am outgoing."

What if I Don't Fit the Beauty Ideal?

It's all well and good saying that aesthetics doesn't matter, but what happens when all you really have is aesthetics? Dating apps are superficial. And what's even worse than that is you aren't even being judged on what you actually look like, but more so on if you know how to take good photographs. This leaves us being even more appearance-focused than we want to be and makes it easy to tell ourselves stories about how our looks are ruining the chance of a good dating life. To prevent being rejected for this very reason, many people feel pressured to disclose what makes them different upfront.

Whether it's writing "divorced" or "diabetic" on your profile, I understand the mentality of wanting to save time by weeding out the people who aren't interested, but you have to ask yourself why you are writing it on your profile. I get the temptation to disclose everything, especially if you have faced rejection for a certain reason. After I broke up with my first boyfriend, my dating profile included a British flag and Hong Kong flag to denote that I was mixed race. I had never met my ex's parents or friends because, in his words, "They were racist." So, in a bid to avoid this situation again, I thought it would be helpful. In hindsight, it actually just attracted people who had a fetish. Those flags were quickly removed once I realized my race didn't need a disclaimer. Let it be their issue, not yours.

We have to understand that our profiles cannot weed out everyone. You will need to actually date some people to find out they are incompatible, in the same way that you could find out something that makes you lose interest on a third date that you didn't know on a first date. We have to be prepared to take that journey without knowing the full picture. Part of the fun of dating is discovering that new person.

The difference is whether your decision for including it is a negative motivation or a positive one. There is a difference between someone wanting to change jobs because they want to challenge themselves versus someone who wants to change jobs because they don't want to get stuck in the same role. The latter is a decision made out of fear, and how it is phrased means you focus on the thing you are trying to avoid. You are leading with what you are most insecure about, in order to scare them away. I used to do the same with my scars. I would blurt out that I had scars before I felt ready to share that information, because I believed I needed to tell people about them upfront. When you are insecure, you almost jump the gun when it's not the relevant stage to reveal something. It's quite a backwards mindset, because if we go on a first date and I decide I don't ever want to see you again, then the fact I have surgery scars or not is unimportant. It hurts when you get rejected for something you are unable to change about yourself, but when you walk through dating apps telling everyone upfront about everything they could possibly reject you for, it is the dating-app equivalent to oversharing – or more specifically, a certain kind of oversharing that Brené Brown calls "floodlighting". It is a way of sharing too much information as a way to protect us from vulnerability. We share the things we are ashamed of too early, as almost a pre-warning to give people the opportunity to run before we get attached. The intentions behind this include trying to soothe your own pain, testing the loyalty and tolerance in a relationship and – specifically in a dating app context – trying to hot-wire a new connection. In her book *Daring Greatly* (2012), Brown elaborates on this:

When we share vulnerability, especially shame stories, with someone with whom there is no connectivity, their emotional (and sometimes physical) response is often to wince, as if we have shone a floodlight in their eyes . . . We then use this disconnection as verification that we'll never find comfort, that we're not worthy, that the relationship is no good, or, in the case of over-sharing to hot-wire a connection, that we'll never have the intimacy that we crave.

You can figure out what your motivation is by asking yourself "Why do I want to include this piece of information?" The clue will be whether your answer is to do with them or do with you. Let's say you ask yourself whether you should include that you have coeliac disease. If your answer is "Because what if they find it intimidating?", that is different to "Because it affects my daily life." The difference in phrasing might be subtle, but it is telling. Once you have figured out your motivation, it is a lot easier to distinguish between privacy and honesty. You aren't intentionally misleading someone if you are not ready to share every aspect of your life. There is a difference between intentionally hiding pieces of your identity and not being ready *yet*.

For example, in one conversation on a dating app, a guy asked what my book was called. This gives him my last name and makes me searchable. I have a public profile and, with my full name, you can find more information on Google than I am willing to share. So I said "Let's save that for our first date", because I was comfortable with him Googling me after we'd met first. It's healthy to let people earn the right to private pieces of information, but be aware that if you decide to hide pieces of your identity intentionally, you prevent intimacy from developing. Nowadays, I would never declare my race, my illnesses or my scars on my profile. But all of those are part of my lived experience, so as much as I don't declare it, I don't hide away from any of it. Since it's a part of my life, it is quite common for me to start stories with "When I was living in Hong Kong . . ." or "When I was in hospital . . ." and that's true for my profile. I wouldn't intentionally put a picture of me in hospital, but if the conversation comes up, I would explain it just like I would to a new friend.

I prefer the approach of explaining it in person on a date because when it's written on a profile, it is ripped out of context. You think the label will tell them everything you need to know and be the deciding factor but it's often *how* you share the information that is more important. A silly example of this is I used to say I would never date a football guy. I hate the culture of it, the violence in it and the racism. If it says something about football on a profile, I would swipe no yet I was once on a first date with a guy who told me he loved football. Being on a date allowed me to ask questions about what mattered to me. I asked him how he reacted when we lost in the Euros in 2021. He said he might have shed a tear. Check! As long as he didn't punch a wall or hurl racist abuse at the players. I then asked whether, if there was a big game on, we could hypothetically still go out for dinner. He said that his life comes first and we would go for dinner, but he might sneak a look at the score when he went to the loo. I could live with that.

It might be silly to use the example of football, but I actually don't see appearance as being any different. If we are going to choose to continue to perpetuate the narrative that our appearance reduces our dating pool, then can we acknowledge that being a smoker also limits our dating pool, as does being really into music festivals. Live a nomadic lifestyle? You've reduced your dating pool and ruled out people who don't like to travel or want the stability of staying in the same place – and yes, being a football person might do the same thing. The crucial point is that reducing your dating pool is not a bad thing. You need to whittle it down to find those that you are compatible with.

The reason these personal aspects feel more important than disclosing whether you like football or not is because of how society reacts to certain disclosures. There is a negativity bias that exists in the media. Without positive media representation of dating experiences, especially those of marginalized people, it ends up looking very one-sided and is fearmongering to the people who haven't got the confidence to date. Let's take weight as an example. It is because of beliefs like this that I have been told that I am a "fat girl with the confidence of a skinny girl" more times than I can count. No, I'm a fat girl with the confidence level of someone who doesn't believe her fat has an effect on her beauty, success or lovability, and firmly believes that your size doesn't correlate to your confidence. Get rid of your outdated belief that fat means no self-esteem and understand that fat people are as diverse in thoughts, beliefs and actions as any other person. People truly believe that they need to lose weight to find love and that without weight loss, people won't find you attractive. The truth is the people who are telling you that are taking their view and applying it to the whole world. *Some* people don't find fat women attractive. Just like some people don't find blondes attractive. It's not about size, it's about having the confidence to know you can thrive at any size. In university, I was dating a guy who never wanted to be official, so I ended things. Three months later, he came back saying he regretted his decision and he wanted to be official. In the intervening time, I had been diagnosed with PTSD and gained three dress sizes. How many times does the world tell us that they would commit if only you were thinner? This is direct evidence to the contrary. You may believe that your body is the cause of your unsuccessful love life but remember that correlation doesn't equal cause. And the only reason it is correlated is because society has convinced us it is and we have bought that lie. If your love life is the problem, fix your love life. Why would you fix your body when it's not the problem?

I would be remiss if I didn't acknowledge my privilege. I can't speak on behalf of all fat women because I'm a size 20, and people larger than me will have a different experience. I can't speak on behalf of all scarred people because my scars are hidden, and people dating with a scar on their face will have different interactions. I can't speak on behalf of all people of colour, all Asians or even all Chinese people because I am mixed race and again, that brings another perspective. I would never undermine anyone's lived experience or speak on behalf of a community, let alone the ones I am not a part of. I have no clue what it's like to date as a trans person or an asexual person, so if you feel safer stating things on your profile, then you have to do what makes you comfortable.

Ultimately, what you decide to include in your profile is your choice. If it feels more authentic to you to disclose information upfront, then go for it. Everyone's line between privacy and honesty will be their own. My rule of thumb is if you wouldn't share that information with someone you meet at a party, then you don't need to put it on your profile. Whether you decide to declare it or not, what matters most is how you communicate it. There are two examples below for someone with a visible disability or someone with a child from a past relationship. One presupposes it's going to be an issue or a turn-off and the other states it as a fact.

Swipe right if . . . you are OK with the fact I have a five-year-old daughter

Typical Sunday night . . . curled up on the sofa watching *Encanto* with my daughter. Don't worry, for our movie nights, I promise a better film selection

I want someone who . . . doesn't mind pushing me around in my wheelchair

Worst idea I ever had . . . confusing my wheelchair for a Formula 1 car at Thorpe Park and tipping over. Won't lie, no regrets, it was more fun than most of the rides there!

Forget Me Nots

- If you wouldn't share that information with someone you meet in the real world, then you don't need to put it on your profile
- It's important to know the line between privacy and honesty – don't overshare just because you are insecure about an aspect of yourself
- Everyone's line between privacy and honesty will be their own
- Whether you decide to declare information or not, what matters most is how you communicate it

---

Take Action Toolkit: You can't love your body if you don't know what it looks like. So it's time to get naked, by yourself, in front of a mirror. I know that sounds like a weird and daunting task, so here's a weirder but less daunting one. Brush your teeth naked every day. It's two minutes every day and you are doing it anyway, so you can't forget to do it. I know when you look in the mirror, your inner voice tends to take charge. The best part about brushing your teeth is when your inner voice is going wild, just focus on the brushing and remember to not believe your thoughts. This exercise is not about changing your thoughts. There are going to be other exercises that target that. This is for you to start getting accustomed to your body in different lighting and at various angles. When you are comfortable being naked alone, you are more likely to be comfortable being naked with someone else.

How Do I Stop Feeling Rejected When We Don't Match?

When you aren't getting as many matches as you would like, people are not responding to your messages, and you are getting unmatched before even starting a conversation, dating apps become a hotbed for rejection. If you already have a rejection wound from the past, it can feel like being kicked in the stomach over and over. The solution to this problem is the combination of two techniques. Feel the rejection that arises and also do not create more rejection than is necessary.

We create more rejection than is necessary when we pay attention to things that we don't need to be noticing. You can't feel rejected if you haven't noticed you've been rejected, so the first thing you can do is to stop watching your matches. You don't actually need to know who matches you, you just need to know who messages you and who replies. Match with people, start the conversation if you want and then go about your day. The easiest way to do this is to mass swipe and then mass message people so that you aren't aware of the specific individual and keeping each one in mind. You can personalize each message without memorizing every message you send out. I find it curious that people will feel more rejection if someone matches and unmatches than if they never matched in the first place. People swipe quickly, we all know this. It's often only when we get a match back that we then have a thorough look at their profile. You are guilty of it too. I remember a client once telling me that she had been rejected 40 times that week alone and my first thought was: "Why are you counting?" Even in non-dating contexts, it strikes me as unusual when an author can recall that their manuscript was rejected 28 times. I've had a bunch of manuscripts rejected too, but I can't tell you how many times, because I wasn't counting them. When you count them, you put your focus on them.

You can't feel rejection if you don't define it as rejection. The reason that people unmatching me doesn't affect me is because I don't label it that way. They don't know me and therefore, they can't reject me. Much like how it's not the author getting rejected, it's the manuscript, I'm not getting rejected, my profile is. I don't personalize it. You are rejecting whatever idea or perception that my profile gives you and I can't control that. For example, if my profile contains the mention of the word "stubborn" and in their last relationship, stubbornness was a constant source of conflict, the word "stubborn" will make them unmatch my profile – or not match in the first place. Them swiping no is not a rejection of me, it's a rejection of them not wanting to relive a past experience. Of course, two stubborn people can display their stubbornness completely differently and could handle conflict differently as well, but the person swiping will be unable to see that because they can't see past the word "stubborn". Do you see how that becomes out of your control? I see this online when people decide they hate me without ever meeting me. They don't actually hate me – they hate what I stand for. If you are uncomfortable with boundaries, of course you are going to dislike a woman who proclaims she is the Queen of Boundaries. If you have an issue being direct, and lack self-awareness, you will project that on to people who are direct, like I am. All of that truly is not about me, though.

Let's go further and explore that rejection hypothetically. Let's say you could talk to that person who just matched you and then decided to unmatch you because that second look at your profile made them lose interest. Imagine you could ask them why. They say they don't like the gap between your teeth and they only noticed once you matched because your first four photos were with a closed mouth. What are you going to do with this information? You have two options: change your appearance based on the opinion of a stranger, or actually find someone who likes what you look like now, as you are. The latter seems like a more sensible solution. Let's say they also say that it's not just that, but from your profile you seem boring because you mention reading and they don't want to date someone who stays in the whole time. If they said this to your face, you might feel the urge to explain that reading doesn't make you boring, someone can be into reading and also love doing things outdoors and that if you were both to go on a date, you are unlikely to bring a book because that would just be rude. Or you could pretend you hate reading, develop an insecurity about how boring you are, and then seek to reassure everyone you know that you are absolutely not boring. Surely, it's easier to just find someone who loves reading too, or simply someone who doesn't equate reading with being boring.

We get tempted to be who we aren't because if you then get rejected, it feels safer because they didn't know the real you. To me, it's worse to be rejected for what you are pretending to be than what you actually are. At least you're never left wondering if they would have liked the real you and you wouldn't have self-abandoned in order to gain their attention. That person has done you a favour by swiping no. When they did so, they decided you two don't align. As much as they don't know you, you don't know them – so trust that they made the right decision for both of you. When we get rejected, we assume something is wrong with us. We don't consider that there might not be anything wrong with either you or them, but simply that you are wrong for each other. I'd even go as far as to say that you want people to reject you. The alternative is being strung along even though they are not interested. Can you imagine if the only reason someone keeps dating you is because they don't want to hurt your feelings? You don't want that.

Unmatches hurt less when you stop seeing them as a loss. Rejection is a redirection. Every no gets you closer to a yes. Going on a date will get you closer to finding a person who will add to your love life, even if it doesn't lead to another date. We think that rejection is the worst option. It's not. The worst option is avoiding it by not trying at all. You have already decided they will turn you down you, so you don't take any risks. If you are scared of someone being uninterested, create a greater fear around the fact that you never take a risk. Being "dismissed" hurts, but losing all potential opportunities because you don't want to risk the potential of pain is worse. Stop rejecting yourself in an effort to not get rejected – you are probably doing it more times than you notice. It's in that moment when you see someone's profile and, even though you are attracted to them, you swipe no because you think they would never be interested in you. It's that moment you cancel a date because "What if they think I'm bigger than my photos?", so you protect yourself and you think that will keep you safe. They can't reject you and therefore you can't get hurt. But rejecting yourself hurts more because, as I said before, they don't know you. You do.

Dating is often a numbers game and perseverance will pay off more than fitting in the beauty ideal will. Let's say you swipe on 100 people a day. Now imagine the last 100 humans you interacted with. How many were actual friends or someone you would actually want to be friends with, let alone have a romantic relationship with? When someone is so focused on rejection, they ignore the fact that they are rejecting people too. You are only looking at the pool of people you liked who didn't like you back, and never once consider the pool of people who liked you but you were not interested in. So if you have a good conversation on an app and have a moment of connection on a date, stop viewing it as failure. Any match is a win. Any conversation is good news. Any first date is a success.

Once you reduce all the stories you are telling yourself about rejection and reframe it to work to your advantage, that still won't make you immune to rejection. Part of the reason I declared myself consciously single at 21 was due to this frustration. When friends would ask, I would say: "I have just started a business and it occurred to me that if my love life was a business, it would be operated at a loss. I am not getting anything back from what I am putting in." As much as I have evolved since then, there was a point in 2021 when we had just come out of lockdown and four guys in a row had cancelled on me because, on the day of our date, they said they had Covid. Who knows how many actually did, but I remember I had grown disheartened with repeated disappointment and was moaning to my social media agent about how I hadn't been on a date in six months. He said that it wasn't true cause I had been on a video date the week before. I amended my statement to say I hadn't been on an in-person date in six months. He said it didn't count because for four months of that, we were locked down so I couldn't physically go on a date. I rolled my eyes. And then he reminded me that I am the same woman who once went to an event full of only women to promote a dating app and walked away with the number of the only man in the room, the photographer. Just because I am a life coach doesn't mean I am immune to those moments of wallowing and self-pity. Thankfully, I have people in my life who won't indulge my negative self-talk.

When you feel rubbish about yourself, you will exaggerate and generalize. One way your brain will do this is using words like "always" and "never". "I'm never going to find someone! I always get rejected!" It will take things to an extreme, and all that will do is hurt and scare you. It will delete every memory that contradicts your generalization and instead, find evidence to prove that you are right. My brain told me that I had not been on a date in six months and I should give up. The truth was I had not been on a date in a week, and an in-person date in two months because we were living through a global pandemic. If you aren't conscious of what you are telling yourself, it is easy to spiral out. What was behind all this noise in my head was hurt. I wake up the morning of a date excited, so when someone cancels the day of the date, it's disappointing. The rise and fall in emotion feel like a big drop on a rollercoaster. I had started chatting rubbish in my head, because I didn't want to feel the disappointment in my body.

Ultimately, if you feel rejected, you need to feel it. You only heal when you acknowledge the hurt that was caused and give yourself full permission to let those feelings hit you – and even let a few tears out. It's really tempting to go down a new spiral of invalidating your feelings with "I didn't even meet them" or "You are being silly", but when you hear those voices, focus instead on finding the feeling of rejection in your body and letting it hurt. Breathe into it and allow yourself to take a moment. You can get back to dating later. For now, you are just experiencing what it is like to be a human. You are not too sensitive or too emotional – you are simply living in a world that has taught you to never let them see you cry. It encourages you to numb yourself and equates feeling your feelings with weakness. Pretending to be emotionally detached will only appeal to people who are emotionally detached, so you need to feel it. Our world only emphasizes strength and resilience, but there is power in not letting the world make you hard and giving yourself permission to heal. So cry, darling. Cry to your heart's content. There is beauty in being soft.

When I got off the phone with my agent, I had realized the story I was telling myself. I let myself feel the physical ache of disappointment after four cancelled dates in a row and the lost potential of what could have been. I accepted that I will never know and put my hand on my heart, breathed it in as the pain worsened and then, when it started to lift, a quote popped into my head. As cliché as it is, it provided relief: "Everything is going to be OK in the end and if it's not OK, it's not the end." And I lived to swipe another day. As I type this, I realized for the first time that the very next person I went on a first date with is now my boyfriend. You are more powerful if you let yourself feel it.

Forget Me Nots

- You can't feel rejected if you haven't noticed the rejection – so stop watching your matches
- Rejection hurts, but losing all potential opportunities because you don't want to risk rejection is worse
- You only heal when you acknowledge the hurt and give yourself full permission to let those feelings hit you
- If you have a good conversation on an app and have a moment of connection on a date, stop viewing it as failure; any match is a win, any conversation is a win, any first date is a success

Take Action Toolkit: When you are in the midst of rejection, it's really hard to see it as a redirection that might work out in your favour. Let's recall your past rejections and use that as evidence for how you benefited from it. For example, using my own life, I was rejected from Oxford University and it was one of my first rejections, so it hurt a lot. I ended up at Bristol and that was the best thing that could have happened. In hindsight, I don't think I could have kept up with the workload at Oxford – I would have either burned out or dropped out, or both. By ending up at Bristol, I found the best friendship group that built the confidence I have today. I already placed too much emphasis on academics. I got my self-worth from my intelligence, and Oxford would have just enhanced that, whereas Bristol made my life fuller and made me a more well-rounded person, something that has served me so well in adulthood. Your turn!

....
....
....
....
....
....
....
....
....
....
....
....
....
....
....
....
....

SHOW THE EVERYDAY YOU

....
....
....
....
....
....
....
....
....
....
....
....
....
....
....
....
....
....
....
....
....
....
....
....
....
....
....
....
....
....
....
....
....

Chapter 6

If You Look at Reply Times, You Have Too Much Time

How to Be Empowered Texting

Do I Message Them First?

From the earliest days of having a crush on a guy, texting stressed me out. This was back in the days when BlackBerries were more popular than iPhones, and exchanging BBM pins was the way you knew someone liked you. As Alain de Botton said, "The telephone becomes an instrument of torture in the demonic hands of the beloved who does not call." You'd wait three hours if they had waited two, you'd notice when their kisses increased from "x" to "xx", and you'd spend hours decoding whether that meant anything or if their finger just slipped. Since then, it's only got worse, as WhatsApp has given us both the function of checking when someone was last online and those dreaded double blue ticks to know when you've been "left on read".

But even in 2012, this was a thing. I was in my second year of university and was dating someone for the first time ever. He was doing computer science and we had just slept together for the first time. We were lying in bed when he told me he was developing an app that would automatically calculate when you should reply to a person based on their average reply time. He also said it would have a function to analyze the average amount of kisses to send so you didn't need to work it out yourself. Being 19 years old, I played along and pretended like this was something I was completely naive to, innocently asking, "Oh, what does the different number of kisses mean?" as if I hadn't been analyzing them myself. He laid out the meaning for me. One kiss was just polite, two kisses are when they start getting interested in you and three kisses is when you are cemented and they want you to like them back. The real goal was to get to the point where you put an indiscriminate number of kisses at the end. That really locked it in! I rolled over and grabbed my phone.

"OK, let's see, then . . ." I said as I pulled up our texts and started scrolling through. Noticing how his in-text kisses did indeed gradually increase from one to two to three, only to return to two before jumping up to 10.

"So what does that mean?" I asked him, with the smallest grain of hope that it would mean we were locked in.

"Oh, that was Halloween, I was just drunk."

As far as I'm aware, his app has never existed and I'm going to assume the statute of limitations has run out on creating it, since he did make me promise I wouldn't tell anyone, in case someone copyrighted it. But that conversation exemplifies how truly stupid it is to try to decode something as uncomplicated as kisses. Everyone now gets a default two kisses, whether I am dating you or you are a work colleague I am sending an email to. We can get really hung up on texting details when we are telling ourselves a story about how our phrasing in a text, or the frequency of a text, will make or break a relationship. This part of dating is not complicated; you are complicating it. If the way you text is the deal-breaker that ends a relationship, then it's not a relationship that would work anyway. After all, if you are going to be in a relationship, especially one that lasts, you will need to be texting that person for the rest of your life. Since texting is relatively new, it's easy to belittle the importance of it, but having incompatible texting styles is a legitimate reason it could not work out. If it doesn't, it is no different than ending a friendship because they consistently turn up late when you make plans.

How to move from dating apps to texting

Usually, the move from dating apps to texting happens from a logistical standpoint. Most people don't have notifications on dating apps in the same way they do for texts, the functionality on many dating apps is slower than an app like WhatsApp, and we check the apps less frequently. This move doesn't need to mean anything. I have given out my number straight away and I have also given out my number a few weeks after a second date. The last time I gave out my number on a dating app, it was the first day we had matched and all that provoked it was a message I received that read:

> By the way, I know this is a bit forward, but can I ask for your number? You can say no, of course. I won't be offended xx

Often, it's just a case of giving out my number when someone asks for it. If they don't ask, I tend to swap numbers soon anyway because messaging on the app starts to annoy me. The only other factor that some people may consider in this step is safety, and they may not feel comfortable handing out their number too early on. For me, if someone starts using my number inappropriately or makes me uncomfortable, I have no issue setting a boundary, asking them to stop. If they persist, I tell them that if they continue, I will block their number, and then I follow through if they haven't listened.

If you would like to exchange numbers and you don't know how to do it without feeling like you are waiting for rejection, it is easiest to bring it up when you are arranging your first date. Again, from a logistical standpoint, trying to find someone at your date location is often more convenient when you have each other's numbers, and that's a great opportunity to do so without making it into a big step. If the date doesn't go well, then you never use that number, and if they would like a second date, they now can be in touch off the app. All you need to say is:

> Here's my number in case you can't find me xx

And if someone asks you to swap to texting and you don't feel ready to do so, then only do what you are comfortable with. You could reply:

> Thank you for your number! I'm good to stay on the app for now and I've got it for the future :) xx

Who should text first?

The old school rules of "playing hard to get" and trying not to seem more keen than the other person are boring and out-dated. You don't need to play hard to get if you *are* hard to get. Keep your standards high and it will weed out a lot of the people you don't want to be dating. You won't need to pre-tend. And in terms of playing games, keep playing them if you want to attract a game-player. If you want to attract someone who communicates clearly and directly, then you must do the same. The simplest way to text a person you are dating is to text them the way you would a friend. For most people, this would be replying to a text when you see it and you are available to reply, and not replying when you are occupied or in the company of others. As a result, you will sometimes reply instantly and you will sometimes be with your friends all day and won't see it until you get home at midnight. If you have the time to be sitting and calculating reply times, my biggest suggestion is to make your life fuller so that you have better ways to use your time. Interesting people do not have the time to sit and stare at two grey ticks and wait for them to turn blue.

Finish that email. Fold that laundry. Focus on your workout. If you are busy, stay busy. Don't drop everything because a text comes in. Ditch the games, start living your life and don't put your life on pause to reply. As much as you think fast replies are a nice way to express interest, it can actually do more harm than good. A great example of this was one of my friends, who got frustrated that her partner dropped everything to reply. If she was in a meeting, she would leave the room. If she was driving, she would pull over to reply. Yes, this was extreme – but what ended up happening is that my friend never wanted to text her because she felt like she was intruding on her day. To a lesser extent, how often do you pause what you are watching to respond to whatever notification pops up on your phone? Stop that. You are teaching your brain to wait on a text.

If you are having a quiet night in, watching mindless TV and scrolling on social media, and you see the text come in, feel free to reply to it and have a back and forth like you would do if a friend had texted. You wouldn't sit there and wait for an arbitrary length of time with someone else, so don't do it with the person you are dating. Treat them with the same respect. Oftentimes, we don't want to reply instantly because we worry, "What if they think I have nothing better to do?" Well, you don't have anything better to do, and that's why you are replying! That's not to say you *never* have anything better to do, but at that moment, on a random Tuesday night after work, you don't – and that's OK. When you have an interesting life, you don't have to create the illusion of one by not replying, because you are already living it. By the same token, everyone hates it when their friend starts dating someone new and they are constantly texting under the table, so keep your phone in your bag. Focus on the people you are spending time with, give them your full attention and reply to your texts later. If you are finding that texting someone is taking up too much of your brain space and your time, then boundary it.

> Hey! I don't text during work hours so I will reply to you when I leave the office xx

> Hey! Having a long week, can we text at the weekend when you can have my full attention? xx

> Hey! I'm just going to the gym and I want to focus on my workout so I will text you tomorrow xx

We have also overcomplicated the rules on who should text who first and whether the man, in heterosexual relationships, should always be the one initiating. At the end of the day, you don't want to be in a dynamic where you are only allowed to speak when spoken to. If you initiating the conversation is off-putting to a man, then it's putting off the wrong man. Text them when you want to talk to them, when you think of them in your day or when you see something that reminds you of them. If you don't have a conversation going, start the conversation. It is OK to show interest in a person who is interested in you too. And if they aren't interested, you will know sooner – and the sooner the better.

Have they lost interest?

Can someone still like you if they never text you? Have they lost interest if they take three days to reply? What about if they used to take an hour to reply and now they take a week? We can spend years asking ourselves these questions and it all essentially boils down to one: what does it mean? Growing up, I remember whole articles dedicated to helping you try to understand this complicated language of texting, with titles like "What does his text really mean?", as if it was a science that just needed to be decoded. Looking back at these articles with wiser and older eyes, this whole idea has a misogynistic undertone. It sends the message that women are the confused party, we are uneducated in the "language of men" and therefore, it is our own fault our love lives are a mess. Of course you don't have your one true love because how stupid do you have to be to not get the message when he stopped texting you with emojis? Long story short, the onus is on you.

But wait, hold up. Where was the accountability for this man who is a bad communicator? Why wasn't there a conversation about how, instead of removing emojis, he should have actually engaged in a conversation to express his lack of interest like an adult? Why are we blaming the woman for not reading between the lines rather than expecting grown men to communicate directly and clearly? And most of all, where are the articles in men's magazines with the title "What does HER text really mean?" Oh yeah, that's right, it doesn't exist, because men aren't sold the idea they are incomplete without a woman. In fact, if you aren't attached, you will be seen as a playboy and a bachelor, not a too-picky, barren spinster.

The idea that we can deduce meaning from an increase in reply time is ludicrous. We don't need to become a culture of "text decoders", we need to become a culture that learns how to communicate. We don't need books on how to analyze "what it means", we need books that encourage us to say what we mean and mean what we say. These blanket rules do not work. In one situation, it could be because they lost interest and in another, it could be because they have been too over-whelmed with work. So what's the solution? Ask instead of assuming. The reason we don't ask is because it feels more vul-nerable, like we are putting our heart on a plate to be rejected by showing that we care. There is no shame in showing that you care, and the only person who will shame you for being vulnerable is a person you wouldn't want to date. You want to date someone who, when you show vulnerability, is able to receive it kindly, even if they are not interested.

> Hey! Haven't heard from you in a while and I was just wondering if you are OK? Would love to see you again xx

> Hey! I've noticed that you've been more distant since our last date and if something has changed, I'd really appreciate your honesty xx

> Hey! We've not been speaking as much as we used to and I wanted to let you know I'm going to need more communication in order to stay interested xx

> Hey! Miss hearing from you every day!
> Are we good? xx

Communicating directly means you are giving them a road map on how you want to be communicated with. The reply you get might not be as direct as yours because, unfortunately, we do live in a world of bad communicators, but let their reply tell you what you need to know. Let their reply demonstrate whether they are the kind of person who understands where you are coming from, acknowledges the distance and makes more effort, or the person who dismisses it and doesn't want to engage in the conversation. There is a difference between this:

> Hey! Miss hearing from you every day!
> Are we good? xx

> Nah, all good. You? xx

And this:

> Hey! Miss hearing from you every day!
> Are we good? xx

> Ah sorry, my bad. Work has been a mess and I know I've been shit at keeping in contact but I really did have fun on our last date. How about I give you a call after work tonight and we can catch up?

Which person would you prefer to date?

What are your texting needs?

We have all heard the "bad texter" excuse. The worst I've ever heard was from the guy who supposedly dropped his phone down the side of his bed for a month and "just couldn't be bothered to pick it up". When we receive these excuses, it is really tempting to go down the rabbit hole of trying to figure out whether it's true. We think about the fact that they are always on their phone when they are with us and truly wonder how plausible it is that someone can lose their phone behind their bed for a whole month. Whether it's true or not doesn't matter. What matters is if you want to be dating a bad texter.

Texting is our most common form of communication. If your communication levels and styles are not on the same page, you will have an issue. Being selfish means you need to honour your needs. Therefore, it's important to clarify for yourself what those are.

Ideally, I want someone I am dating to text me _ times a day/week/month	
At a minimum, I need someone I am dating to text me _ times a day/week/month	
How often we are going on dates would affect how much I would want to text	True/False
I care that they text me after a date	True/False
I want a person who will ask me how my day is every day	True/False
Texting shows me they are thinking of me	True/False
I care more about the quality of interaction than the frequency of interaction	True/False
The quality of interaction would affect the frequency of texts I need	True/False
I would prefer a phone call to a text	True/False
Voice notes are more meaningful than texts	True/False
If they called more, I would need fewer texts	True/False
It's important to me that we text more as we get more serious	True/False

As humans, we often make the assumption that everyone else thinks like us. We put that into our dating communication with statements like "If only they would just call me." Some people like phone calls and others don't. The person you are dating won't know unless you tell them, and you can't tell them unless you've asked yourself the question. Once you know what you need, you can communicate that.

> Hey! Communication is really important to me and for this to work, I need us to be texting more between dates xx

> Hey! I know texting isn't your thing so is there another way you prefer catching up? Why don't we FaceTime later? xx

> Hey! No pressure on replying, texting actually isn't that important to me. If you ever want to voice note, I'd love to hear your voice though! xx

Why you keep checking your phone

There is a reason you can't stop checking your phone. You aren't crazy! It is a psychological effect called intermittent reinforcement. In one of the most well-known psychology studies concerning this effect, the researcher B.F. Skinner proved this with rats and a lever that produced food. If the lever reliably produced food and one pellet would come out every time it was tapped, the rat soon lost interest. However, if the food came out at a variable rate, releasing a pellet after six taps and then 15 taps and then one tap, the rat kept returning to the lever and pressing it. The lever is more engaging when the response is unreliable – and that's exactly what happens in casinos, when you don't know when the slot machine is going to reward you. It's also what happens when you check your phone and you don't know if you are going to be getting a dopamine hit or disappointment.

That lack of reliability will make you check your phone even more. That's why, when you text your best friend who always consistently replies to you, your brain will not respond in the same way. It's why, when the person you like only replies every so often, it will make you more addicted to it. It's why, when your crush likes your Instagram photos but never actually sends you a text or makes any effort to see you, you still get a rush. When you do actually get a reply, not only do you get a rush with the notification, but you also experience a relief from the fear of rejection or the fear of being ignored, alongside whatever external validation is sitting within the actual body of the text. Altogether, it's a very intoxicating combination that can keep you returning to your phone over and over.

In the days when we weren't tied to our phones, this effect still existed, but it was less all-consuming. Of course, you could sit by the phone and wait for it to ring, especially in the age of no answering machine, but if you were out, you couldn't run home in a second to see if someone had called – to receive the call, you had to be there. Without an answering machine, you would never even know if they had called while you were out. With the increased accessibility we have today, the instant gratification hits are immediate. What's worse is that there are elements on these apps to get us even more hooked – namely, the read receipts and "last seen" status found on WhatsApp and iMessage. These are breadcrumbs of interaction, without having to say a word. Make these apps less engaging by turning off your read receipts and your last seen. What is misleading about both of these things is that we think it means some-thing that it doesn't always mean. It's important to separate a behaviour and the meaning you give it, and to be able to see them as two separate things.

Let's use the example of being left on read (the stimulus). Before you get to your response, in the middle, there is the meaning you give it. If the meaning you give being left on read is that they are busy, your response will be to go about your day and not think about it. If the meaning you give it is that they are ignoring you because the relationship is over, then your response could be firing off an angry text or calling a friend in tears. The meaning you have given it alters the response but, more importantly, both meanings are actually stories you are telling yourself. The only fact is that you have been left on read and therefore it's important to become aware of how the meaning alters our perception and behaviour. For example, if they go online and don't respond to you, you might deduce that they have lost interest, they are texting other people and you are unimportant. It might even open up your rejection wound because you have told yourself that they are rejecting you. You will often deduce the meaning that will hurt you the most and not the one that gives them the most grace. You take one thing and you run with it and create a whole narrative to hurt yourself. So what can you do instead?

If you find yourself constantly checking your phone, there are practical solutions. I hate the word "discipline" because it's so connected to self-hatred and the message that you are not "strong enough" – instead, I admit who I am. Self-awareness is more powerful than self-discipline. I accept my weaknesses and, out of a loving and compassionate place for myself, I make it easier for myself by setting better phone boundaries. One of the ways I do this is I have a no-texting-boys rule during the workday. It means I can focus better. And because I work for myself, without good work boundaries, I would end up texting all day because that's a lot more fun than filing my invoices and updating my website.

When I create any rules, I believe in rules with flexibility. While this is my rule 90 per cent of the time, if we are meeting up that day and you text me at midday saying you are going to be late and ask if we could meet at the restaurant instead of the station, of course I will reply to that when I see it, because it's logistics as opposed to casually chatting. If this ever becomes an issue or a guy brings up that I seem to be online a lot of the time but not replying, I explain that I don't reply to texts during working hours but I will get back to you at the end of the day. Alongside this, I have phone boundaries in place for everyone that I text, whether they are romantic, platonic or professional connections. I turn my phone off an hour before I go to sleep so there's no late-night texting, I don't take my phone out when I'm with people or at the table when eating, and when I am writing, my phone goes on airplane mode so I can focus. These boundaries do not change depending on who I date. These boundaries are set for me and they are not personal to the person I am texting. Therefore, as much as they are not owed an instant reply if I am busy, it is important to reciprocate this mentality and understand that I am not owed an instant reply either.

This is a muscle I have built over time to have stronger boundaries with my phone and with others. How you start is by breaking the cycle of bad habits. In order to change your behaviour, you need to start catching yourself the moment that you do it. So let's say you catch that moment when you click on WhatsApp for the sole purpose of checking when they were last online. Swap it for something that is productive or you want to do more of. Go empty the dishwasher or get yourself a glass of water. The more full your hands are, the better. Something that gets you up and changes your physiology will assist your brain in doing something different. Want your brain to stop thinking about them? Give it something else to do. I often personally resort to mundane but quick household tasks because I rarely have time to clean but always have time to scroll on my phone. Even if all you do is take your phone, walk into a different room and put it down, that's enough. Pick one thing and stick to that one thing so you create an association. If it's making yourself a cup of tea, do that repetitively until your brain gets the message that the thought "I wonder whether they are online" won't get the result that it is searching for.

Is it really about texting or is it about control?

As much as texting and good communication is important, it's also necessary to consider if it is really about texting. Often, when we feel insecure in a relationship, we will try to manage the details because we feel out of control. We think if we text regularly enough, we can control the outcome of the relationship and feel more certainty in a situation that is, frankly, always uncertain. You will hear people say that replying to texts with "yh" or "yeah" is an ick, or hear them judge others for the type of emojis they use. Do they truly care whether someone uses "haha" or "hahahaha", or does it feel safer to keep a person at arm's length and judge them for their grammar, spelling or emoji usage?

Believing people owe you a reply the instant they see it is a form of entitlement. If you are a new person that they are dating, it is not only understandable but healthy that you are a lower priority than their friends and family. This means they might go online to reply to their best friend and not you. A healthy relationship develops over time, and how much someone prioritizes you in the beginning is not an indication of how they will in the future. We have become so accessible because of our lack of boundaries with our phones. You are not owed constant access to a person as much as they are not owed access to you. Them replying to a text when they are ready to, and not when they first see it, is not an indication of lack of interest, it is an indication of good boundaries and should be treated as such. We take their lack of reply personally because we assume if they can reply to a text, then they should. Our egos take it as a personal insult and we tell ourselves the story that they are clearly on their phones and therefore intentionally ignoring us. For someone to ignore you, they have to think about you and choose otherwise, but what if they aren't thinking about us at all? What if they are thinking about the other million and one things going on in their lives? There is a psychological theory called the spotlight effect, which states that because we can't escape our own world, we believe we are the centre of other people's worlds. We overestimate how much other people notice us, our appearances and behaviours. The world doesn't revolve around you – so stop assuming it does.

Think back to how you might have felt differently about texting when dating other people. Have there been differences between how often you checked your phone with one person you were dating than another? In my own life, there was one person I remember I felt most at peace with about texting and around my phone in general and it was because he was always consistent and reliable. When I sent a text, I knew I would get a reply, and so the intermittent reinforcement pattern never existed. In another situation where I felt calm, it was because he used to see me multiple times a week and so the importance of texting diminished. Yet another was actually with a guy who declared he was a "bad texter" even before the first time we went on a date and, before the days of Zoom, we used to Skype once a week instead of texting. All of these guys provided security and certainty in different ways. It isn't about the texting, it's about the effort they make. Instead of looking at the minutiae of texting details to try to determine whether they care or are interested, look at the broader picture of how they are making effort. Texting is not the only way to make an effort or to show interest. Texting is never going to be a 50:50 relationship where you both start the conversation an equal number of times, send texts of equal length, and have equal reply times, in the same way that a relationship as a whole is rarely 50:50. Sometimes it will be 20:80, and other times that will reverse. But if you look at the overall effort being made and you do find you are starting more conversations than you would like, communicate that. If no change takes place, then validate your needs, understand your need for more communication is important, and end it.

As a person who views communication as one of her highest values, when someone is a bad communicator – whether that is because they raise their voice, can't apologize when they are wrong or take a week to reply to a text – I genuinely lose interest. It is now a turn-off to me because I associate good communication with good emotional intelligence, and that is what I am looking for in the people in my life. Once I validated that need, I flipped my mindset from getting insecure anytime someone stopped communicating with me to acknowledging that they couldn't meet my need, and I would express that kindly.

> Hey! It's been lovely chatting to you over the last few weeks. I think the way we communicate is too incompatible, though, so thank you for the great chats and take care xx

Forget Me Nots

- If you play games, you will attract a game-player
- Reply to the text when you see it and you are available
- Communicate how you want to be communicated with
- If your communication styles are too incompatible, you have voiced this and nothing has changed, then that is a reason to end a relationship

---

Take Action Toolkit: Let's unpack this idea of stimulus → meaning → response in the context of texting. When a meaning is not immediately provided, automatically assigned by a person explaining why they do the things they do, our brain will create stories. The majority of the time, the stories we tell ourselves will paint the worst version of events in order to make us feel bad about ourselves. It is important to realize the stories you make up about a person in the absence of a reply may not be accurate.

When someone texts me a lot, I think
....

When someone texts me a lot, it could also mean
....

When someone doesn't text me, I feel
....

I feel that way when someone doesn't text me because I am telling myself
....

When someone sees my text and doesn't reply, I tell myself
....

When someone sees my text and doesn't reply, it could also mean
....

Is It OK to Talk to More Than One Person at a Time?

Dating more than one person at a time is a strategy that revolutionized my way of dating. This strategy is not for everyone, and you have to listen to your own body when it comes to how it feels when you are dating multiple people. But for me, and for people who fall on a spectrum of getting attached earlier than they should, I found dating more than one person was the best way to slow things down, protect my heart a little more and force myself to evaluate the person in front of me, as opposed to just getting hooked on the first person who came along. It selfishly reminded me that my needs and my opinions were more important than theirs. As a person who used to romanticize and fantasize a lot, this worked for me, but I can't say it would be the ideal strategy if you are more avoidant; in fact, it might reinforce distancing strategies. Therefore, I want to offer this as one possible approach and make a case for it as something that worked for me. That doesn't mean it will work for everyone. Within life coaching, a core principle is that everyone actually already has the answers to their own problems, it is the life coach's job to ask the right questions to get you there. If the below resonates, great. If it doesn't, then leave it. Take what helps and leave the rest.

Dating more than one person raised my standards. When I was dating one person and they started treating me badly, it was really easy for my brain to feed into the narrative that all men are trash. My scarcity mindset would tell me to lower my standards because "He's the best we are going to get." By dating more than one person at once, it was easy to remind myself that my brain was lying. I had direct evidence that other people do meet my standards, which made this one person the anomaly. It also meant my communication got better. I learned how to end a relationship as soon as I wasn't feeling it or they started getting flaky – because when you have other offers, you recognize that you don't deserve that kind of treatment. You don't let men mess around with your schedule so when they bail on a date with no notice or explanation you tell them that:

> Hey! Sorry about last night, should we try again next Thursday?

> Hey! You missed your chance. You wasted my time last night and that doesn't work for me. Take care xx

As a result, it means that if one person stood out from the crowd, you also noticed them faster. More than anything, I got better at dating because, ultimately, the only way to do this is to go on dates. Having multiple first dates a week lowered the pressure of each one and it meant I could be myself more and so enjoy myself more. It was also just a lot of fun! I got to have many life experiences with different people while exploring London more than I had ever done. Meeting fascinating people – and realizing they were interested in me too – gave me a confidence in my dating life that I never had before, and cemented my belief that I bring a lot to the table.

When I talk about dating more than one person at a time, I don't mean as a polyamorous or an open relationship. I see this as the dating stage, the talking stage or the pre-exclusive stage. Unless we have decided to be exclusive, we aren't. I understand it can be confusing with all these new terms and it can be particularly frustrating when you want more commitment than the other person is willing to give, but dating this way made me realize how important the talking stage was. The stages before becoming exclusive are critical periods of time that provide you with valuable information and, more importantly, allow you to figure out whether they deserve your vulnerability.

Men have been dating like this for years, yet when I started doing this and would talk about it, there was one word that was constantly being thrown in my direction: "fuckboy". The truth is, I wasn't dating like a fuckboy. The definition of a fuckboy is one that is dishonest, leads people on and doesn't care who they mess around. Instead, I was being transparent and upfront, and not making assumptions that we were exclusive before we had the conversation. I was meeting people at the level at which they were investing and wasn't in a rush to expedite the exclusive process.

I used to get really frustrated in university that there was a stereotype in straight relationships that women are always the ones that want more commitment, even when that hasn't been communicated. In my second year of university, I kissed a guy that was on the outskirts of my friendship group at a mutual friend's birthday party. When we returned to university after the summer holidays, this guy would go around our whole friendship group and hug each person and purposely miss me out. It was rude and, more importantly, it was obvious. I had not told anyone about our kiss, so my friends were understandably confused as to why he was suddenly ignoring me. On one of these occasions, one of my guy friends turned to him and said, "What's up with you and Michelle? Why are you acting like she doesn't exist?" He told him that we had kissed and he didn't want to lead me on. When this was passed on to me, I laughed. Who said I was interested in him? I wanted to forget the kiss so much that I hadn't told anyone – meanwhile, he had told himself a story in his head that he was so irresistible that a cordial hug would leave me picturing our wedding together. It's archaic and frustrating, and I believe it's this kind of mindset that leads to fuckboy behaviour and more ghosting than is necessary. In my experience, it's also why women don't tend to date more than one person.

Before I started dating more than one person, I realized that men were dating one way and women were dating another. A woman would match with someone and stop swiping or talking to others. At a push, some women wait until a date is confirmed and then they stop swiping. However, guys keep swiping past the first date and beyond until there is an exclusive conversation (and sometimes after!). Until we both start dating in the same way, it is never going to be fair or equal, and the woman will always be the more attached party. Instead, when I started dating more than one person, I normalized not making assumptions. Most men have a rotation; I simply got one as well.

The main distinction between the way I was dating and a fuckboy is the fact that I communicate. Dating selfishly doesn't mean being a dick. It means honouring your needs and treating others how you would want to be treated. When I date two people at the same time, they both know. I don't go out of my way to tell them before the information is necessary, but I don't hide it. If they ask me out on a night that I am going out with someone else, I say, "I have another date that night. How about Monday instead?" Their reactions often tell you a lot. One guy voiced the fact that he was uncomfortable with it even before our first date. I responded that I had actually started talking to the other guy first and booked in that first date before his. I said that I didn't know if he was dating other people, I didn't want to know and we hadn't even been on a first date yet, so it was peculiar to me to want an exclusive relationship with someone you've not even met.

Then there are the conversations I have at a later date. I had just gone on a fifth date with a guy when he said he wasn't dating anyone else. I said that I was dating one other guy, and he asked whether I was sleeping with him too. I don't personally like sleeping with two people at the same time and I believe in the importance of being transparent if you are. I told him I wasn't and then he said that it was starting to make him uncomfortable that I was dating someone else and I needed to make a decision. I thanked him for his honesty, said I needed some time and then made a choice. I actually ended up choosing him, and the choice was an easy one to make – but with clear communication, no one gets messed around. Even with the other guy, he knew I was seeing other people, so I said that one of the guys I was dating wanted to be exclusive and that I'd been having a great time with him but I really wanted to give it a shot. He thanked me for my honesty and we made a brief attempt at trying to stay friends. When you practise transparency and good communication in your dating life, you will be amazed how much more open the people you date will be with you. Your directness gives them permission to be direct back, and in a world where ghosting is the norm, people are often appreciative of your candour and being able to know that you are on the same page. Most people I dated never had an issue with this because they would be dating others too. When they wanted more commitment, it was never assumed but directly communicated. We can kvetch about how dating has changed, no one wants commitment these days and everything is so complicated or we can be the clarity we seek in our dating lives.

Forget Me Nots

- The only way to get better at dating is to go on dates
- The main distinction between dating nonexclusively and a fuckboy is communication and transparency
- It's not healthy to immediately become someone's top priority – the talking stage allows you to slowly become important to someone
- Unless we have decided to be exclusive, we aren't

Take Action Toolkit: One way you can strengthen your boundaries is to control who has access to you. Inherent in notifications is a demand for you to see a message as soon as it arrives, and that sends the implicit message that it should be your top priority. I don't think this should be the case. People can rise in your order of priorities over time, but if you are still communicating on a dating app, then they shouldn't get priority yet. A way to do this is to change your notifications for dating apps. I personally have no notifications for any dating app. I choose to go on the app once a day and reply to those messages at a time that is convenient for me. If I happen to be on the app when someone replies, I write back because I have seen their message, but dedicating a specific time to it means you don't let your phone dictate your priorities.

What Do I Actually Say on Dating Apps?

One of the common complaints I hear is about how boring texting is on a dating app. You have the same conversations over and over again and, because so many don't lead to in-person dates, it can quickly feel like a waste of time. One way I avoid boring conversations is using a technique that I do when I'm talking on panels. The questions that I am asked on stage or in interviews tend to be quite repetitive: "What's one tip for someone who wants to start setting boundaries?" and "If you could tell your younger self one thing about boundaries, what would it be?" It got pretty boring for me to keep answering those same questions, so I wouldn't. I would answer the question with what I wanted to talk about instead. That way, I wasn't bored and it benefitted my audience because they weren't getting the same content. I didn't answer the question I was given, I answered the question I wanted to be given. How does this apply to dating? I never answer "How are you?" directly. It's a rubbish question on a dating app. I either become a needle in a haystack by saying "Yeah, good. You?" or I become an emotional dumper and tell you how awful I am feeling and reel off every single problem in my life. I don't like either of those options and so I don't reply to the question literally.

I can use the question to simply say what I did that day:

> How are you?

> Good, I just came back from the gym and I've collapsed on the sofa and I'm doing that thing where I am trying to mentally scan my fridge and decide what I want to eat before getting up to actually check what food I have in the house. Tell me you've done that before!

Or I can use the question to discuss something I'm interested in and have no one to talk to about:

> How are you?

> Good, I am just watching *Inventing Anna* and I don't know how I feel about the fact that the original con artist got paid for this show. Have you seen it?

Or I can even turn it into a silly conversation:

> How are you?

> Good. I'm just sitting in a coffee shop and the person in front of me has both a glass of wine and a cup of tea and I'm horrified at the combination. It's one or the other! It's just wrong to have both at the same time. Please say you agree with me

In all of these examples, you will also notice there is an air of confidence to them. I've taken a stance without knowing their opinion and I have offered enough information to start a different conversation without much investment. The key with this is that you get to decide the trajectory of the conversation; you don't just have to accept the one you are given. When you enter the conversation as an interesting person and not the bog-standard "yeah, good" replier, it then becomes easy to weed out the boring people. Let's see how these play out:

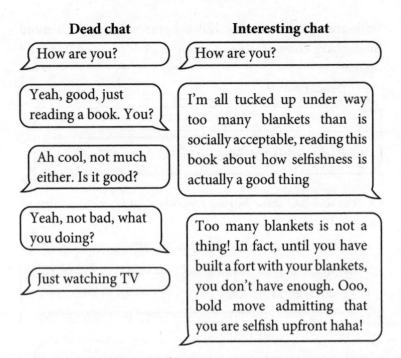

Dead chat	Interesting chat
How are you?	How are you?
Yeah, good, just reading a book. You?	I'm all tucked up under way too many blankets than is socially acceptable, reading this book about how selfishness is actually a good thing
Ah cool, not much either. Is it good?	
Yeah, not bad, what you doing?	Too many blankets is not a thing! In fact, until you have built a fort with your blankets, you don't have enough. Ooo, bold move admitting that you are selfish upfront haha!
Just watching TV	

Now, could you respond with the interesting chat and be met with an "ah cool"? Absolutely. But then at least you know it's not you. If they just reply with "good", that's the end of the conversation. If you enter the chat excited about life and enthusiastic to be there, and then get a dead response, at least you know sooner rather than later. By having your bio filled out and a complete profile with prompts, you increase the chance of having a more interesting conversation. Even without that, a good opener can help. As an example, I once received the following messages on the same day from two different people:

> What are you most passionate about?

> Your profile is great! You are really cute!

Both are sweet messages, but the one will lead to a more interesting conversation. During lockdown, this was my opener:

> Hey *insert name*! At what stage of lockdown are you? I'm at a struggling-to-see-the-end-and-loving-my-sofa-a-little-too-much stage

Of course, I had some boring responses, but here are some of the good ones:

> Hey Michelle! Oh I'm wayyy past that point. Today I woke up at midday, got UberEats to deliver me a McDonald's and have yet to actually properly get out of bed! My only excuse is I'm on gardening leave

> Oh, I entirely understand Michelle, I'm at the "I can understand my cat's specific meows" and "Blankets are my friend" stage

If you are reading this and thinking that you are boring, you are wrong. I truly believe that boring people do not exist. "Boring people" are simply people who live boring lives and once you start creating an exciting life, it is impossible to be boring. An interesting life doesn't mean you have to be in a club and partying all week, it means you have to be interested in your life. As I have shown above, you can be reading a book and make it interesting. There was a quote I saw on Instagram many years ago that said the best people are those you can ask a ridiculous question like "A hippo is chasing you, what do you do?", and they'll say "How big is the hippo?" instead of telling you that you are being silly. I take that same energy into dating apps. The first ever conversation I had with my boyfriend, he had responded to the prompt I mentioned earlier in the book – "The key to my heart is ... ambition, emotional intelligence and passion in whatever you do. Someone who can handle a little sass, a lot of deep chats with cuddles in between" – with the following:

> Deep chats and cuddles are the best thing on the planet :) Maybe with a cup of tea and some blankets?

> Well, I don't just share my blankets with anyone ... it depends how you would make my tea?

We spent the first few messages debating how a perfect cup of tea was made, and I teased him, saying that I thought sugar in your tea was only a thing that kids did. Was how he made his tea really a deal-breaker? Of course not, but it showed me his sense of humour and it was a light-hearted, fun conversation that demonstrated both of our personalities. Plus, it was far more engaging than pointless small talk! And if we could talk about tea that long, it implied we weren't in danger of a silent first date.

If you don't know where to start, use their bio. If they don't have a bio, then I won't message first because it implies they fit into the category of "time-wasters". My pet peeve is profiles with no bio except "Don't just say hey." I think it reeks of entitlement to judge someone for starting a conversation in a boring way when you aren't even willing to do the basics of filling out your profile. I actually think it's OK to start with "Hey! How are you?" – again, the difference is in the next response, and my follow-up will be interesting too. When I have the energy to, I will often try to add more and start a conversation with something like: "Hey! How are you? I've just spent the whole day cleaning my apartment and now I'm not sure I know where anything is", so they have something to comment on. Sometimes it's commenting on a travelling picture with a simple "Is that Australia?" Here's an example of a conversation that led from a caption about how he was always too full for dessert:

> I'm not a big dessert person anyway. Much more of a multiple starters that we can share kinda person

> Get over here now 🤩

> Hold up ... I need to know whether we are getting bread for the table first

Whether you are questioning what to text or what to actually say on a first date, this requires practice. It's not about whether you were gifted a personality at birth, it's about being able to lead a conversation and engage people on topics that are interesting both to you and to them.

Forget Me Nots

- Don't answer "How are you?" literally
- If you enter the chat with boring energy, you often will receive boring energy

- Decide the trajectory of the conversation yourself, not the trajectory you are already on
- You don't have to be good at dating, just good at being a conversationalist – and that's a skill worth practising, as it's useful in more than one area of life

Take Action Toolkit: It is easy to overthink the texts you send and tell yourself that how you phrase it will decide whether you last or not. Telling yourself this will make your body stressed and that will reinforce what you are thinking. When you find yourself overthinking, the best thing you can do then is to relax your jaw and look up. This works because it utilizes eye patterns. According to Neuro-linguistic programming, a model I am trained in, in order to get in your feelings or to talk to yourself inside your head, you need to look down. When doing this with a trained professional, you can decipher which is on your left or your right side but for the purpose of this section, all you need to know is to access the visual representation of the world you have to look up. This will happen naturally mid-conversation when trying to recall something visual like what your car looks like or even imaginary things like what your front door would look like with yellow spots on it, but you can use eye patterns intentionally too. Therefore when you intentionally stop looking down your brain will have increased difficulty accessing your kinaesthetic (feelings) or your auditory digital (talking to yourself) areas. The reason it is important to relax your jaw is because we clench it when we have a conversation with ourselves. Overthinkers tend to have very strong jawlines as a result! If you want to relax even more, do a long in-breath and let out a long audible sigh. Sighing is associated with relief, so your body will experience that relief even if nothing has changed.

How Do I Turn Texting Into a Date?

There is no point being on dating apps if you have no intention of actually getting off the app and meeting in person. I don't need to be having endless back and forths when we could just be doing this face-to-face, or at the very least, in a phone call. We have all been trapped in conversations with these time-wasters. In fact, over the course of years, I matched with the same guy on five different apps and had conversations that spanned weeks on each app. We even planned a date twice – and yet we never went. Now, I would never let this happen. I nip it in the bud early. There are many people who will text you for weeks without any intention of following up with a date or following through on the plan they set. This is why I take it off the app as soon as I can, even if I am unsure if I will like them. I don't believe you need to like someone to go on a first date; you just need to be curious.

I won't spend ages texting unless we have a date already organized and, until we reach that point, I keep communication to a minimum. From the very first text, I set up the assumption that we are going to eventually meet. I set it up as a "when", not an "if".

When they ask a question that requires a long answer:

> So how did you become an author?

> Long story, I'll tell you in person

When they ask for information that's too personal:

> Oh, why were you in the hospital?

> I'll explain one day – that's a Date Three story

When you discover something in common:

> I'm such a foodie

> Now I'm excited to see where you pick for our first date!

Or even include the prospect of a date in a light-hearted way:

> Wow, I thought I was clumsy!

> I should warn you, I'm even worse in person

If you assume we are going on a date, it exudes confidence. I very rarely ask people out myself. Instead, what I prefer to do is make it easy for them to ask me out. In the same way that I talk about how you make yourself more approachable when you introduce yourself at the bar, you are making yourself more approachable by implying a date. The reason I do this is because I find it's a great opportunity to see how interested the person is – and also how proactive they are. One of the top values I look for in a person I am dating is that they are proactive. I make enough decisions in my work life and, among my friends, I am always the planner and the booker, so in my love life, I don't want to have to always be initiating. When you make comments like the ones above, what you are doing is taking out the vulnerability of asking you out. It's telling them: "If you ask me out, it will be a yes." In the past, I would do all the legwork, and what ended up happening was a lot of people saying yes and then cancelling on the day. In the bestselling book *He's Just Not That Into You*, the authors say, "I know it sounds old school, but when men like women, they ask them out." It's quite sexist to suggest you wait for them to ask you, so I'm not saying that. If you want to ask them out, do. No one is stopping you. What I'am saying is if you ask them out and plan the date, you actually don't give them the opportunity to take the lead. Create space for them to make more effort. If they ask me where I want to go, I will often say "I don't mind, you pick" or "Surprise me!" If they don't make a plan, I am happy to, but I give them a chance first. It doesn't matter who asks who out, or who makes the plan. It matters that there is effort on both ends. If there is a discrepancy in effort at the beginning, it will likely be there throughout. Allow them to meet you halfway.

As controversial as it is, doing it this way has served me well. It's not about being feminist or anti-feminist, it's about reciprocity and matching the level of investment they are making. How the first date is planned also provides you with a lot of information based on what they pick. Do they pick a location close to you or to them? Do they ask for your preference or just make a decision? Do they pick a bar, a pub, or something a bit different? Do they suggest a free date like a walk in the park or one of the most expensive restaurants in London? There are no right or wrong answers to these questions – they're just providing information on whether you are compatible with each other.

There are a number of dating experts who would disagree with the above. More recently, there has been a bigger conversation about how we should only be going on "high-investment dates" (a subtle way of saying expensive dates) as compensation for the inequality in the world and how, due to things like the gender pay gap, in straight relationships, them footing the bill is equity. In theory this may work, but practically, you can't apply the rules of a system on an individual basis. Systemically, men get paid more than women but with two individuals on a date, the financial disparity could actually go the other way. This way of thinking goes that if you are offered a walk in the park, you are meant to retort with "You need to give me a better offer for me to leave my house", and some go as far as to say that if they aren't taken to a high-end restaurant, it's a no. It is a great technique if money is your highest value within your dating life, but even then, it creates cause for concern.

The way some people use money is to control others. They will pay the big checks, take you to the fancy restaurants – but then there is an entitlement to what they believe they deserve in exchange, whether that's sexual acts or control over your appearance. In fact, one of the principles of "strategic dating" is that you present the best version of yourself – but to the extent that you are portraying a level of wealth (by carrying expensive handbags) that you don't have, in order to attract a certain kind of person. Money can make the relationship quite transactional. Without intending to, you can put yourself in a position where you're distracted by the expensive, shiny things and not paying attention to the person in front of you. Personally, if someone can't recognize my worth without designer trappings, that is not someone I want. There is no judgement within this; if it works for both parties, then good for you.

If a sugar daddy/mummy relationship is what you are after, and it works for both parties, then good for you. I want to be clear there is no judgement on these types of relationships, but "strategic dating" is not this. Strategic dating elicits strong feelings in me because of the level of deceptiveness. In most cases, one person is not aware of how transactional the relationship is, and is seeking out connection and intimacy within the relationship. It's important to note that this way of dating will attract a superficial man. It is close to impossible to have a healthy dynamic when this is the precedent. If you are toting luxury handbags that you can't actually afford in order to portray yourself a certain way, that's manipulation – that version of you doesn't exist. Healthy relationships don't include manipulation. A number of the ways of thinking within strategic dating feed into the messaging around the beauty ideal, especially because the beauty ideal targets straight women. They say that if you want to attract a "high-value man", then you need to be wearing make-up and if you aren't good at doing make-up, you should invest in lessons. It follows the school of thought that a high-value man is one that is deemed by society to be the beauty ideal – and therefore, you also need to make "an effort" with your appearance. If you are plus size, you should lose weight to become high value. It's quite a toxic school of thought because our value doesn't lie in our appearance. Our worth isn't determined by the world declaring us "high value" but by us recognizing our own value, even if it doesn't fit with the world's definition of what should be of value. Furthermore, if you have to pretend to be someone else to keep a partner, that's not someone you should keep.

My preferred first date is drinks. I prefer a low-investment date – and not just low investment in terms of how much money they spend, but in terms of how much time I have to commit. If you commit to a meal, what if you decide you don't like them after the starter? Even with a fun date like minigolf, what if you've run out of conversation by hole four? I am so opposed to the idea of strategic dating that when I went on a first date and the guy offered to buy me both a Rolex and an iPad, it made me uncomfortable. A stranger should treat you like a stranger; that experience made me feel bought. When a guy asked me out and then proceeded to name three of the most expensive restaurants in London as options for our date, my first thought wasn't about how "high investment" that sounded, it was: "What are you compensating for?" It doesn't tell me that he is investing a lot in me specifically, but rather that he invests a lot in all his dates – because ultimately, he does not know me. This could just be a nice gesture, but it implies they are not secure enough in what they bring to the table that they need to make sure it's an expensive table. As you can probably tell, money is not one of my values in dating and it is not a reason I would or wouldn't date, so I don't care who pays on a first date. However, I do have a value for reciprocity, so I would care if I always end up paying – not because of the money, but because of the fairness. If you get one drink, they get the other. If they want to pay for it all, I let them, but I am cognizant of it over the course of our dates, so that we maintain a balance.

When organizing the date, pay attention to the information they are providing. I never blame a human for trying to make it as convenient for themselves as possible; that's them being selfish and putting their needs first, but you can be selfish too. Place a value on your own convenience, say no and offer an alternative. Communicating standards is about telling them that it doesn't work for you and that you have higher expectations.

If they pick somewhere close to them and far from you:

> That doesn't work for me. Let's pick somewhere in the middle xx

If they give you a last-minute offer with little notice:

> I need more notice. Make a plan and I'll consider it xx

If you accept what you are given, it reads as "I want to see you, no matter what, whenever you squeeze me, no matter how little you give me." Planning implies that you are a priority. It's not about making it a red flag or cancelling the date, but notice it. Set a precedent for the effort and respect you deserve. This is also when people can stand out. For example, when my boyfriend booked our first date, I noticed that he not only chose to have it near me but he also picked the closest bar to me. There are next to no options in my neighbourhood, and despite the fact it would have taken him two hours to get there and I could walk there in less than five minutes, that's what he chose. This information is valuable because it's often a sign of things to come. If he isn't even doing the middle ground on the first date, when people are usually on their best behaviour, what makes you think the effort will be there in a few months?

Within *The Joy of Being Selfish*, I used an example of a time when I was making plans for the next day with a guy I was casually seeing, and he said he would let me know in the morning. I shared the following text exchange:

> That's not how this works. Let me know now if you are free, and if not, I'm making other plans

> Alright, Miss Sassy. 3 p.m. it is

When you set a boundary, the person can either step up and start behaving better because they know they will lose you, or they don't – and that means they are willing to take that risk. Let them lose you. Communicate your standard and how you deserve to be treated. I also don't allow strangers to have the pick of my week. They have not earned it. I pick two dates that are convenient for me and let them decide. In the past, if they chose a date that didn't work for me, I would change my plans to make it work. Dating selfishly means to stop rearranging your life for strangers. You shouldn't be making sacrifices this early on in a relationship.

A note on safety here: taking things from online to offline can be nerve-wracking from a safety perspective and while I am adamant it is not the victim's responsibility to not get murdered or sexually assaulted, there are a few things that I personally do that put my mind at ease. I will look up their social media profile to verify they are who they say they are. LinkedIn is often the best site because it's easy to find someone without a last name (if their job is on their dating profile). Through that, I am usually able to find a last name and verify their identity. If I am unable to find a profile, I will call the place they have made a booking and ask for the last name. It might sound paranoid, but you are meeting a complete stranger and I would rather be safe than sorry. The reason I don't ask the guy directly for the information is because most men, no matter how feminist they are, do not understand the everyday safety concerns that go through women's minds; if that is not your lived experience, it likely comes across as suspicious. Most of the time, after we've met, I will tell the person that I have looked them up. Until that point, it's just unnecessary information.

With a job and a full name, I have a way of keeping them accountable, whatever happens on the date. Unfortunately, people are often held more accountable by their workplace than the dating app, mainly because the greatest consequence a dating app can do is block you, whereas a workplace can fire you. That is likely to be of higher importance to the person and therefore provides greater accountability. I give their last name and job to a friend who is free that evening, who will also have me on Find My Friends so they know my location. I usually arrange for them to call me an hour into the date to check that all is well. In the planning of the date, there have been a number of instances that have sent alarm bells off. In those instances, I don't risk it. In one situation, I asked a guy what he did for a living and when I found out my friend worked near him, I asked him which company he worked for and he refused to tell me. I am direct in those situations.

> The fact you are being so adamant about not telling me where you work is concerning. You know all the details about my job, and reciprocity is important to me xx

He dug his heels in and I cancelled our date that was planned for the next day. With another guy, we had planned to go for a walk as it was the week that lockdown lifted and restaurants, bars and pubs were still closed. I asked him to give me a location to meet and he said Richmond Park. I said Richmond Park was huge and we needed to pick a specific location. That's when he offered to pick me up at the station in his car. I said that I didn't want to get in his car and suggested we just name a place, so I picked a pub outside the park where we could meet. He said that it's hard to park around there. I asked him to give me a street name where he could park. He said it was too complicated and if I just stood outside the station, he'd swing by and pick me up. The insistence of picking me up in his car made me nervous and I never went on that date. Follow your instincts. If there is even a little doubt in your mind that they are acting strange, don't go on the date. It's not worth the risk.

However, to balance out the negative press about them, I refuse to buy this narrative that all dating apps are dangerous. The number of successful encounters way outweighs negative ones, and the negative ones only make the news because they are rare. With eight years on dating apps, and some safety precautions in place, I never felt like I was taking more of a risk than I was with the people I met in bars. There is the potential for danger, in the same way that dangerous things could happen if someone asked for your number in a pub. It's important to remember that correlation does not equal causation, and in the instances where a man has raped or killed someone on a dating-app date, that is down to the perpetrator and not the dating app. People were killed and sexually assaulted on dates before dating apps. They would have been just as dangerous even if you had met them another way. One way some people feel better about meeting a stranger is doing a pre-date phone call or Face-Time. This is another way to verify they are who they say they are and can serve as a chemistry check to see if you get on. If you are still concerned about your safety, the Safer Sounds Partnership has set up a safety scheme called Ask for Angela. If you feel unsafe on a date, you can go to the bar and ask for "Angela" and they will get you out of the situation. Be sure to select a place where they are aware of this campaign – the posters are usually located behind the doors in the women's toilets.

Forget Me Nots

- You don't need to like someone to go on a date, you just need to be curious about them
- Text as if it's assumed you are meeting up eventually
- A stranger should treat you like a stranger
- When you set a boundary, the person can either step up and start behaving better because they know they will lose you, or they don't – and that means they are willing to take that risk. Let them lose you.

Take Action Toolkit

If you dread first dates, it's time to inject some pleasure into it. Forget the person you are going on a date with – how could you make the evening more pleasurable? For me, the part I dread most about a date evening is figuring out an outfit, so I prevented this by creating a go-to first-date outfit so I didn't have to faff. After all, you aren't going to ever go on a first date with the same person twice, so no one will know it's a repeat outfit. Remove the misery and increase the pleasure. For you, it could be going to that museum that you've not had anyone to go with or choosing to go to a pub instead of a bar. It could be that you hate putting make-up on, so either remove this aspect entirely or just keep it to a quick swipe of your favourite lipstick or mascara. It could be that you have a craving for ice cream, so when they ask you what you want to do, say:

I don't mind, but all I know is it must involve
ice cream

Choose a date that suits you and it will create a pleasurable evening even if you don't end up being interested in the person.

IF YOU LOOK AT REPLY TIMES...

Chapter 7

Stop Impressing Them, Let Them Impress You

How to Be Empowered on First Dates

What if They Cancel?

There is a certain kind of person who exists on dating apps who only wants to chat on the app and never meet in real life. Except this person is even more of a coward: they follow through on the planning of the date only to cancel the day of. And sometimes they don't even bother to let you know. Unfortunately, this is very common and it is beyond frustrating. I hate having my time wasted and I very rarely give them a chance to waste my time twice. I have only ever given someone a second chance once. He said a family member had died and – because I had been on dating apps long enough to receive every excuse under the sun – I assumed it was a lie and moved on with my life. Turns out his grandma had actually died and, three months later, he got back in touch after he had processed some of his grief. It ended up being a wonderful first date. Of course, real-life things happen, but if it's a genuine excuse, you will know because of what happens next. There is a difference between:

> Hey! Can't make it anymore! Sorry! xx

> Hey! So sorry I know this is last minute, but something came up with work. I would really like to see you. I'm free next Tuesday and Thursday. Let me know when works for you and I'll sort something fun xx

It might have taken him three months (understandable, given how draining grief is), but he reached out again because he always had the intention of going on the date. (I myself have only cancelled a date twice. But when I do that, I offer an immediate alternative date, put in the extra effort to organize it and often foot the bill as an apology for the inconvenience caused the last time.) Whether the excuse is valid or not doesn't matter, because time will tell. How they rearrange demonstrates how they treat humans and how much respect they have for other people's time. The key here is to not take it personally and regardless of how last minute or ridiculous the excuse is, I respond politely:

> Hey! No worries, thanks for letting me know. Have a lovely evening xx

The ball is then in their court. More times than not, that ends up being the last text and I put them in the category of guys who are "time-wasters", who only want online interactions. Then there are the ones that go even further. If you haven't been stood up, then you haven't dated enough. I have been stood up twice. Thankfully, both times it didn't involve me waiting in a public place alone. With one, it was a first date and he had started acting off a few days before, so I had texted him the morning of to see if we were still on to meet at the bakery he had booked at 12 noon. He never responded, so I didn't go there. As soon as I started to feel he was getting flaky, I prepared myself for the inevitable. And when I hadn't heard back by 10 a.m., I made other plans. What would I have said if he ended up replying last minute?

> I didn't hear back so I made other plans xx

I don't wait around to be annoyed and I also didn't pretend to make other plans, I actually did. I went swimming with a friend and had a fun day in the sun so that, regardless of his decision, my day was unaffected. Previously, in my self-less days, I would have been overly understanding, spent the day waiting by the phone, obsessively checking it and getting increasingly more disappointed. I would have then got sad and seen it as a reflection of me, and questioned whether I did anything wrong. When he eventually texted, I would have jumped at my phone and replied so quickly, saying that it was OK. We would make plans only for it to happen again. I ended up getting a text from this guy at 3 p.m., three hours after our booking, asking me how my day was, ignoring my previous texts or even the acknowledgement that we had a date. Take me for granted and watch how quickly I end things. Here was my response:

> Hey! I find it really disrespectful that you didn't let me know or even acknowledge that we had a date today, let alone apologize for it. This doesn't work for me and I'm not interested anymore. Thanks for the chats and take care xx

His apology came later that evening at midnight. We had planned to go for lunch as he was starting work at 5 p.m. and was doing a night shift:

> Hey! Sorry, I've been flat out at work this evening. That's understandable. Apologies for wasting your time today, hope you find what you are looking for xx

This reply was interesting. He knew he had behaved badly but I guess he was testing his luck to see if I would ignore it? I found it curious that he didn't even try to convince me otherwise – and that's why I keep these kinds of people as a separate category. They don't have an intention of meeting and I'm not sure they ever did. If someone cancels, bails or even stands you up, do you think they have done it before? Of course they have, and they will likely do it again. He owns his shitty behaviour – that doesn't belong to me and I'm certainly not going to be carrying it. It's got nothing to do with me. If you don't date in an empowered way, it's really easy to believe it is you, but being stood up happened to me just twice in eight years of dating. Why would I pull eight years of positive dating experiences out of context to make myself feel bad? The other time I was stood up, it was a second date. I had just come back from an incredible photo shoot and he was meeting me at mine to go for a walk. He never got in touch, but if he had resurfaced at a later date, I would have declined his offer:

> No, thank you. My schedule is pretty packed and I think it's best we just leave it xx

I had scheduled the date for the two-hour window that I had free that day and so instead spent that time relaxing. Then I went on my way to my next event, where I was speaking on a panel about my favourite thing: boundaries. This is why you cultivate a life that you love. I'd had an amazing day without our date and my first thought was: "It's his loss."

Forget Me Nots:

- It doesn't matter if their excuse is fake or genuine – if it's real, they will rearrange
- If you need to cancel, offer an alternative time and make extra effort to plan the date
- Don't wait around to be annoyed – make other plans so you aren't watching your phone
- If someone cancels, bails or even stands you up, they've done it before

---

Take Action Toolkit: When someone cancels, it can lead you to spiral into negative and unhelpful thoughts. One thing I use if I am thinking something I don't want to be thinking anymore is I yell "Next!" in my head. If you are alone, it works even better to say it aloud. I imagine it's like hitting the next button when listening to music. Once the word "Next!" has broken the spiral I caught myself in, I then do what I like to call an appreciation spree, in which I focus my mind on things I can appreciate. Focusing on the gratitude in your life might sound cliché, but it works. You can appreciate things about yourself, like the fact that you are willing to take risks even if it didn't work out or general things in life, like the sun shining today. This combined with yelling "Next!" is a two-pronged approach to changing the direction of your thoughts.

How Can I Be Certain It Will Last?

Stop dating with the goal of a relationship. When you are dating for a specific purpose, it becomes a means to an end, and that sucks the fun out of the entire process. In the same way that I only started enjoying exercise when I removed the goal of weight loss, you measure your happiness in a different way. Whether it's weight loss and exercise or dating without the goal of a relationship, it gets squeezed into a pass or fail mechanism. When you measure a date's success or failure based on whether you get another, and a relationship's success or failure on whether you become official, it removes the ability to stay present in the moment and enjoy the person in front of you. The response I often get is: "But what if I do want a relationship?" Well, if you are actually having fun, the chance of you getting a relationship is higher – but that's not why you should do it. You should do it because when you skip ahead in life, you miss the fun in the moment.

I learned this lesson when my housemate told me she was going to move out to live with her boyfriend. I have always been terrified of living alone and, faced with the prospect of that, I asked one of my friends if I should fill my housemate's room or whether I should actually face my fear. My friend lived alone and she said the reason she decided to was because "One day, I will be living with my boyfriend and there will be a day I have a house full of kids and I long for an empty house. So why not treasure it while I have the chance?" I had the financial privilege to be able to not worry about the increased cost, so I kept the room empty. After two years, I made that decision final by converting the room into the office I am writing from right now. After five years of living alone, I can say I am no longer scared of it and actually love solitude.

I see my single period the same way. I treated it like a finite period of time that I didn't want to waste away. How would I act if my goal of one day being married and having kids was inevitable? I would be making the most of this precious time where I'm not attached to anyone and have no responsibilities. Ultimately, one of my life goals has always been a relationship. I am the type of person who has known since they were seven years old that they want to get married and have kids, but there is a difference between that being my life goal and seeing every date I go on as a stepping stone towards that goal. Just because I know I want to get married someday doesn't mean I want to get married to the person I am dating.

If you think this is impossible, I hate to break it to you, but you already form relationships in this way. Every time you make a new friend, you don't have a goal in mind and you are able to enjoy the time you spend with them. When you arrived at a new school, you didn't make a condition on your first day that you would only become friends with them if the friendship survived at least 20 years. If that friendship were to end, you wouldn't label it a "waste of time", because there was no hidden agenda. It's the reason people hate networking events, because you go into those events with a purpose and if you don't make the necessary connections, then it actually is a waste of time. Can you imagine if every time you went to a house party and started a conversation with a stranger, you were assessing if that person is friendship material? House parties would quickly stop being fun. I'm simply asking that you see dating the same way.

Have you ever had someone buy you a drink with an expectation of something in return? Or have you ever had a person in your life who will do nice things for you but they will keep count and ask for a favour at a later date and use that nice thing as a bargaining chip? Everything given becomes a tit for tat. While you might not be able to pinpoint it in the moment, it feels different to someone buying you a drink because they want to or doing a nice thing because they care about you. It feels icky and you would have rather known to say no to the drink or favour if it came with strings attached. When you go on a date with the goal of getting a relationship, you exude the same energy. It's the idea that they only deserve your time and energy if you get a relationship in exchange.

If you struggle to remove the idea of a goal around dating, then set a new goal, one that is focused on yourself and improving your dating skills. After all, you can only get good at dating if you actually go on dates. We want confidence before we take action, but taking action builds confidence. When I first started dating without the goal of a relationship, I would set an intention prior to each date. This could be that I wanted to be better at listening because I noticed I had spoken a lot on my previous date but didn't ask enough about them. It could be setting the goal to be more comfortable in silence and allowing the awkwardness to exist, instead of rushing to fill it. For one date, I even remember just setting the very basic goal of not laughing when I didn't find things funny. I still had left-over habits from people-pleasing – I felt pressure to perform on a date rather than be authentic, and staying true to myself was something I wanted to work on. Instead of pretending to laugh, I would simply smile and continue the conversation, and that felt more authentic.

It's small things like this that make a big difference over time, because if you laugh at things you don't find funny, the other person understandably gets the impression you have a similar sense of humour, and that's not accurate. When you are authentic, you allow both of you to see if you are actually a match. I've had dates where my intention was to interrupt less. It's a bad habit that I've always wanted to get rid of, so going on the date would help make me better. I've had dates where my intention was to learn something new from the person. You can learn something from everyone you encounter, and by going on a date with this intention, it encourages me to get more curious. As a result, each date not only makes me more authentic but actually makes me better at dating. Even if it doesn't lead to another date, there are wins there because these dates have allowed me to improve my communication skills and get closer to figuring out what I want. I use dates as a training ground because the person doesn't know you. You can be whoever you want to be, and if that's a better version of myself, my date gets to meet that person too. Setting goals that are based on yourself are more fulfilling to achieve, whereas the goal of a relationship depends on both parties.

I only did this in the beginning of my dating experience to distance myself from the idea that a date should lead to a relationship. For me, it quickly evolved into simply dating because it was fun and enjoyable. I loved getting to know new people, and each one brought a different point of view. Whether it was me learning about songwriting from a guy who had a song that went platinum or exploring a food market with a pastry chef, dating made my life fuller and, by extension, the guys I was dating were making my life fuller too.

See each date as an experiment. When an experiment is written up and nothing is found, it is said to have "insignificant findings", but it is not deemed a failure. Insignificant findings provide us with information that is needed as well. Whatever the outcome of the experiment, significant or not, we learn something new. Apply that to dating. I remember being asked out by a guy I felt unsure about but, following my rule to stay curious, I accepted. An hour later, a restaurant was booked and I was sent the time and address. I was impressed. I was actually so shocked at how impressed I was that I told all my friends about it. Many said it was bare minimum and "HE BOOKED" is now a running joke in my friendship group. It ended up being an average first date, but it showed me something I didn't know about myself. I like guys who are proactive and initiate, make plans and organize – and I actually found it a turn-on. As much as my friends make fun of me now, I'm glad I had that experience because it showed me something new to look for in the next person.

A lot of the time, when you set a goal of a relationship, every date you go on is a potential partner and, unconsciously, you commit earlier than you intend to. Stop seeing every first date as the last first date you are going to go on. You put up with more because you want it to work out so badly. You put your blinkers on because you want the relationship more than the person. That's when you can fall in love with their potential and not the reality. You don't even know if they are reliable, if your values match or whether or not they can apologize when wrong. This is why I find the question of "What are you looking for?" frustrating, especially when asked on a dating app. It's too narrow, and you can't know what you are looking for until you know the person. When I get asked that, my two responses are:

> I love my life and I'm looking for someone to add to that

> I am looking for a relationship, but I would rather be single than be in a bad one

For brevity, I sometimes will just say a relationship, but that still doesn't mean I date with the goal of a relationship. I have ended up in many fulfilling casual relationships and had great one-nighters from dating apps, but I would never sleep with someone before meeting them for a date first. When you state that you are looking for something casual, they tend to invite you over straight away, and that's not my style. For me, the only time when casual relationships have worked is when there is something about the other person that means I don't want something more. I don't actively seek out friends with benefits, but if we go on a date and they aren't what I am looking for long-term, I am open to something less exclusive. The reason I say I am looking for a relationship is because I have noticed that when you state you don't want a relationship, they treat you worse. They see it as permission to pick you up and drop you as they please. For me, regardless of how casual the situation is, I don't like being treated like an option. It's wrong and it shouldn't change their behaviour but, more often than not, it does. I deal with the world how it is, not how I want it to be, so if you put me in a double bind with that question and make me choose between whether I am looking for a relationship or something casual, I'll say the former. That conversation actually came up with my boyfriend when we first matched:

> It's a bit awkward but since we are on the topic,
> I am not looking for a relationship by the way

> For full transparency, I am

> OK, should we stop talking then since
> we are looking for different things?

> Respectfully, I am looking for a relationship but I don't know I want a relationship from you. We haven't even met yet haha!

Our long-term goals might not have aligned, but since I don't date in terms of goals, I still saw the benefit of a date. This communication is actually an example of how healthy his communication is. I appreciated his honesty and reciprocated with my transparency and it set a precedent for our relationship. It's how we have communicated ever since. The same way I didn't know whether I wanted a relationship from him until I was actually dating him, he didn't know he wanted a relationship until he met me. I stayed conscious about the fact he wasn't looking for more and I didn't entertain any illusions that I would change his mind. Instead, I had the mentality that I would enjoy it for as long as it lasted. It's not a waste if you are enjoying your time together. Remove the mentality that it needs to be your forever person. Detach from the outcome and take the pressure off. Take it for what it is: an evening with a stranger. It's either a good date or a good story ... and this book would be empty without both. There is something you can learn and experience from everyone, even a one-night stand. But you won't appreciate these good things when the end goal overshadows it.

Forget Me Nots

- When you measure a date's success or failure based on whether you get another, it removes the ability to stay present in the moment and enjoy the person in front of you
- See each date as an experiment
- Either it's a good date or a good story
- When you date with the goal of a relationship, you unconsciously commit earlier than you intend

---

Take Action Toolkit

Your challenge is to go on a first date and not talk to your friends about it afterwards. When you recall how the date went, you alter the memory of it. In order to tell the story, you have to cut bits out and without meaning to, we romanticize and embellish the reality in order to make a better story. More importantly, you become vulnerable to the opinions around you. Stop asking your friends and trust yourself. Their opinions do not matter; they were not on the date. They are hearing a version of the date that was already filtered through your lens, so it makes it biased. When you tell them about the date, it cements your feelings rather than letting them change, shift and develop. You don't have to do this after every first date – but by trying it, you might find you prefer it. Similarly, stop letting your dating life be your first conversation topic when meeting up with friends. When I stopped dissecting my dates, I found I preferred only talking to one friend about it until the third date, usually the same friend who had my location. It made me realize that your friends often don't know better than you do.

How Do I Get Them to Like Me?

The first time I met my boyfriend's parents, I told him that I was nervous and warned him that because he has never seen me nervous, I might talk too much. He looked at me, confused.

"Surely you were nervous on our first date?"

"No, you were a stranger. Why would I care what you think?"

I responded a bit quicker than I should have, but it was true. Eight years into dating in an empowered way and with too many first dates to count, first dates were low stakes to me.

We put so much pressure on first dates – from saying the perfect thing to wearing the perfect outfit – that we forget that the person in front of us is a complete stranger. Their opinion of you doesn't matter because they really don't know you. Even by the end of the date, just because they have spent three hours with you doesn't mean they know you. Compared to the rest of the people in your life, they are still a relative stranger. Being selfish is about putting your opinion first. But, at the very least, you should be putting your opinion above a stranger's. We are taught that love means putting someone else first, but that's wrong. It leads to resentment and you losing yourself. We place too much focus on what they think of us, and as long as you are wondering what is going on in their head, you lose awareness of what's going on in your own. If you spend the whole time wondering whether you are ticking their boxes, how are you meant to know if they are ticking yours? The way to remove the focus of their opinion is to flip the situation from trying to impress them to asking yourself if they impress you. You need to know what you are looking for. As much as you shouldn't be going on a date with a checklist and seeing if that person fulfils it, it's important to ask yourself whether you are actually interested. Far too often, people get so preoccupied with wanting to be liked that they never think to ask if they like them back.

The use of gender-specific terms like "needy" trains us to understand that having needs makes us less desirable. We must keep our requests small so as not to be intimidating. The irony is that if someone gets intimidated that easily, that's not someone you want. When we tell women they are being demanding, we learn to communicate indirectly through passive aggression, sarcasm or talking behind each other's backs. It's why there is a stereotype of women being gossips and saying they are fine when they are not. Men, however, are given the permission to speak directly, because they have never been taught to be agreeable, polite – or any other way. When a man has an opinion, they are assertive. When that opinion is unpopular, they are outspoken and an independent thinker. Men get praised when dealing with a situation head-on, but when a woman does it, she is being confrontational and difficult. Women have not become indirect communicators by accident. We have been taught to be this way in order not to be ostracized by society and ultimately to be good enough as a woman.

We dishonour our needs for as long as we can bear and then we explode. It serves no one. Dating selfishly is knowing that your needs are valid, and you deserve to have needs as much as everyone else. Learning boundaries meant realizing I would never get those needs met unless I communicated directly. Say what you mean and mean what you say. When you learn to ask for what you need in a straightforward way, it not only simplifies your dating life, but your whole life. They can trust what you say. So when you say that nothing is wrong, they know it is the truth because if something truly was wrong, you would voice it.

There is a difference between someone expecting you to meet all their needs, and someone stating their needs and knowing that if you can't meet them, someone else will. One says, "This is what I need, meet me there or not." The other says, "I need you, and only you can fulfil my needs." The solution is to be direct in your communication. One person feels challenged to meet your standards, and one feels pressured. One tells the person directly what you need and the other implies that whatever they do, it will never be good enough. Here's the difference between trying to impress them and letting them impress you:

Needy	Has needs and knows it
I never heard from you after our last date, I thought you had lost interest	Hey stranger! Nice to hear from you. Would love to hear from you more between dates
Why don't you ever call me?	I'm bored of texting, give me a call if you want to talk
You never want to hold my hand, it's like you don't want to be seen with me	I'm an affectionate person and it's important to me that I can be like that with the person I am dating
I feel like you never want to see me!	I'm starting to lose interest as we only see each other once every few weeks and I need a change to happen if you want to keep dating
Why haven't I met your friends? Are you embarrassed of me?	If I'm dating someone, it's important to me that I am a part of their lives. You have met my friends; when am I meeting yours?

We have been taught that we should change ourselves to be dateable, rather than be ourselves and decide if the other person is a match. Much like how I say to present the everyday you on dating app profiles, you should do the same on the date, even down to what you wear. Dress how you would normally dress. If you never wear high heels, don't wear them. If you are normally in leggings and a hoodie, wear that. A good first impression is often a more perfect, polished version of yourself than truly exists. Any time you are trying to project perfection, you will fail because no human is perfect. So instead of aiming for a good first impression, aim for an accurate one. You never want to project an image you are unable to maintain, because the moment you slip up and actually act like yourself is the moment they lose interest – all because you've been projecting a false version of yourself. You should not have to work at getting someone to be interested in you. That's an entry-level requirement.

Once you take the focus off whether or not they like you, and start examining if you like them, you will notice the first date nerves drastically reduce. This is because you've now put your focus on something you can control. In terms of first dates, your level of enthusiasm for meeting a stranger is allowed to fluctuate. There were many times before a first date that I would drag my heels to get on the Tube – but once I was there, I would have a great time. If you are out of practice, it's normal to feel jitteriness before a date. Anxiety and excitement are very similar physiologically – both arouse the nervous system – but how you label the feeling will change your interpretation of it. Reframing it as excitement can help you look forward to the date more. You can settle your nervous system by mentally scanning your body and finding your safe space. We all have a safe space in our body. For me, it's in my heart. Focus on that, breathe into it and that will help ground and centre you before your date.

If you are still nervous, say you are nervous. There is nothing that dissipates the nerves faster than calling them out. Nerves only consume so much energy because people try to hide them. Instead, name them. If you feel awkward, then simply say that you feel awkward and it will dissipate any tension. When I first began being open about my scars, I would often skirt around the topic. And then I just embraced it messily. When they would ask, I would simply say, "I don't know how to say this, so don't judge me if this comes out clumsily." On one date, I was approached by a follower and it made me feel really awkward because I hadn't told them about my social media yet so I explained that with an "I'm feeling quite awkward now, so I should probably explain. This hasn't really happened before, so I'm just going to blurt it out." On the way to another first date, I was followed down multiple streets and harassed in a way that really threw me off. By the time I bumped into my date, I was frazzled and I told him, "I know I'm being weird so I just need to say this. I was just followed down the street by a man who wouldn't leave me alone and now I'm feeling quite jumpy." He validated how I felt, gave me a moment and asked if I was OK. Once I had a moment, I was able to have a good date because I was honest and his understanding demonstrated a great quality in him.

A person trying to project perfection would never admit how they are actually feeling. But if you are authentic and admit how you feel, you can see the person's response. They are either going to make fun of you (in which case, that's not a person you want to date) or they will make you more comfortable and may even reassure you that they are nervous too. I want you to get the idea that you can say the wrong thing out of your head. You can't. On my first date with my boyfriend, he had booked a Prohibition-style detective bar. I'd heard of it and knew they ask you questions on entry and that it could be quite awkward. Instead of worrying about it, I just told him. The fact my message was met with reassurance, not judgement, told me a lot.

> I'm worried about the questions at this detective place haha. I don't want to navigate that alone

> Oh, we were always doing that together haha

> OK, but you can't judge me on that cause I've been to a place like that before and I just get awkward

> Don't worry! I'm sure it will be fine!

> I've decided the date starts when we sit down. Until that point, I'm just a stranger standing next to you

> So what you are saying is I get a free pass for half an hour?

All the supposed first-date rules are nonsense. I will take them back to mine after a first date if I want to. I will mention exes on a first date. I remember one of my first dates where we actually spent the whole date telling each other the worst first-date stories. As much as most dating experts would say that's a bad move, it became a wonderful date – by talking about the worst first dates, we realized ours was one of the good ones. There are no blanket rules. Add some nuance into every rule you get told. For example, the classic rule of not drinking too much on a date. Of course, it's not a great idea but if your drink affects you a little more than you expected, it happens. You don't need to beat yourself up over it. I'm a lightweight so while I now know I can't drink more than two glasses of wine without getting tipsy, there were many dates where I crossed that line. I'd apologize, ask for a glass of water instead of the next round and often we'd end up laughing about it. More times than not, I still got a second date anyway. This rule should mean that getting too drunk means game over, but I've even had friends who have thrown up on a first date and gone on to have a relationship so while it is a guideline, we don't need to punish ourselves for not being perfect. I truly believe if it's the right person, there is no one thing you can say that will become a deal-breaker. There was a running joke in my friendship group that I used to say the ditziest things on dates and somehow would always get a second date. At the time, my friends and I couldn't understand it, but looking back, I believe it was because I always felt I was in on the joke. If you feel like someone is judging you or laughing at you, you will shut down, but I would laugh along because I do think it's funny how ditzy I can be – and it's a really quick way of getting rid of judgemental people. One of those dates was in my final year of university. We had matched on a dating app and he was a little bit older and worked in Bristol. When we met up in a bar, we sat down, got drinks and then I realized I had never asked him what he actually does.

"Part-time shark dentist," he stated matter-of-factly.

"Wow, that's so cool! How did you get into that?" I said with genuine excitement.

I was met with a blank stare, at which point he explained that it was a joke and that I was really gullible. Instead of letting it go,

I doubled down. "But who cleans sharks' teeth?" What made it worse was that to move the conversation on, he asked me what I look for in someone I date. I gave my three responses and when I asked him the same question, he replied with "intelligence" – and then paused.

I said, "I have to stop you there. You just said 'intelligence' and I have to ask, after the shark dentist comment, why are we still on this date?"

"Well, you go to University of Bristol, so I figured I would give you the benefit of the doubt."

We still went on a second and third date after that. You can say stupid things. Give other people grace to say stupid things as well. This was an accurate version of me. I say ditzy things all the time. I am smart in the things that I know, but there are also a lot of things I don't know. I often don't think through what I say, so if ditziness is a turn-off, then you don't want to date me and it's a good thing I showed you that on a first date.

The first date is there to give you information. If you are able to get out of your head, you are able to pay attention to whether the person in front of you meets your criteria. I remember on one first date, someone mentioned that one of their goals was to own a house by the time they were 30, and that impressed me. Less so about the house specifically, but that he had goals that he was working towards – it implied a level of ambition that I found attractive. The first-date conversation doesn't need to be any more complicated than a conversation you have with a stranger. It's easy to overcomplicate it if you believe you have to be flirty or ask bigger, broad life questions. Keeping it simple works. Even just asking them what they got up to that day is not a bad question. It either flows or it doesn't. If you are running out of things to say, people love to talk about themselves, so ask questions. Listen to what they say and pay attention to whether they ask you questions back or not.

If you are enjoying yourself, feel free to tell them. If the date isn't flowing and the awkwardness sticks around, then have the confidence to end it after one drink and be grateful that you decided on a low-investment date. When I started dating after my single period, leaving a date after one drink for the first time was incredibly empowering. It meant choosing my authenticity over a moment's discomfort. Selfishly, I didn't want to waste my time, but it does the same favour for them. When we finished our first drinks and he asked me if I would like another one, I responded: "I have a lot of work to catch up on, so I should get back to it. But it was lovely to meet you, and thank you for the drink." He said "No worries" and that he would go up and settle the bill, and then we went our separate ways.

It's actually kinder not to fake interest when you aren't interested. It was a week when I had two other dates lined up, and when the conversation was stunted, my mind kept focusing on the fact that the series finale of *Jane the Virgin* had just come out. I realized that if I was on a date and thinking about a TV show, there was no potential with this man. People avoid ending a date early and will endure it because they are focused on the other person's feelings – but whether you reject them now or you reject them later, their feelings may still get hurt. I will always be polite and finish my drink, but agreeing to another drink would have implied interest. This could lead to greater hurt later, when they realize their interest is not reciprocated, so be selfish and embrace the moment of discomfort.

Forget Me Nots

- First dates are low stakes
- The way to remove the focus of their opinion is to flip the situation from trying to impress them to asking yourself if they impress you
- You should not have to work at getting someone to be interested in you
- You can say stupid things, and give other people grace to say stupid things as well

---

Take Action Toolkit

This is a technique I use to get my head in the right mindset before public speaking. I want you to picture yourself coming off of a date and feel how you would feel if you knew it was the best date ever. Would you be feeling relief or excitement? Actually feel it in your body as if it's already happened. How would you be breathing? How would you be standing? And what would you be saying to yourself? Really feel it in your body. How would you go on the date if you knew you were brilliant at dating? What would you be thinking right now? Perhaps you wouldn't be thinking about it? Let yourself be a person who loves dating. Now, how would you be acting now if you knew with 100 per cent certainty that you were about to have an amazing date and that it was a foregone conclusion? Embody that feeling and let it exist.

Should I Go on a Second Date?

When you are a recovered people-pleaser, it can be confusing when you start dating in a healthy way and the intense emotions that used to come with dating disappear. Occasionally, I would go on first dates and not be sure if I wanted a second date because I hadn't over-romanticized them or jumped into our future and imagined our wedding the moment we met. With narratives of "love at first sight" and "sparks flying", we can be convinced that the first date should tell you all you need to know. For some people, yes. For others, you may need more time to decide, and that's OK. There is no rush to make a decision after the first date. The people-pleaser in me would be concerned that if I said yes to a second date but was unsure, then you would be leading them on. But leading them on is when you know you are not interested and you are intentionally misleading them. If you are unsure, you are allowed to take your time to figure it out. A large part of this is also about control. When we are unsure about how we feel, we can feel pressure to make a pre-emptive decision based on a first encounter, because saying "I don't know" seems too vague. Dating doesn't need to be full of big decisions and you don't need to put people in distinct categories of "casual" or "serious". You can just want to see where it goes.

Are you still curious about the person? If you are, go on another date. Even easier than this is to ask yourself if you want to spend another evening with the person. If you do, then there is no loss because you know you will have a nice evening together. In our hyper-independent culture, we can be too abrupt with cutting things off and moving on, unable to recognize that no one is perfect. If there was something that was done on a first date that you didn't like, but the rest of the date was great, then communicate that rather than ending it. Give the person an opportunity to change on the second date and if they don't, end it. Of course, there will be red flags that are non-negotiables. In those instances, listen to your gut.

In my early twenties, I remember going on one date and not being interested. The guy texted shortly after our date when I was on a night out. I was going to respond saying I was not interested in a second date, but the group of women I was with said that it was unnecessary and I would hurt his feelings. They told me to just leave it instead and he would get the message. They said it was weird to be so serious and end it because if you've only been on a first date, you don't owe them anything – I was making it into a big deal by sending a message. They convinced me that it was kinder. Being 21, I ignored my own opinion and followed what they said. All those women were wrong. This is an example of why your friends don't always know better. This guy proceeded to text me four more times over the next few days and with each text message, I felt worse and worse. Not only because I believed it was meaner but because I was going against my own code of morals to follow the crowd. On the fourth text, I realized how stupid it was.

> Hey! Sorry for the lack of reply. It's been great getting to know you but I don't think this is a great match. Take care! xx

It's not about "owing" people anything, it's about owing yourself good communication and treating people how you want to be treated. I once dated a guy who complained about having no friends. It made me so sad but, by the end of our time together, I understood why. He was an awful friend to them. Dating is no different. You can't expect to have people treat you well if you treat them badly. As the Queen of Boundaries, I am the first to say you don't owe anyone a reason for saying no, but they do deserve a no. You don't have to give the reason that you aren't interested, but you do have to say you are not interested. It doesn't need to be explained or justified – it just needs to be communicated. And the more you do it, the more practiced you become and the more your communication improves overall. Before one first date even happened, I discovered we lived really far away so I communicated that I wasn't looking for a long-distance relationship.

> Just noticed where you live. I've tried the long-distance thing and unfortunately, I don't think I can do it again

> That's a pity, you seem lovely. Bloody geography getting in the way

If you want clear communication from others, it starts with you first. We all know the pain of ghosting, so don't be the perpetrator of that pain. You don't have to end it perfectly, but you do have to end it.

When deciding how much information you want to include in the text where you end it, be selective about what information is necessary. You don't have to be unnecessarily unkind or harsh for the message to be received. Honesty never needs to be brutal. For example, it is never necessary to say "I don't find you attractive." Similarly, do not give a reason that is subjective. Telling someone that you found them boring is hurtful and pointless, because who says you get to be the measure of who is interesting enough? They are boring *to you*. That doesn't mean they are boring or you are right. You may believe your reason could be constructive, like "I didn't like the fact you were on your phone the whole date." But even then, I would rarely include it. Leave the constructive criticism for the people who actually want to continue dating them. Saying less is more.

People avoid ending it because they worry about the response. When people who lack self-awareness are rejected, they can get mean, hurtful and even abusive. I personally do not retaliate because it escalates the situation and I am always in control of how I act. If they respect you, respect them. If they disrespect you, still be respectful because you are responsible for your own behaviour. That doesn't mean you have to tolerate it. Once you have communicated your point, that is all that needs to be said. If the conversation escalates and becomes mean, then what you need to say is:

> I will not be spoken to that way. This conversation is over, and I will be blocking you now

If you are the one who wants a second date and you've not heard from them since the first date, the best way to find out is to ask. You don't need to ask them out directly, you could just start a conversation and see how their day is going (none of this "three-day rule"). When I go on a good first date, usually I have received a text – either checking that I arrived home OK or saying they had a nice time – by the time I get home.

Forget Me Nots

- You are allowed to be unsure and you are allowed more time to figure out your feelings
- If you want clear communication from others, it starts with you first
- If there was something that was done on a first date that you didn't like, but the rest of the date was great, then communicate that rather than ending it
- You don't have to give the reason you aren't interested, but you do have to say you are not interested

---

Take Action Toolkit

One of the ways I stop myself from making up stories is I write things down. A blunt pencil is better than a sharp mind. Our minds have a tendency to forget, and if we have romantic tendencies, our brains will erase any things worth noting, filter out the bad and glamorize the whole evening as perfect. After the date, or the day after if they spent the night, write down everything you are thinking. Write down the positive things that you noticed (like the fact you both have the same sense of humour) and the negative (like the fact he was on his phone a lot during the date). Keep the full picture of the date written down; it creates a resource you can look back at later, to remind yourself of the things you notice. You don't write these things to hold it against the person but, rather, to ground you in reality.

Chapter 8

There Is No Rush

How to Be Empowered in the Dating Stage

What Even Are We?

Enter the most frustrating stage of dating – or, at least, you think you are dating, but does that mean you are dating or are you *dating dating*? There would have been a time where if you said you were dating, you could assume exclusivity and the labels attached with it, but not anymore. Now it's a lot more complicated than that. Whether you call it the dating stage or the talking stage, you are in the murky middle – or what my friend Honey Ross calls "the perineum" of dating. You are both clearly interested in and learning about each other, yet you don't know whether it's going to last or even whether you want it to. I used to hate this phase. I'd want to jump from a date to automatically exclusive. But the part of me that wanted that was the same part of me that made friendships too quickly, only to then get hurt because I had shared pieces of myself without checking that the friend was trustworthy first. It's not healthy to immediately become someone's top priority, and the talking stage allows you to slowly become important to someone. The more you get to know a person, the more you start to see under the hood of the perfect exterior. People get lazy in this stage: they stop trying to impress you and more of their human side shows through. The mask they present to the world will start to drop. It's really easy to be charming on the first, second and third dates, but how about a month later? Two months into dating a guy non-exclusively, I was invited on a holiday with two of my university friends to a cabin in the woods in Norway. The guy I was seeing at the time had a huge issue with it because the two friends I was going with were male.

He gave me an ultimatum: "If you go on this holiday, we are over."

"We are over, then."

This is why I say the talking stage is vital. In this one conversation, I was able to foresee a future where I had to defend myself any time I wanted to hang around my guy friends, and that is not a future I want. I have no interest in justifying my time spent with friends and, most of all, I don't like being threatened. The way it was put to me was controlling and demonstrated the lack of trust he had in me. I would have reassured his concerns, but the line was drawn when he stated his demands without so much as a conversation. If I am dating someone, I am owed the decency of a discussion – at the very least – and the fact he resorted to an ultimatum showed me that we weren't a match. People tell you who they are if you are listening. And in this stage, more than any other, it's important to pay attention. Insecurities also arise around this time. Everyone has insecurities and these in and of themselves are not a reason not to date someone. But how they manage their insecurity might become a sign of a longer-term issue. As you continue dating, you are able to see how this manifests in the relationship.

I like to see this phase as a trial period. It's data collection. It is the time to see whether you both work. In order to do this, you must be honest about your needs and wants. Being selfish is about voicing that and having the opportunity to see how you communicate when you need to work through issues. Issues are inevitable. I personally love the Buddhist teaching that difficulty in life is inevitable. Dating is no different. It's usually in this phase that it arises, because the more time you spend with a person, the higher the chance you will cross someone's boundary, often without knowing you have. What is different about my empowered approach to dating is I don't brush an issue under the carpet. Instead, I'm direct about it. I stopped hiding aspects of myself that I deemed "too much", "too difficult" or even just weird. I even stopped hiding my two stuffed toys on my bed when a guy came over. You either accept me with my two toy dogs or not at all. In the past, I was so worried about losing them that I would try to be a cooler, more palatable version of myself. Now I see this period of dating as an important step that provides me with vital information. Here are just some of the ways I stayed authentic both in-person and over text:

When it was moving too quickly:

> Hey! You made a comment the other day about our future and I'm not sure I'm ready to talk about that kind of commitment. It made me feel pressured and if you want to discuss it, I'm happy to have a proper conversation about it.

When I felt he was being evasive:

> I feel like this is becoming quite one-sided. I've shared quite vulnerable things and I need that to be reciprocated.

When I wanted more affection:

> Hey! Affection is really important to me and I was wondering if there was a reason you aren't more affectionate?

When talking about personal things related to sex:

> Hey! I want to talk to you about something privately. I feel really vulnerable right now, so I'm going to need you to not laugh.

When our dates only took his schedule into consideration:

> Lately, I feel like our dates have been on your terms. For this to feel more equal, I need you to ask me about my schedule more.

Dating selfishly is about having more loyalty to your needs than their opinion. What that means in practice is if you feel that you don't see each other enough and they think you do and suggest that you are being needy for wanting more, you are able to stand behind how you feel. You remain loyal to your needs and reiterate the point:

> You are allowed to think that. But if I am dating someone, I need more dates in person. If you are unable to fulfil that, let me know.

Loyalty means not letting them persuade you that your needs are unimportant or too much.

When you communicate directly, you give others permission to do the same. With one guy, he hated PDA and communicated that before our first date. I love PDA, and we found a line that works for both of us. Everyone has different boundaries and you can't assume you know what you've not been told. The area where boundaries differ the most in romantic relationships is around jealousy. From sharing a bed with a friend or saying another person is attractive to flirting with someone else, everyone has their own lines. It's not about one being wrong or right, it's about being suited to each other. While I was in this murky territory with my now boyfriend, he was contacted by an ex to go for a drink.

> Just been asked to go for a drink with an ex. Not asking permission per se, but are you OK with it? If not, I don't mind saying no

> Go for it! Thanks for asking

> Cool cool :)

> I'm just being nosy, but can I ask out of curiosity which ex it is?

We had both been very open about exes from the start and when we became official a few months later, he actually recalled this situation. I'd made a joke saying "I back myself", and he said that my confidence was a contributing factor to wanting to become official. I wasn't saying it to seem "chilled" or to impress him – I said it because it was true. It's the way I've always been. Even at 19, when I was with my first boyfriend, I remember seeing him flirt with someone else in a club. My friend saw it happen as well and said I should go and say something. I explained that it didn't bother me: "At the end of the day, he's coming home with me." I shouldn't have to convince someone of my worth and I'm not competing with someone he just met in a club. My point of view is if someone wants to cheat, they will cheat. So I don't feel the need to mark my territory. A decade on, I still believe the same. If meeting an ex for drinks had bothered me, I would have said so. For example, a friend told me about how her partner wanted to watch *Bridgerton* with an ex while they were still in the pre-official stage. She said no unless she was present. That works for them. It wouldn't work for us. Jealousy is a big turn-off for both me and my boyfriend. In other relationships, it is a turn-on and feeling that threat means they don't take for granted the person they are dating. One relationship is not stronger than the other. Both relationships were strong because we were able to be honest and authentic to how we actually felt. It's about compatibility.

I want to be clear that the talking stage is not what some people refer to as a "situationship". A situationship is different. It is when one party wants commitment and the other doesn't, and the latter keeps kicking the commitment ball down the road with droppings of promises they can't keep and sentiments that allow the other person to attach to them even more. Chasing someone who doesn't like you back is like playing a game of tennis and the other person deciding to pull out a sun lounger. They have declared they are not playing. They are not in the game. If you force a tennis racket into their hand and swing the racket for them, you still don't have a game of tennis.

A situationship hurts because you dishonour your needs for commitment out of fear of losing the person, and therefore settle for less than you deserve by ignoring what you want. The difference between a talking stage and a situationship is communication. The latter involves someone misleading you and selling you false promises. It is created by one person convincing themselves the other will change their mind – and both people ignoring the emotional unavailability present. There is a vagueness when you bring up issues, whereas in the talking stage, you might be pre-commitment, but there is still transparency and respect when concerns arise.

The talking stage is not just about noticing the friction, it's about noticing the good stuff too. If you continue focusing on red flags, no one will pass this stage because everyone has red flags, including you. I don't love the terminology of red flags because humans are more complex than that. But if you are going to play that game, then at least notice the green flags too. It's often small things: when you are talking, they put their phone down to give you their full attention, or they call when they say they will. In 1992, Dr John Gottman, a leading psychologist in research on romantic relationships, demonstrated this when he found that how much you responded to a partner's "bids" determined whether both partners were satisfied in their relationship and could predict divorce with 94 per cent accuracy. He refers to bids as "a fundamental unit of emotional connection", when one partner makes an attempt to connect with the other. He found that it didn't matter how deep the conversation was, but whether the other partner paid attention. In less intense examples, this could be them asking about your friend and actually remembering their name from when you mentioned it the other day. On the flip side, ignoring bids can be as simple as when you ask them to pass the salt and they are too busy on their phone to notice or have even heard you. These micro-moments build up over time, for better or for worse. For me, it was when we got a takeaway and, despite me telling him to leave the packaging because I would clear it in the morning, it was cleared up while I was in the shower. It was even old-school things that I thought I wouldn't like, like him always walking between me and the road, or the fact that on holiday, he will always offer to carry my bag for me. The small things turn into big things, and that was proved more than ever the first time I got ill. I have an extremely complicated medical history and people often get intimidated by it. He was unfazed.

The most important thing to notice in this stage is how you feel around them and how you feel once you leave them. If you feel depleted after spending time together, pay attention to that. There is a lot of talk about feeling "butterflies" when you are around someone, but people often confuse "butterflies" for fear and anxiety. You should be comfortable around someone you are dating, especially after a while. The greatest sign of a healthy relationship is when you feel calm around each other and, most importantly, safe.

Forget Me Nots

- More commitment and exclusivity is not always best
- The talking stage is your trial period to see whether you both work and how you communicate when you need to work through issues
- If you continue focusing on red flags, no one will pass this stage because everyone has red flags, including you
- The greatest sign of a healthy relationship is when you feel calm around each other and, most importantly, safe

---

Take Action Toolkit

When you are in this complicated stage, it's really easy to turn small decisions like whether to ask them why their text replies have got slower into make-or-break decisions. My greatest principle in terms of this is: do both. "Ask him or don't" is too all-or-nothing. Instead, sit with it and ask

---

yourself why less frequent texts make you anxious. Sit in those feelings and explore the question. Use it as an opportunity to teach yourself how to gain distance from your phone. Then give yourself a deadline: in three days, if the discomfort hasn't improved, then honour your needs and send that text or have that conversation. You can work on yourself while receiving relational intimacy and affection. You can get the reassurance you need and also show yourself that you don't need to be reliant on it. It's not one or the other; you can do both.

Is It a Bad Sign if We Fight?

There are many schools of thought when it comes to arguing when you are dating. On the extreme end, I have seen TikTok videos saying that being around a new person should be as easy as breathing and if it isn't, they aren't your person. The people espousing that are in the camp of believing it should be effortless in the beginning and if you are already having conflict, it is a bad sign. Then there's the other argument that says fighting is a sign of passion and that you should only start worrying when you stop fighting, because that means you no longer care. As we know, extremes don't work. So let's find somewhere in the middle. The difficulty with any conversation around love life and fighting is that people define fights, arguments and disagreements in different ways. Two people can be in the same conversation and one person can think it was a fight and the other didn't even notice there was an issue. So when we discuss fighting, we could actually be discussing different things. Whatever you want to label it, I categorize it all as conflict – and conflict is normal and expected whenever two humans interact.

One of the best things I learned while dating is seeing conflict as a sign I was finally being honest. My past relationships never had conflict because I was such a people-pleaser that, if there was a disagreement, I would change my mind to avoid conflict. If one person doesn't feel safe or comfortable enough to be honest about their needs, you end up avoiding conflict – but exchange it for resentment instead. Back in my selfless days, the first guy I liked asked me if I minded if he didn't stay over after we slept together for the first time. I said I didn't because I wanted to come across as chilled and relaxed. Of course, I wanted him to stay and when he left, it felt awful. I even convinced myself it was for the better because I can snore and at least he wouldn't find out. He ended up never staying the night and I never vocalized how rubbish that made me feel. If I was selfish enough to communicate my needs, what I would have said was: "I know I said that it didn't bother me when you left after we slept together, but it actually does. Next time, can you stay over?" Instead, I told myself that it was too early in our relationship to make requests like this, and I buried my sadness and feelings of rejection. The reason I believed that conflict was something that was reserved for people in more serious and long-term relationships was because my fear of abandonment had told me that if you argue in the dating stage, that's it, game over.

Learning to not cut and run at the first instant was a game changer when it came to my dating life, and this lesson came in the form of boundaries. As I write in *The Joy of Being Selfish*, "Boundaries are the way we teach others to treat us. They are how we communicate what is acceptable and what is not." You can't teach boundaries without teaching good communication alongside it. Without it, people think boundaries are cutting someone off as soon as a boundary is crossed. That's not a boundary, that's a wall. What if they didn't know your boundaries? What if you never communicated them? You need to give them an opportunity to change, no matter how vulnerable that feels. If we are too busy calling everything gaslighting, we fail to learn how to have the difficult conversations. Stop expecting perfection and then running as soon as you find out the person you are dating is human. Sometimes we use this "Don't settle, you deserve the very best!" excuse as a way to avoid being vulnerable. It's easier to end it under the guise of having "high standards" than admitting that having to communicate makes you feel exposed.

Being able to be vulnerable is a sign of strength. If you can communicate in the early stages, you set a precedent for communication early on and are able to assess the other person's ability to resolve conflict. If we keep glorifying this idea that we want perfect humans who worship us and will move mountains for us, we are setting ourselves up for failure. What actually happens if a person worships you is that they will put you on a pedestal. And when you mess up, like all humans do, the crash down to Earth – when you don't live up to the expectation of the illusion they created – will be painful. Any relationship where one person worships the other is a relationship where they will be unable to be honest about how they feel because they don't feel they deserve you. Because of this, they keep their needs small for fear of losing you. It creates an imbalance. You don't want a person who pursues you no matter what, moves mountains for you and worships you, you want someone who respects and values the reality of who you are. Those in a healthy relationship have the self-worth to know what they deserve. If I'm putting mountains in between our relationship, they also have the self-awareness and self-respect to go, "You know what? I don't deserve this. I need you to treat me better." A healthy relationship means knowing you can set boundaries with them, but also that they can set boundaries with you. No matter how long you two last, if you can communicate clearly, calmly and compassionately from the beginning, it can often be a way that someone you date separates themselves from the crowd.

The flip side of this is if you are in constant conflict. An unhealthy pattern can arise if one or both individuals are used to creating problems to foster a sense of closeness. Intensity can be easily confused for intimacy when, in reality, intensity is a way to avoid intimacy. This is often the case when someone grew up in a household where fights were the only time they were given attention and therefore, fights are the only way they know to be intimate. If chaos and intensity were the norm at home, the version of love that is most familiar to them is often a turbulent one. If they are in a situation where the other person is safe, calm and stable, they may start fights because they don't know another way. If you are always searching for a problem, you will find one. We also need to be cautious about when disagreements escalate to unnecessary arguments. The normalization of this under the guise of "passion" is unhealthy. We should be holding our standard of behaviour no matter how passionate our emotions make us.

I am a reformed hothead. It's what happens if you grow up not being allowed your anger, if you weren't listened to until you got louder, and if you have trauma where you were unprotected as a child. A pinprick will often feel like a punch to the face, so you learn a defence mechanism: to attack before you get attacked. The problem is that if you see every squabble as an attack, you don't realize that a conversation doesn't need to escalate into an argument. If your only tool is a hammer, everything looks like a nail. The reason I am so passionate about the way we communicate is because I was awful at it and, over many years, I have figured out ways to do better. I now have a few basic ground rules when it comes to any kind of disagreement.

Arguments are not an excuse to hurt the other person

Words said in anger count and cannot be forgotten. The problem with saying something in anger is that in order to say it, you must think it. It's really hard to repair the trust if arguments become a place to unleash harboured feelings. An argument is not a competition in who can hurt each other the most. If someone says something hurtful, pause.

Once something is resolved, don't bring it up again

We all know those married couples that are still having the same fight about something that happened 20 years ago. Nothing was ever forgiven or forgotten. While I don't believe in "forgive and forget", I do believe in letting things go. Stay in the conversation until it is resolved. If we need to take breaks, we take breaks and the alone time we need. But we continue the conversation – and once it is resolved, you have to let it go. Stop defining your relationship by its worst moments and stop defining your partner by their mistakes. Allow them to move on and, in so doing, give them the opportunity to grow.

Focus on the one issue that has arisen

When someone feels backed into the corner, it is really tempting to equal the score by reminding them of something they've done. You never resolve everything if you throw every issue into the same conversation. When you start turning it into a tit for tat, both parties end up feeling invalidated. Instead, hear out the other person and apologize if you are in the wrong – in the same way that you would want them to admit their wrongdoing. When that is all sorted, you can say, "You know how you felt ____? Well, I also felt that way when you said ____ the other day." You enter the conversation from mutual understanding of feeling the same way rather than invalidating how they feel because you once felt that way too.

Me and you versus the problem, not me versus you

You are on the same team. One of the ways conversations become hurtful is when you see the other person as the problem. If you are able to see the issue as the problem, you then become two problem-solvers on the same team trying to find a solution. Now, there is no winner and no loser; you both win if the problem is resolved. Conflict can actually bring you closer as a couple if you see the problem as a challenge to overcome, as opposed to a threat to your relationship. When you target the problem together, you figure out what is important to each other in order to resolve it in a way that pleases both parties.

No yelling, name-calling or making it personal

These are basic boundaries around communication. Just because you are in a disagreement doesn't mean the rules of engagement change. Any form of labelling and name-calling is off the table. In the reality TV show *Bethenny Ever After*, Bethenny's partner consistently used the facts that she "doesn't have a family" and was "damaged" from her parents abandoning her as a point in his arguments when she didn't prioritize his family. Not only did it weaken his points, but it's also unkind. When you label someone, you ignore all the nuances of their situation.

No bailing at the first sign of difficulty

Break-ups should never be used as an empty threat – it can trigger feelings of abandonment in the other person. Part of commitment is not running from a hard conversation, even if the only commitment you have made to each other is a friends-with-benefits situation. Even in the most casual situations, difficult conversations will arise. If you flee because it's uncomfortable, there is no element of safety, even if the safety is only necessary for a sexual relationship. If you do decide to end it, it should be a thought-through decision, not one made in haste out of intense emotions.

*   *   *

How someone responds when you bring up an issue tells you a lot. Their response can either be receptive, wanting to listen and open to being wrong, or it can be invalidating, dismissive and wanting to shut down the conversation as soon as possible. The difficulty is because the majority of us were not taught to communicate, it's hard to measure someone on their communication skills. Instead, measure someone on their willingness to learn. We all bring our bad communication styles that were handed down to us from our caregivers, but it is our responsibility to learn to do better. As the saying goes, we marry our unfinished business. When you date someone new, you are given the opportunity to rewrite the past. Here are some tools to help your communication:

Listen to hear, not to respond

Howard Markman's Prevention and Relationship Enhancement Program (PREP) that started in 1988 highlighted that when people are in conflict, they don't listen to more than 10 seconds of someone's argument before they start building their rebuttal. This is why it is important to keep it to one issue at a time. When we feel insecure in conflict, it can be really tempting to bolster our argument with multiple reasons. However, you should state your issue without justification. Keep it short.

The more you say, the more the other person can nitpick. Say one thing, pause, and even ask them to repeat back what you said if you feel it has not been heard.

It's about understanding, not blame

Blame divides. If you view conflict as a medium for both of you to understand each other better, you can look underneath the surface argument to see what's really going on. As psychotherapist Esther Perel says, "Behind every criticism is a longing, behind every anger is a hurt." When you seek to understand someone else's point of view, you are able to see their behaviour in context.

XYZ approach

This is one of the key tools of communication, and it has the following format: when you do X, in situation Y, I feel Z. It allows us to describe how we feel in a specific context and helps us avoid generalizations.

Whenever I discuss teaching someone you are dating how to communicate, I will often get told that they shouldn't have to do the emotional labour of teaching someone to communicate. If that's what you believe, fair enough. I won't try to convince you otherwise. In my world, though, a relationship, whether romantic or platonic, is about you both mutually teaching each other and learning and benefiting from the other person's strengths. It is emotional labour, but there will be times when they do the emotional labour of teaching you something *you* are less skilled at. It requires two people for a dynamic to take place, but it only takes one person to change it. For example, if they struggle to ask for what they need, you can ask them:

> Do you want advice, a distraction, to be alone or for me to listen?

You can see it as you teaching them communication, or you can see it as you asking for a road map so you know what to do. Next time, they will know what options they can ask for. If you communicate well, it becomes easier for the other person to do so as well. Honesty begets honesty. Vulnerability begets vulnerability. To expect someone you date to be perfectly designed to complement your style of communication is unrealistic. Communication between two individuals rarely comes perfectly formed – rather, it is often something you learn to navigate together.

The next step, after a conflict has occurred and a resolution has been found, is for the behaviour change to occur. There is only so much an apology can do unless the behaviour follows suit. An apology without behaviour change is manipulation. It can be used as a way to get the conversation over and done with, rather than you hearing what changes your partner actually needs to see from you. As Socrates says, "To be is to do." It doesn't matter how much they love you if their behaviour doesn't match up. If you characterize people by their actions, you will never be fooled by their words.

What's more important than the conflict itself is how you repair it. Have a conversation about what you would do differently and instead of the behaviour you do not want, ask for the positive alternative. When you tell the person what you want, you give them a road map for what they can do next time. As Dr Gottman puts it, "Happy couples are not so very different from unhappy couples; they are simply able to make repairs to their relationship easier and faster so they can get back to the joy of being together." Change takes time, and having a bit of patience for people to create that change is important. The change doesn't need to be instant, but gradual, incremental improvements create huge change over time.

Forget Me Nots

- If you are always searching for a problem, you will find one
- It doesn't matter how much they love you if their behaviour doesn't match up
- An apology without behaviour change is simply manipulation
- We need to stop focusing on the conflict, and instead focus on how we repair it

---

Take Action Toolkit

As early as the playground, we were taught to give instant apologies even if we didn't think we did anything wrong or weren't actually sorry. Instead, I wish we emphasized understanding over apologies to children. You might not be sorry, but you can learn to understand why someone is upset. I don't believe in fake apologies. I don't believe in accepting them or giving them; it's inauthentic and it means choosing someone else's comfort over my need to be honest. If I am giving an apology, I will seek to understand the situation better in order to make the apology sincere. And if I'm on the receiving end and I haven't actually forgiven them, there are ways to acknowledge this without lying. My favourite phrases to use are: "Thank you for your apology", "I really appreciate your apology" and "Your apology means a lot to me." All of these can be true, and then I can process the forgiveness in my own time. I see apologies as gifts, in that they should be freely given and not in exchange for instant forgiveness. So thank you for the gift; I will return the reciprocal gift of forgiveness in my own time, when I have processed my feelings and am ready to move on.

Are We Official Yet?

One of the changes in modern dating is that there are now more stages than we know what to do with. Just like in the noughties, when you would get confused with the differences between "hooking up" and "making out", the words have changed but the confusion remains. Now, the main differentiators are the talking stage, being exclusive and being in a relationship. These don't mean the same to everyone, so you need to clarify this with the people you are dating.

I dated a guy for months in university without knowing if we were exclusive, if we were in a relationship or whether we were just friends with benefits. I didn't have the confidence to actually ask him. Instead, I started reading into things and deducing meanings from things that weren't there. I remember saying to a friend at the time: "This can't just be sex to him – he wouldn't be texting me all day if I was just a friend with benefits." I assumed he wasn't dating anyone else because between a master's degree in London, a full-time job in Bath and commuting back and forth three times a week, I just didn't see how it was feasible that he would have time for anyone else. So all these questions remain unasked and unanswered in my brain until one day, my best friend matched with him on Tinder and started a conversation just to see if he would reply. He did, and all my assumptions were shattered in one painful blow. Amateur move on his part, though – if only he had swiped two pictures along, he would have seen I was actually in one of her profile pictures. We would now call this a situationship, and the worst part of giving this a label is that it confers validity on the situation when it's actually entirely avoidable. None of the above needed to happen if I could have just asked him if he was dating anyone else.

The main query I get around this topic is "How do I know if we are official/exclusive?" There isn't a checklist that proves you've reached this stage. You actually have to ask. In the past, I settled for boyfriend-approximation because I was too scared that seeking clarity would result in the end of the relationship. We put off this conversation because we are scared of the answer. We sometimes think it's better to live in the endless denial of "not knowing", but we need to shift our mindset. Instead of worrying about being too needy, validate your needs and realize that you deserve to get those needs met. Unlearn the idea that if you had no needs, you would be easier to love. Remove the idea that if you have fewer needs, your partner is less likely to leave. Finding a love that is conditional on you suppressing your needs is not love. Dating selfishly means being honest with yourself about what you want. Ask yourself what the label would give you. If you want a label that they are not willing to take on, then you need to make a decision about whether your need for a label is important enough to end it and find that elsewhere or whether you can be OK without a label, if you gain certainty in other ways. If the latter, ask for your needs to be met differently, whether through more communication or some reassurance. In all aspects of dating, get used to asking for clarity when you need it. Communicate when you want to check you two are on the same page. This principle of clarity actually applies to everything. Want a label that you don't have? Ask for it. Worried that you are bothering them when you text them at work? Ask them. Unsure if they are still on dating apps? Ask them.

I have always treated being exclusive and being in a relationship as two separate stages. I treat being exclusive as a decision you can make individually – it doesn't have to be mutual. There is a difference between when I decide I want to be exclusive and when I will care whether the other person is. For me, the point at which I become exclusive is if I'm dating multiple people and my focus is always on one. I will end it with others because I think that's the respectful thing to do. It's not fair to anyone involved to go on dates where you wish the person across from you was someone else. Sometimes one person fulfils me enough that I don't feel inclined to use my dating apps, and sometimes I only have time to be dating one anyway. I decide to be exclusive with no expectation for reciprocity. Often I won't even inform them that I have become exclusive because it's a decision I made for myself and is what is working for me in that moment. If more time goes on and I want reassurance they are feeling the same way, I will ask:

> Hey! I'm really liking where this is going and I've personally stopped seeing other people. Would love to know if we are on the same page

I won't demand they stop seeing others, but I let their response tell me all I need to know and I ask any questions that I might have. When a person is saying no to being exclusive, and you want to be exclusive, you need to listen to that.

> I am at the point where I want to be in an exclusive relationship and if you are unable to give me that, then I think I need to find what I'm looking for elsewhere

Some people, like my boyfriend, conflate it and see being exclusive and in a relationship as the same thing. As a result, he thought we were in a relationship when we became exclusive and when I brought up the conversation of a relationship, he was confused. In my mind, we had been exclusive for months, but not in a relationship. So when it came up randomly, I said that we hadn't spoken about it and we needed to have a conversation. Not wanting to do it over text, he asked if we could speak about it at the weekend and I agreed. The conversation resulted in him saying he's never cared about labels and as plainly as he stated his views, I stated mine – that I do care about labels. Calling each other boyfriend and girlfriend gave me the certainty that I wanted and so in that conversation, we decided to be boyfriend and girlfriend.

If he hadn't wanted the label in that conversation, I wouldn't have ended it there because I wasn't needing that security at that stage – but I knew at some point, I would do. The conversation came up by accident, but if a few more months had passed and I hadn't got the commitment I wanted, I would have brought it up myself. It's best to have a conversation about this before it becomes a deciding factor because waiting until it's an ultimatum can create pressure where there didn't need to be any. Instead, bring it up with curiosity when it starts being a question in your mind. If you are able to ask their thoughts when it's a "want" not a "need", this gives you time to say:

> I know I'm going to want more commitment soon, but it's OK if you aren't ready for that yet and we can talk about it in a few weeks

In fact, my boyfriend knew this and reminded me of it months later. Early on in dating, we were watching a TV show where someone says "I love you" and it isn't reciprocated. I moaned about how that's unrealistic because people don't always feel the exact same way at the same time and that it's the same with being exclusive or in a relationship. When he recalled this conversation, he said that's why he never felt pressured to say yes, because he knew I would voice it when it became a deal-breaker. When you communicate that, include why the label is important to you – whether it's the external perception of the label or an internal one.

> Hey! We have been dating for a few months and I want to know where your head's at when it comes to us. I'm starting to feel uncomfortable when we go to parties and I don't know what to introduce you as, so can we have a conversation about that?

If you don't get the outcome you want, thank them for their honesty and then recognize that your needs are not being fulfilled with this person. The reason clarity is needed is because different terms and phrases mean different things to each person. To some, labels don't matter. To others, they do. To some, it would be more important to have the boyfriend/girlfriend labels and to others, meeting their friends is a greater sign of commitment. For me, my greatest sign of commitment is meeting my friends, but I will not do that without the certainty of a label. Different stages can also bring their own worries or insecurities. It's important to ask yourself why you actually want the label. Society places such an emphasis on it that we can sometimes covet it because we can't have it. You gain a lot from being official, but without recognizing this, you forget that you lose things too. It might sound silly, but when I was single, I used to love a night out and the potential that came with it: that you could get with someone new. Clubbing is a different experience in a relationship. Of course, the girlfriend label fulfilled me in other ways. For example, I felt I could plan more into the future. But commitment should be a decision and not just the default next step. We have to remember that getting into a relationship is not the end goal, it's a new beginning. Securing an official label is not the finish line. In many ways, no matter how long you've been dating, it's the starting line.

Forget Me Nots

- We put off defining our relationship because we are scared of the answer
- Be honest with yourself about what you want and if you want a label that they are not willing to give you, then you need to make a decision
- It's OK if someone doesn't want the next stage as fast as you want it, but you have to stay true to what you need
- Securing an official label is not the finish line, it's the starting line

---

Take Action Toolkit

Knowing your love life values is so important. Within *The Joy of Being Selfish*, I run through a more thorough version of eliciting your values, but I will give you a shorter version here. Note that the values you look for in a casual situation versus dating versus a relationship versus being married can change. This is often why people can be happy in a relationship, get married and become unhappy, because what they find is that the person met their values for a relationship but once they got married, they perceived them as family. Your family values and love-life values don't always match. In completing this exercise, make sure you use the situation (casual, dating, relationship, marriage) that applies to you (or soon will).

Ask yourself what dating (or being in a relationship with, marrying, etc.) someone would give you. Come up with as many answers as possible, and then find the top eight and rank them in order of importance. As an example, if two of your values are excitement and affection, ask yourself, "If I could have excitement without affection, would I be happy?" Then flip it around and ask, "If I could have affection without excitement, would I be happy?" In order to do this accurately, you need to remove any judgement. It's OK if money is in your values and it's OK if kindness sits lower than sex. These are your values and no one else needs to see them. At the end of the exercise, you have a list that becomes useful when assessing whether the person in front of you actually meets your values in dating or in a relationship. It should look something like this:

1) Fun
2) Excitement
3) Understanding
4) Passion
5) Emotional intelligence
6) Sex
7) Kindness
8) Spontaneity

....
....
....
....
....
....
....
....

Chapter 9

Your Body Doesn't Need a Disclaimer

How to Be Empowered Sexually

How Do I Respond to a Sext?

My introduction to sexting came with my introduction to dating apps. Perhaps it shows my age but, prior to dating apps, we would only really text once a day to ask if we each were going out, and then we would meet in the club. Dating apps were the first time you got to know someone over text before you got to know them in person, and it was easier to make it sexual earlier on, especially as it felt more anonymous.

In my era of dating, when I was so keen to impress them that I forgot whether they were impressing me, I sent many nudes I regret and sexted people even when I felt uncomfortable. This is what happens when you aren't selfish. In order to take care of yourself, you have to put your needs at the top of your list. As a result, everyone else's needs have to be a lower priority. In this instance, I placed a random person's request for a nude over my own discomfort. I placed my desire to be liked over my sexual boundaries. I was so concerned with being judged as a prude and was so desperate to convert the conversation to a date that I would oblige and then feel shame and guilt after. There is nothing shameful about wanting to sext or send pictures; the shame I was feeling wasn't because of the action but because I was living outside of my own integrity. Now I look back with a lot more compassion for myself in those years. After all, she grew up in a world where if a woman said no to any sexual act, she would be called a tease, but if she said yes too easily or too often, she was a slut. It's a fine line to tiptoe. While we have made improvements in bringing double standards to light in the last decade, it's unsurprising that teenagers today still feel the same pressure around sex. I wish someone had taught me how to communicate that I was uncomfortable and told me what to say if someone asked for a picture and I wanted to say no. Instead, I learned it the hard way and, through empowered dating, I found my voice and began to set boundaries. This conversation followed on from the prompt on my profile about *Love Island*:

> You need to invite me over so I can watch my first episode of *Love Island* then . . .

> You are skipping a few steps. Before I invite you over, you need to invite me out

There is nothing wrong with asking for a picture, but there is also nothing wrong with saying no. The problem is if you combine this with a culture where women are never given permission to say no, and men are taught that a "no" is just a challenge to try harder, it leads to a lot of sexting being a result of coercion. When saying no, make your boundary firm. If they persist, notice it. If they won't take your first no to sexting, they won't listen when you say no in person either.

> Nice try but no

> Maybe if you survive a first date . . .

> Wouldn't want to ruin the surprise, would we?

> No, you'll have to wait and see

> Patience is a virtue

> No thanks, pictures aren't my thing

Similarly, if a person on a dating app is sending pictures of themselves without asking for consent first, notice that. Unsolicited nudes are bad boundaries and – more importantly, at the time of writing – due to be illegal. If you would like to send a picture, all you have to do is ask first:

> I just got out of the shower. Would you like to see?

> Bought some new lingerie – want a glimpse?

> Want a preview of when I next get to see you?

When it comes to sexting, it can feel like there is an expectation for you to be an erotica author overnight, but it doesn't need to be that difficult. The easiest way to sext, if you want to, is to describe what you would like to do to the other person. Here are some phrases to help you out:

> If I was there right now, I would . . .

> I have this fantasy that I've always wanted to live out. Do you want to know what it is?

> I had a dream about you last night and now I keep having filthy thoughts

Sexting can be a great opportunity to tell the person you are sleeping with what you like in detail by talking about it hypothetically. It is an easy way to give specific instructions about what you want them to do next time – without egos being bruised – because it focuses on what you want, not what they are doing wrong. If you are new to sexting, you can let them lead the conversation:

> If we were alone, where would you start?

> Tell me more

> I like the sound of that, keep going

One of the greatest frustrations I hear about dating apps is that people want to make it sexual too early and if you are looking for something more serious, that can get annoying. In fact, I got so curious about whether asking for sex out of the gate really worked that I once asked a guy who asked me for a nude before having a conversation:

> Does this line usually work for you?

> Haha, the responses I get are a bit all over the place. Being honest, I can't read you. Too much of a one-way, so it's hard to gauge

> So basically if I sent a picture, this would be going better?

> Yeah, it would help

A picture was never sent. My personal boundaries are that I will always want a conversation, and a date first. For me, it's not about sex as much as it's about respect and that I wouldn't allow anyone to have access to me in that way. Assuming respect is there, casual sex, fuck buddies and friends-with-benefits relationships are wonderful options for people exploring dating for the first time. There is an ability to be more honest and selfish in casual sex that allows you to discover what you like. Some people often find it easier to vocalize their needs because there isn't a pressure of a more long-term relationship. However, it is not for everyone and it is important to know if you are one of those people. I actually believe that when it comes to casual relationships, the communication needs to be clearer in order to make sure you both are on the same page. Casual relationships don't work if they are treated like a consolation prize for when you can't get the commitment you want. They are not something you settle for when they say no to any more commitment. They must be treated as a separate category.

If you are unsure if you are the kind of person who can do sex with no strings attached, then the only true way to find out is to try it. Try it and know you are capable of handling whatever the fallout is. Go in fully prepared to take the risk. Promise yourself to continually check in with your feelings and that you will end it if it starts draining your life rather than adding to it. I think sometimes we want to pain-proof our lives, especially our love lives, but life requires risk. Risk it, and if you don't feel safe or comfortable enough to take the risk, then you have the answer you need – casual sex is not for you. Listen to those feelings, they will tell you more than any self-help book can.

Sometimes we equate casual sex to treating each other like trash. We believe because we are casual, we aren't allowed to ask for anything, but we actually are. As I say in *The Joy of Being Selfish*, "The seriousness of a relationship shouldn't determine the respect you receive." I still want my time to be respected, I still want there to be transparency around other partners for my own sexual safety and I still want clear communication when it stops working for either of us.

Your feelings during casual sex or even while sexting might change. It could be working for a certain period of time and then it can stop working. If it stops being fun, stop doing it. I had this happen in my own life when we entered the first lockdown. I had started a casual situation with a guy I had previously gone on a few dates with when we both locked down in different parts of the country. We kept sexting for a few months, but when it became clear that the lockdown was going to last longer than expected, I sent the following message:

> I've been thinking and obviously, this is not what either of us planned for. The pandemic has made this more frustrating than fun. Since we don't know when this is gonna end, let's not drag this out. When you are back in London, give me a shout and we'll see where we're both at xx

> Hey! I completely understand. I agree that it's been a great distraction, almost too good in fact, and this situation is definitely very frustrating for us. I'd definitely like to see you when I'm back – I mean the frustration goes to show how much I'd like to be there with you right now! I'm happy to leave texting until we know when we can see each other again, although of course if you do fancy a catch-up every now and then I'd be cool with that and hope you're having a lovely Easter weekend! xx

We need to remove the hierarchy in dating that ranks sexual relationships and romantic relationships. One is not better than the other. One is not more impactful than the other. There are some casual situations that have ended with more heartbreak than official exes, and some from which I've learned a lot about myself and what I want and need. Different people have different needs. Different times in your life might mean you want a different thing in your love life. The key to all of this is self-awareness. If sexting or casual situations aren't for you, then honour that.

Forget Me Nots

- There is nothing wrong with asking for a picture, but there is also nothing wrong with saying no
- If they won't take your first no to sexting, they won't listen when you say no in person either
- If you are unsure if you are a kind of person who can do sex with no strings attached, then the only true way to find out is to try it
- We need to remove the hierarchy in dating that ranks sexual relationships and romantic relationships

---

Take Action Toolkit

These journal prompts came from Esther Perel, who is one of the greats when it comes to relationship and sex psychology. She asks you to complete the sentences "I turn myself on when . . ." and "I turn myself off when . . ." I love these questions because they put the responsibility of arousal on you. More importantly, they make you realize you could be

---

the one turning yourself off. For example, your answer could be: "I turn myself off when I can hear notifications on my phone." This tells you that if you want to enjoy sex, you need to put your phone on silent. On the flip side, one of your answers might be: "I turn myself on when I spontaneously start dancing and not caring what I look like." Allow your lists to be as long as possible and include things that aren't sexual. The erotic isn't simply the narrow window of what we define as sexual.

I turn myself on when...

....
....
....
....
....
....
....
....
....

I turn myself off when...

....
....
....
....
....
....
....
....
....

When Should I Sleep With Them?

One of my earliest memories of an adult talking to me about sex was a family member reminding me that you shouldn't "open your legs so easily". After all, "No one will buy the cow if you give the milk for free." Nowadays, I would simply respond, "Thank God I'm not a cow, then." But at the age this was said to me, it really shaped my point of view on sex. What the saying means, for those who have had the good fortune of never hearing it, is no one will marry a woman if she is sleeping around without the intention to marry her partner. It's a stupid saying, because are we really arguing that the only reason to get married is for sex? While that is the direct explanation of this saying, this outdated phrase sent me broader messages about sex in general. It taught me that sex was something that was given and could be taken away. Sex could be used as a power play and a chip to gain control. Worse than that, it taught me that sex in a heteronormative world was just for the man and – because men can't control themselves – women were responsible for controlling their urges. It taught me that women lose something when we engage in sex and men gain from that loss. You were responsible if you caved to your desires and you were even responsible if men caved to theirs, because clearly you were being a tease and provoked them.

It also sends the message that the only reason a man would want a woman is for the sex; the implication is that women can't want sex too. Ultimately, summing up: if you have sex, it cheapens you and lowers your value, and therefore women who have sex a lot are worth less than those who keep their legs together. And this is just the tip of the iceberg of awful advice that surrounds sex and dating. God forbid you would want to engage in casual sex. Anyone ever been told, "You have to test-drive the car before you buy it?" We love women being referred to as property that you buy. Then there is the misogynistic idea that sleeping with many men will give you a loose vagina. But sleeping with the same man multiple times won't? Doesn't make a lot of sense, does it? When we start to unpick all the things we get taught about sex, they fall apart quite quickly – but unless you know to do that, you accept them as fact and let them warp your idea of sex.

How this plays out in the dating world is that we give the timing of sex a lot more weight than it deserves. If a relationship lasts, then we credit our patience and willpower to wait for its success, and if a relationship doesn't, we either tell ourselves that we shouldn't have made them wait so long or that, if we had waited longer, they would have been more tempted to stay. Either way, it's our fault, our responsibility – and no wonder you can't keep a man! The truth is that when you sleep with a person doesn't determine the longevity of a relationship. When you decide to have sex won't make the right person leave and the wrong person stay. We need to remove the illusion that if we had taken the other option in this pivotal decision, it would have had a different outcome.

We are told that if you sleep with someone on a first date, the other person will assume it's casual and that if you wait longer, they have time to build an investment in you and therefore will perceive you as higher value. While I understand the psychology behind this, I also believe the kind of people who think that way are also the kind of people who like playing games. So if you don't sleep with them until the fourth date, they will wait until the fourth date to sleep with you. It still doesn't guarantee that they will stay after the fourth date. If sex is all they want, they will wait you out to get it. If you make them wait for the sake of it because of sexist messaging you have been taught, all it does is prolong the game. The unfortunate thing that isn't said enough is that there is no straightforward way to make sure they keep wanting to see you after you sleep with them. If you are concerned about the impression it is sending to go home with them earlier rather than later, the solution to this – unsurprisingly – is communication. I have no qualms about having a conversation about whether what we're doing is just sexual or not.

Much like I have touched on in this book, there is no "one size fits all" answer to when to have sex. It is, understandably, very dependent on each person and there is a case for waiting and there is a case for sleeping with them on the first date. If you are a person who takes a while to feel safe and comfortable with a person, then wait until you do. If you are a person who is often wrong about first impressions and has a history of not being a great judge of character, again that is an argument to wait a little longer. If you are a person who confuses love and sex, that is also a strong suggestion to wait. If you are a good judge of character, trust your intuition and ultimately, if you want to sleep with them on the first date, then do. The problem is, because of all the sex negativity, shame and patriarchal double standards, it's a lot more complicated to know whether you want to or not. This is not a moral decision and it doesn't determine how good a person you are. When your patriarchal training pipes up, wanting to call you "easy" or a "slut", remind yourself there isn't a single man in the world sat there asking his friends, "Do you think it's too soon to sleep with her?" because they are not judged in the same way.

Personally, I fall all over the spectrum. There are guys I have slept with on a first date and there are guys that I have waited to kiss until the third date. In hindsight, I seem to date people longer if I sleep with them on a first date, but I think it's important to see this as correlated information rather than the cause. It does not mean sleeping with them on the first date made us date longer; it is likely correlated because, if I felt an instant connection with them, then I would sleep with them sooner – it's related to the instant connection more than the timing of sex.

Sex can be as meaningful or as fun as you make it. What's more important than the timing of when you sleep with them is understanding your relationship to sex. Decipher the meaning you are attaching to it. What does it give you? Does it give you connection, intimacy, a chance to relax, attention? There is no wrong answer to this. When you understand your relationship to sex, you can make decisions that are based on what you truly want and not what the other person wants from you. One way you can explore your relationship to sex is by asking yourself why you want to sleep with that person: do you believe that it will make them like you more? Do you believe it will make them stay? If neither of those things are true, are you still able to enjoy the sex? And ultimately, do you want to have sex? If you don't know the answer to these questions, then err on the side of safety and wait until you can answer them.

There was a time in my life when I struggled to differentiate between love and sex because sex gave me a brief respite from feeling unlovable. Therefore, I would often feel pressure to sleep with them earlier than I felt comfortable. As a result, I challenged myself to try the alternative. The only way to unlearn something is to do something different, so as an experiment, I forced myself to wait to see if it felt more authentic. By trying the alternative, I could tell when it felt right and when it was due to me wanting to please the other person. I was also able to grow in confidence with communicating when it felt too soon. Asking yourself what your motive behind sex is means you can remove the societal shame around this decision. By asking myself that question, I know how I feel before putting sex in the mix, and if I'm feeling unsure, then that's a no.

The most important thing about sleeping with anyone, either casually or on a date, is that you feel safe with them and, at a bare minimum, you have trust and respect. You need to know that they will respect your first "no" and that together you will create a safe environment to be vulnerable, as sex inherently is. In our society, women are shamed for having sex – and also for not having sex, so you can't win. The ludicrousness of the idea that having sex makes you a dirty woman actually implies that what makes you dirty is the man you slept with. If anyone dares judge you for sleeping with them so early, remind them that they also took part in the activity. If a guy pressures you to sleep with them sooner than you feel comfortable, that is a person you don't want to be sleeping with. It's OK for them to want sex on a first date and it's equally OK for you not to. Rather than judging them on whether they want to get sexual on a first date, assess their reaction when you set your boundaries. I don't believe in placating people when setting boundaries:

> I need to know you better to feel comfortable with that

> Hey! This is moving too quickly. We need to slow it down

Many dating books out there give you special sentences to avoid bruising their ego, and I also don't believe in that. If they take your no as a personal insult, that tells you everything you need to know. We spend so long worrying about people judging us rather than asking ourselves if we want to sleep with a judgemental person. Remember that you can withdraw consent at any moment, even if they are already in your apartment, even if your clothes are already off and even if you are in the middle of a sexual act. One time, I was crying outside a club and a guy I had spoken to earlier in the night offered to walk me home. I agreed and when we got there, I went to the loo. When I came back, he was naked on my bed. He claimed he thought we both knew what "walking you home" was "code" for; regardless, I only gave him long enough to get dressed again before he was kicked out. You are also allowed to have a no-tolerance policy on body shaming or around sexual safety. One of my rules is no condom, no sex. Whatever your boundaries are, you are allowed to set them:

> I need us to use a condom if we are going to sleep together non-exclusively

> My sexual health is important to me, so I'm going to need us to go for an STI test before we start sleeping together

There are many situations prior to having sex in which a conversation may need to take place. This could be if you have a stoma and need to explain that anal sex is off limits. For me, if I remember to, I have a conversation about the fact I have a shunt in my neck that can't be touched. I tend to start this conversation when we start kissing and will say something like, "Can we just talk about something first?" I often forget, though, so will bring it up when they put their hand on my neck or go to kiss me there and will explain it with: "Long story, but I have a tube there, so just be careful around my neck." If they ask questions, I answer them – but that's often all I need to say. You can choose to have this conversation whenever feels most comfortable. If you know that you are going to sleep with them on that date, even if it's at the end of the date, then bringing it up earlier could work for you so you don't have to worry about it. If it feels presumptive to bring it up, then you are allowed to pause while you are kissing and have the conversation then.

It's your information that you are disclosing and you have every right to disclose it at a time that feels good to you. What will likely happen is that each situation will differ slightly. With one guy, we had gone back to mine on a first date to order a takeaway because all the restaurants near me had shut, and we started talking about how I like painting. One of my more recent paintings I had done sat in my home office and I went to go show him it. It was a picture of a naked woman, and he held it up and jokingly asked if that was an accurate representation. I responded "minus a bunch of surgery scars", and that's how the conversation happened. When you stop seeing it as a big deal, you allow for it to come up naturally. Don't worry about "ruining the mood". If they turn it into an issue or make you feel like you are an inconvenience, use that as an indicator that you don't want to sleep with them.

When you choose to have sex with someone, be confident in your decision. None of this taking someone home with an "I never do this" to justify your actions. If you want to sleep with them on the first date, then do, but own it. The phrase "I never do this" is one that is rarely believed – and why does it matter whether you've done it before, anyway? The perception we have when the words come out of our mouth is that it will make that person seem special by virtue of being the exception, but it still feeds the narrative that sex is more special if it is rare. This idea that they are your exception to your rule doesn't make sense because after a first date, they are essentially still a stranger. What exactly can you learn about a person in one date that makes them the exception to the rule? Stop caveating your decision and own your decision. If you can't stand firm in the certainty of your decision, then wait until you can. Raise the benchmark to feeling alright about sex to enthusiastic consent. If it's not a hell yes, it's a no.

Forget Me Nots

- The timing of when you sleep with a person doesn't determine the longevity of a relationship
- How soon (or not) you sleep with them is not a moral decision and it doesn't determine how good a person you are
- The most important thing about sleeping with anyone, either casually or on a date, is that you feel safe with them and, at a bare minimum, you have trust and respect
- If it's not a hell yes, it's a no

Take Action Toolkit

We need to lose the concept of "good sex" and "bad sex". There is simply sex in which our tastes align and sex in which we are incompatible. Even when they don't align, there is sex in which both parties are willing to learn and listen to preferences, and sex in which each party remains stuck in the way they have always done things. In order to be able to communicate what you want, you need to know what you want. These are prompts that Emily Nagoski, a brilliant sex educator, suggest you ask yourself:

– What do I want when I want sex?

....
....
....
....
....
....
....
....
....
....
....
....

– What do I not want when I want sex?

....
....
....
....
....
....
....
....
....
....
....
....

The answers to these could be specific acts, like you don't
want someone fingering you like a jackhammer, or external
factors, like you want a broad enough span of time so you
don't have to watch the clock.

How Do I Get Over My Insecurities Around Being Naked?

Sex is us at our most vulnerable, so it only makes sense that even the most confident people will have insecurities when it comes to the bedroom. In university, I was in a large corridor of 40 people and I had a strong policy of not shitting where I ate. The rest of the corridor ended up being quite incestuous, and because I opted out, I became the person that everyone would come to, to discuss their neighbours their neighbours. I would be the first to know if two people were getting together and I would also be the first person to know when it would go wrong. Because we were newly independent young adults, there was a lot that went wrong.

Being the one that was never involved meant these conversations ended up being quite formative in how I viewed sex, especially as I was privy to a level of transparency that those entangled in the web were not. You'd think having access to this higher level of detail would be a good thing, but it often just left me picturing this graphic conversation taking place about me, just on another corridor with a different friendship group. The horrible ways in which the guys would discuss the girls – in front of me, and often in front of many of them – made me increasingly insecure. Whether they were comparing the blow-job technique of my friends or announcing something sexual that should have stayed private while in the middle of a drinking game, it made me turn inwards rather than question what was going on in the room. Now that I am much further into adulthood, I can see that all the conversations that took place in that room were games in trying to come across as the most experienced. Every time they put down the women they slept with, it was to hide their own insecurities. The problem is that once you've sat in a room where your supposed friends have compared your sexual skills, that's an insecurity that will stick around. So it was unsurprising that, when I first started working as a life coach and the majority of my clients were coming to me for body image issues, the main concern was taking their top off in the bedroom. They worried that they would look fat.

When I first started dating, I had actually been OK with my body for quite a while, so when body wobbles started creeping back, I was caught off guard. Unconsciously, I had started viewing my body through the lens of who I was dating and this was placing my body confidence outside of what I could control. It began affecting how I saw myself, and I realized I held their opinion of my body in higher regard than my own. This actually wasn't wholly negative. It worked in a positive way too but, positive or negative, it made me vulnerable. If that vulnerability was placed in hands that shouldn't have been trusted, it became a problem. When a guy told me that he thought that my glasses made me sexy, my 10-year insecurity about wearing them disappeared instantly. However, when the same guy said "ew" to the story of my illness, I didn't tell another person that story for another four years.

My self-esteem revolved around him, which meant he had the power to give me confidence – but could also take it away. This is why it's important to have a solid sense of self, because otherwise the rise and fall of their moods dictates your own perception of yourself. Once I ended that relationship, I told myself I'd never let the same thing happen again. It took a few months, but thankfully, I was able to return to my former certainty in my appearance. One of the most harmful things that he embedded, and the one that took the longest to unlearn, was that he was with me despite my body. I hate that I couldn't see it at the time but both my body and I deserved better than that. I deserve someone who wants all parts of me, and so do you. It became the wake-up call I needed; the stubborn part of me kicked in and refused to let him affect how I viewed my body long-term. I had spent so long to get OK with my scars and my appearance and out of pure drive to not let him win, I worked just as hard to get back to that. By the time I got to the end of my dating detox, I was the most confident I had been in my body.

Thankfully, I have never given another person that power since – and no matter who I date or for how long, I never will. It is your job to believe you are beautiful. It is your job to be in your corner and know what you bring to the table. It is not the job of the person you are dating to make you feel beautiful or fix your body image. Yes, they can help by supporting you, but if it's all external validation, it's a double-edged sword. Beauty is not a big deal unless you believe you don't have it, in the same way that money is not important unless you have none. You do not need to believe you are the most gorgeous person in the world, but you do need to believe you bring beauty to the table. It doesn't have to be a kind of beauty that everyone is able to recognize but, at the very least, accept that the person you are sleeping with or dating can see it.

Today, I struggle to remember the last bad body image day that I had. I am pretty certain it hasn't been in the last decade. Any time I say this publicly, I am accused of being arrogant. But as someone who spent so much of their life insecure, I will take the label of "arrogant" over how I used to live. I say I haven't had a bad body image day in a decade because it's the truth. I have had bad body image thoughts, but you are not your thoughts and you can't control your thoughts. Many of those thoughts are old programming from buying society's lies for too long. What I can control is whether a bad body image thought spirals into my whole day. The reason it doesn't is because I don't give it air to breathe. A thought like "Wow, you have a lot of cellulite on your thighs" will pop into my head and I will not attach to it. It's as if the thought that appears in my head doesn't feel like it belongs to me. Then my next thought might be: "I really need to send that email." We have useless thoughts all the time, and it's as if the thought that pointed out my cellulite was as useless as my brain saying "You have blue hair." Well, I don't, so my brain moves on. I don't say it aloud, and I don't feed it by trying to create a solution to the cellulite and I don't think about the thought. I am more than my body. I have more important things to think about than my body, and whether I have cellulite on my thighs or not doesn't impact my day. It doesn't impact how much I write that day, it doesn't impact how well I slept last night or what food I am going to put into my body that day.

If you are fat with your top on, you will be fat with your top off. If you aren't fat with clothes on, you aren't going to suddenly become fat with your clothes off. Even with the best Spanx and push-up bras, you cannot look that different in person. They already know what you look like. If you are naked with another person, accept that the other person finds you attractive. Questioning this does not serve you. What we should be questioning instead is why looking fat is such a bad thing. We live in a fatphobic world, where being fat is the worst thing a woman can be. We have talked about how this message was created to capitalize on our insecurities, but how that translates into the bedroom is trying to portray the perfect vision of beauty – whether that's been formulated by the porn you watch or simply by the media's version of what is sexy. We need to cement the idea that all body types can be seen as hot and that you don't need to appear as the thinnest, most done-up version of yourself in order to be sexually attractive. With such an emphasis on physical appearance in women, it's no wonder that during sex, women suck their stomachs in, concern themselves with which sexual position is flattering or feel the need to turn the lights off to give their minds a brief respite from being aesthetically pleasing at all times.

Sex is not flattering. That is a fact. You will not look the thinnest you have ever looked. Your make-up will not be flawless. Sometimes your body doesn't do what you need it to do and sometimes you are cock-blocked by thrush or a UTI. Sex is messy. It involves body fluids. Some of the best sex can involve you both ending up in a laughing fit. When there is naked person in front of you, you aren't going to be examining their imperfections. You will be thinking about the sex you are about to have. They are the same, and they might even be thinking about their own insecurities. If you are concerned about how many stomach rolls you have while you are in doggy style or whether they are going to be turned off by your pubic hair, you are not going to enjoy sex. If you focus on what you look like, you are not focusing on what you are feeling. If you are in your head, you won't be able to focus on the incredible sensations sex brings. As Dr Karen Gurney states in *Mind the Gap* (2020), this is due to objectification theory:

"Objectification theory proposes that we have internalized the (very gendered) social scripts that self-worth is highly dependent on how we look. Therefore, when we feel we have to be naked in front of another person, we are overly focused on seeing our body from that other person's perspective."

The more negative thoughts you have, the more you will be in your head throughout sex. Unsurprisingly, poor body image is associated with lower sexual satisfaction, avoiding sex, struggling to have orgasms and having less desire to masturbate or have sex with a partner (Dosch et al., 2016). The best way to reduce your negative thoughts is to stop vocalizing them. The less you say it aloud, the less time you give it. Eventually, your brain learns that thinking that thought doesn't result in anything, and it creates that thought less. The problem is we spent so much time colouring in the details of our insecurity instead of colouring in the details of what we want instead. I'm not saying you have to be confident. I'm saying stop talking about being insecure. Not just in the bedroom, not just on dates, but in life. When you talk about how ugly your thighs are, the first thing anyone does is look at your thighs. You are drawing attention to the thing you don't want anyone to notice. If you can't love your body, at least stop thinking about it. Think about anything else. Focus on where they are touching you and concentrate on the sensations.

Forget Me Nots

- You are more than your body
- Sex is not flattering, and it's messy; sex is not about looking good but feeling good
- If you are naked with another person, accept that the other person finds you attractive
- Stop vocalizing your negative thoughts about your body

Take Action Toolkit

When someone has a poor body image, they tend to segment their body into parts. They will see their saggy boobs or their stretch marks rather than seeing their body as a whole. When we objectify others, we do the same. Adverts include a picture of a woman's legs without the rest of her body – or just her arse, to promote the latest beer or diet shake. This allows for nitpicking and not seeing our body parts in context. To help combat this, make your vision peripheral before looking in the mirror. You need to stop reading in order to do this (foveal vision is needed to read), so read the rest of the paragraph before doing this exercise. To start, find a spot on the wall in front of you. Put your awareness on the two front corners of the room without moving your eyes from that middle spot. Hold that spot, and bring your awareness to the two back corners behind you. Obviously, you will not be able to see them, but you should now be able to sense all four corners while still looking at the middle spot. This forces your vision to be peripheral. Now, if you look in the mirror, you will see your body as a whole.

How Do I Prioritize My Own Pleasure During Sex?

One of the greatest myths about dating is that if you are with a compatible person, sex should be magnetic and effortless instantly. Good sex often requires work, communication and time to get to know each other's tastes, preferences and bodies. Of course, there are the rare magical times when the first encounter is incredible, but this is the exception. For me, this usually happens only when sex is all I am expecting from them – that is the one and only criteria they need to meet. If you want a person who you actually want to date and who meets your needs emotionally, then it's going to be a lot harder to find. Even the people who just "have a way to them" didn't accidentally become good at sex, they had more practice than others. Much like how you can't get good at dating without going on dates, you can't get good at having sex without having more sex. I once asked a guy I was sleeping with whether he was always confident in the bedroom. He told me he used to be shy and nervous and then one day, he went on Google and started reading up on how to be good at sex. He said he spent hours on Reddit threads, where he realized that if you actually ask women out politely and with confidence, most tend to say yes. It made me understand that everyone is on their own journey sexually. No matter how confident someone comes across when having sex, you don't know what it took them to get there.

A lot of the difficulties women face in the bedroom are more indicative of broader societal issues that aren't confined to sex. Women are judged for asking for what they want more than men are. When you are a woman who knows their boundaries and communicates their needs, you are often called harsh, blunt, aggressive, mean, selfish and even a bitch. As a result, as mentioned previously, some women have learned how to communicate indirectly to avoid being judged or disliked. Along the way, women then find it harder to know how they actually feel and what their needs are. How this translates into the bedroom is that they also can't ask for what they need sexually because they have never asked themselves what they need. Since they don't have practice doing so in the world, it feels impossible in the bedroom, when they are at their most exposed. Whatever problem you have in the real world is likely to translate into the bedroom. For example, if you struggle to let anyone help you with the housework, you will struggle to let anyone help you climax. If you don't know how to communicate your needs in general, you may have difficulty communicating your needs sexually. If you struggle to believe you deserve good things in life and are the kind of person who saves up their favourite skincare products and candles (often until they expire!), you may also find it difficult to allow yourself pleasure within the bedroom. If you feel guilty when someone gives you a gift and you've not got them one back, you may have difficulty allowing yourself to receive in the bedroom. You will want to reciprocate instantly and may feel guilt if you are unable to return the favour sexually. And as much as you can improve your sex life by working on the elements outside of the bedroom, lessons from other parts of the relationship can improve your sex life too.

An example of this for me was when I got ill when I was first dating someone. I've always been quite independent, but especially when it comes to my illnesses, I have veered closer to hyper-independence. I have often gone to hospital alone and not told anyone – not even my housemate in the room next door. So when the guy I was dating offered to send me supplies, the hyper-independent part of me wanted to shoot it down. But there was a quieter voice in my head – the wiser part of me – that whispered, "Let him."

When someone I love is going through illness, I sometimes feel helpless – so if I'm given a way to help, even if it is small, it can relieve my helplessness. I realized I was depriving him of that. Why was I arguing so strongly to do everything alone when I didn't have to? What was I trying to prove? If I was honest with myself, it made me feel vulnerable. What if I let you help and then you disappear? Now think about this in terms of the bedroom. How do you think this way of thinking translates into sex?

Feeling guilty around receiving pleasure is a common problem I see in women. One way to reframe it is to understand that by not allowing your partner to go down on you or pleasure you, you are actually preventing them from experiencing pleasure too. You know when you give someone a gift and they light up and it makes you happy too? Or when you give someone a blowjob and you like seeing them enjoying themselves? It works the other way around, so stop depriving them of that. When you fake orgasms, you are doing both of you a disservice. You prevent them from ever learning how to actually get you off, and you are ignoring your needs to boost their ego. When they ask you if you've orgasmed, and you haven't, stop saying yes and start saying "not yet".

Part of the guilt is also that women have been sold on the idea that it is harder for a woman to orgasm than it is for a man, when it's simply because 80 per cent of women can't orgasm through penetrative sex and need clitoral stimulation. Emily Nagoski said it best when she said: "For centuries, male sexuality has been the 'default' sexuality, so that where women differ from men, women get labeled 'broken'." It's been shown that women who have fewer orgasms tend to blame themselves rather than external factors such as the type of sex they are having or societal influences (Bell and McClelland, 2018). In fact, I remember multiple times in my teenage years where my friends believed they physiologically couldn't orgasm – as in they anatomically were unable to – only to discover masturbation and then be able to do it instantly. The research echoes this. When women and men have sex with each other, the rate of men usually or always orgasming stays at 95 per cent and for women, it drops to 65 per cent (Frederick et al., 2018) with only 18 per cent of women usually or often orgasming during casual sex (Armstrong et al., 2012).

We live in a society that encourages us to constantly be thinking to the point of overthinking, and the bedroom is no different. We stay in our heads thinking about if the other person is enjoying themselves, that email you need to send and whether they think you are taking too long. Research found the "quality of being entirely alive in their bodies with no mental interference was the hallmark of great sex" (Kleinplatz and Menard, 2007). If we are unable to get out of our heads in the bedroom, it becomes impossible to enjoy ourselves. Instead of thinking, you should be feeling.

So how can you get back into your body so you can experience pleasure in the bedroom? By controlling your attention. When your attention moves to your thoughts, you need to give your brain something else to focus on. The best thing for you to focus on is your breath, not only because it will bring your awareness into the body, but also because the deeper you breathe, the calmer your nervous system becomes. The autonomic nervous system comprises two parts: the sympathetic nervous system activates the flight or fight response in times of stress and the parasympathetic nervous system returns your body to a state of calm. When your breathing is short and shallow, or you hold your breath, your body perceives it as stress and sends adrenaline and stress hormones around your body. When you breathe deeply, you tell your body you are safe and you can return back to the parasympathetic nervous system so that you can relax. If your mind is still being loud, then focus your mind by counting your breathing in your head. Count to four as you breathe in, count to four as you hold that breath and then count to eight as you breathe out.

As your mind quietens down, scan your body and notice the feelings that are there. Follow those feelings around. If your mind gets loud again, either return your focus to your breath or put your focus on where they are touching you or where your skin touches theirs. As feelings of pleasure arise, allow yourself to make noises. We censor ourselves due to self-consciousness, and when we do so, we enter back into our thinking brain. If we actually let ourselves moan, it allows us to get deeper into the sensation. As much as it sounds counterintuitive, if you are able to remove the goal of orgasm completely, it often actually helps you climax. When we see a climax as a necessary end to sex, it can lead to increased pressure. We end up persevering even if we are tired or if we are actually already satisfied. Stop centring sex around an orgasm and enjoy the pleasure throughout. Normalize telling them what you need – sometimes you will need to show them by demonstrating it yourself. You should be able to have open communication with the person you are sleeping with.

Forget Me Nots

- Good sex often requires work, communication and time to get to know each other's tastes, preferences and bodies
- When you fake orgasms, you are doing both of you a disservice
- Focus on your breath, not only because it will bring your awareness into the body but also because the deeper you breathe, the calmer your nervous system becomes
- Normalize telling them what you need – sometimes you will need to show them by demonstrating it yourself

---

Take Action Toolkit

A lot of the ways we limit the pleasure we can experience in the bedroom is to isolate it to merely our genitals. When we look at pleasure more broadly, we are able to recognize that sensual things can be a turn-on as well. Take some time to discover where you like to be touched. It could be a light finger brushing along your collarbone or it might be a firmer stroke down your thigh. You might enjoy the sensation of a fingernail tickling its way down your jawline or a gentle pull on your earlobe. Set a timer for 15 minutes and allow yourself to explore. Sensuality is all about your senses, so experiment with different lighting, put a candle on to discover which smells turn you on, pop some music on or even have a play with hot and cold items.

Chapter 10

I Don't Deserve This

How to Be Empowered When It Ends

What Do I Do if They Ghost?

We often convince ourselves that ghosting is a new-age thing that only arrived with the advent of dating apps, but this is false. People were ghosted before, we just didn't have a word for it. It's not isolated to dating apps either. My experience with being ghosted is extensive, but it began long before dating apps, at 19 years old, when I went into hospital unexpectedly. There seems to be no factor that prevents being ghosted. I've been ghosted by people who promised they never would and when two of my university friends happened to match on a dating app in the middle of a pandemic, that ended in a ghosting three months later. A 10-year friendship between them was supposedly not enough to give someone the decency to end it properly. Ghosting might be modern terminology, but it is no different to plain old rejection – it is just a more cowardly form. Because of our desire for "cognitive closure", it can feel more frustrating than a break-up that is communicated properly. The psychologist Arie Kruglanski explains that the higher the ambiguity, the stronger the impulse to want an explanation. Whether we like it or not, ghosting is here to stay. If you can't change the culture, you have to change your response.

The first thing you must do is remove the idea that doing something different would have resulted in a different outcome. Stop replaying conversations. There is nothing you could have done to change the ending. Even if you could, it's not a helpful belief because it was out of your control. Even if you did do something wrong or they did want to end it, a person who can communicate would tell you, and end it with words rather than silence. If they have ghosted you, they have done it before, and the likelihood is they will do it again and again until they learn how to have difficult conversations. As much as it feels personal, it isn't. It is not about you; it's a reflection of them. It indicates poor communication skills and I, for one, wouldn't want to be with someone who can't communicate their feelings.

Let's imagine your hypothetical future together. Imagine the silent treatment being a main feature of your relationship: you'd have to be prepared to be left on read and have to guess why they are annoyed. Effortless things like deciding where to go for dinner could take hours. That is the future you are signing up for when you are with someone who can't communicate their feelings. When a person communicates badly in the early stages of dating, it's like a light switch that goes off in my brain. Any form of attraction is gone because bad communication is a turn-off. Ghosting is cruel and cowardly; any interest that I had in them pre-ghosting dissipates instantly.

At my worst, I would try to get their attention again via social media. Social media exacerbates the pain of ghosting by being able to see they are both on their phones and still alive. We can do a lot of damage by stalking their page and posting passive-aggressive quotes. We have all done it. One of my low moments was putting up an Instagram Story of me at dinner with a picture of a guy's hand on the night the guy I'd been seeing cancelled our date. It wasn't even my picture – it was a picture a friend had sent to me to use. The guy's hand in the background was her date. Within a minute, he had viewed it. Within two minutes, he had sent me a text asking me out again. While technically it worked, you shouldn't have to work this hard to get someone's attention. Don't let someone tell you that they don't want you twice. This is not the behaviour of someone who has self-esteem. I might have got a response, but it just delayed the inevitable.

Do not use your time and energy to send another text or ask for reasons why. You are asking to get your feelings hurt when they will likely ignore you again. No one ever changed their mind about someone because they got a second text. Let's say the double text is what convinces them to tell you why they were actually uninterested in you. How does that help you? If they told you they thought you were boring, would that help? No, because their opinion isn't an objective fact. Just because they believe you are boring doesn't make it true, and now you've got a brand-new insecurity that you didn't need to have because you asked a question you didn't want to know the answer to.

If it's really going to bother you to not send a second text, then send that text, but send it for you. Remove any expectation of a reply and keep it short. Do not empty your heart out into the contents of that message, as this will train your mind that when you are vulnerable, you will get rejected. Instead, save your vulnerability for people who have earned your trust and shown that when you are vulnerable, they will keep you safe.

> Hey! Was wondering if you wanted to go on another date? Either way, it would be great if you could let me know even if you aren't interested anymore xx

I am personally against the second text because you can't make someone care. You have an underlying assumption that if you cry, yell or tell them how upset you are, they will feel guilty or change their behaviour. Unfortunately, not everyone who hurts you cares. Texting them again won't force a reply. It's putting time and energy into someone who doesn't deserve it.

Reappearing ghosts

When people ghost, it's usually a case of when, not if, they will resurface. When you train yourself to lose attraction for bad behaviour, you will be resilient when they re-emerge because you will have moved on. Their reappearance doesn't mean what you want it to mean. It just means they are bored, lonely, drunk or horny. These breadcrumbs keep you as an option and they like the power of knowing you will always be there no matter how much they fuck you about. You want to be dating someone who is consistent and reliable. No more revolving doors. They have shown you who they are – now listen.

In the past, I would take a lot of satisfaction from when they would resurface and I'd respond to "I miss you" texts with "of course you do" or "duh". Sometimes I would go the smug route and respond with a "Who is this?" to twist the knife, and sometimes I genuinely had to respond with that because I had already deleted their number. This approach came from my ego. Nowadays, I go the more mature route because I don't let other people's behaviours dictate mine. I always want to have good communication and be proud of how I acted in the situation. Therefore, I don't ignore their text when they reach back out. I show them exactly how they could have behaved by demonstrating how easy it is to be clear and communicative without being hurtful:

> Hey! This disappearing and reappearing thing doesn't work for me. I've enjoyed getting to know you and I am no longer interested xx

You may notice that in most of my texts, I avoid using the word "but" and am very intentional when I use it. This is because "but" is a word that nullifies everything that comes before it. It's why if someone says "I love you, but ...", all you hear is what comes next. I use "and" more often because I don't care about being grammatically correct as much as I care about wanting both statements to be heard. If both things can be true, then I don't use "but" because they don't oppose each other, as in the example above.

Slow ghosting

Slow ghosting is the act of gradually becoming more and more distant. They haven't fully disappeared but they reply at a slower rate than before. In a lot of cases, this is after a period of intensity at the beginning and then, as soon as you become comfortable, that's when their texts slow, the dates become sparse and there is generally less effort – until, one day, they fully disappear. We can take something like viewing our Instagram Stories to mean more than it does. You see their name there and deduce that it means they care about you, yet when you are tapping through Instagram Stories yourself at lightning speed you know how little that truly means. At the most, all it means is that they are curious, and at the least, they are tapping through while sitting on the toilet.

The last time I was slow ghosted was by a guy I had nicknamed "therapy guy". My favourite types of conversations are about psychology: how people think and interact with each other and yes, you guessed it, therapy. On his dating profile, he mentioned tarot cards, so in our first conversation, I said I had never tried tarot cards but I loved angel cards. He asked me how I found out about them and I said that my life coach introduced me to them. This is what I mean by being authentically who you are, and letting them decide whether that's for them. I could have lied and said it was someone else, or I could have stated with some fake embarrassment that I have a life coach, in the same way some people shy away from saying they have a therapist, but I am too tired of the stigma that personal development holds. I was honest.

> Lucky! I wish my therapist believed in angel cards

Be who you are, and let them decide if they like you. We ended up going on around five dates and, while our sexual chemistry wasn't quite there, the conversations we had were fascinating and it really filled a void in my life I didn't even know was there. I didn't realize how much I had missed psychology chats until we started dating. Because of the lack of sexual chemistry, I waited until the fifth date to sleep together and it was after this date that his texting changed. It's too easy and lazy to use the correlation of sex and pulling away to create a cause and effect. Instead of making my own assumptions, I asked. This text, unlike some previous examples, is composed with a marked openness because we were further into the dating process. We had earned more vulnerability and therefore, he deserved some benefit of the doubt and an opportunity to change his behaviour:

> Hey! Are we good? This has started feeling different and if something has changed, I'd rather just know because this is making me feel a bit shit

The key to texts like this is to watch the behaviour afterwards. Most will deny that they are ghosting or that anything has changed. This guy didn't do that, he even acknowledged that he had been acting more distant, apologized and made a plan for another date. But the distance continued to grow. The dates started getting further apart and the texts never returned to the previous frequency, and that's when I decided to end it. Who knows what changed for him. Ultimately, the reason didn't matter – the distance told me everything I needed to know, and I moved on. Sometimes slow ghosting is a way of monkey-branching: not wanting to let go of one branch until they have found another. But you don't want to be someone's option. Instead, cut the branch off yourself:

> Hey! I'm not sure what changed over the last few weeks. This isn't working for me and I need more communication. While that was there in the beginning, I am not getting my needs met anymore, so I think it's best if we just call it a day. Thanks for the fun and great chats. Good luck with the rest of your Masters and take care xx

When they start to pull away, it's tempting to want to protect yourself and pull away first. Pulling away can take the form of starting to play games, waiting longer, matching their reply times or even just pretending not to care. This doesn't work. You are running a test, hoping they will notice, but the problem with tests is that the person doesn't know they are being tested. You might feel the urge to stop texting first to "win" the break-up, thinking that they can't dump you if you dump them first. This is protective behaviour and it doesn't work because no one wins a break-up. No matter who dumped who, it will still hurt and if you try to pre-empt being dumped by behaving badly, then that bad behaviour could actually be the reason for the break-up. This is a risky and inaccurate way of doing it. Their increased distance might not be personal – it could be due to an increased workload, some family drama going on or something else that you are unaware of. The only way to find out is to ask. When you are being ghosted, it is obvious what is happening. Slow ghosting is more confusing and the only way to alleviate the confusion is to get an answer. When it's further down the road and a few dates in, I will give someone the grace of not assuming the worst. This guy had cancelled our fourth date together and then texted me the night after, wanting to reschedule, but everything had been a little off, so I communicated that:

> Hey! Hope you had a good night tonight! Wondering if you fancied doing something tomorrow/Thursday? :) xx

> Heya! I'm going to be honest and say this is all becoming a bit of a game. I'm getting a bunch of mixed signals and it's quite confusing. I'm up for something and also really don't appreciate being messed around xx

> I know, so sorry! I've just been incredibly busy. Just getting back from work now and I really want to do something. It's been mad, had to be at work for 8 as well, so I'm pooped! I don't want you to think I'm messing you around because that's the exact opposite of what I want to do! xx

Sounds like a perfect response, right? Sounds like someone who was genuinely busy and that as I said above, it wasn't personal. Well, we never ended up going on another date – he booked a date only to cancel again, and then I ended it. It's impossible to know from a response whether it's true or not. Part of empowered dating means taking that risk, being happy with the decision you made and then calling it a day when their behaviour doesn't improve.

You are not allowed to ghost either

One of the reasons I avoided dating in university is because I didn't know what to do if they liked you but you didn't like them back. The thought of potentially hurting someone's feelings was a reason I didn't date as much as I wanted to. At one point early on, I remember my life coach Michelle Zelli having to help me construct a text. Eventually, like any skill, you get better at it. I guess I have come quite far considering I'm not only writing a book on it but this book is littered with so many texts – and I couldn't even include them all. As you may have noticed, I don't reinvent the wheel every time I send an ending-it text; I use similar language because I want to send the same message: this is over. I do think it's important to make it personal and in your own language. This was a text I sent after a first date where there wasn't much chemistry. I had a great experience trying a pub quiz for the first time, but I didn't want to spend another evening together, and he had already reached out to make plans for a second date:

> Hey! Hope you didn't have to get up too early today? I was hoping you would like to see me again. Maybe Saturday night or Sunday during the day if you are free xx

> Hey! No, thankfully, I could sleep in ... I probably could have slept all day. Had a really lovely time yesterday! Unfortunately, I don't see this going anywhere romantic, so I think it's best not to take it any further. Thanks for last night though, take care xx

The people who tell themselves that ghosting is kinder are lying to themselves. It's not. You don't have to end it perfectly, but you do have to end it. You don't need to be mean to get your point across and, if you can do so calmly and maturely, most people appreciate you letting them know. I know I appreciate the honesty and transparency when I receive a final text and will often return the kindness with a personal touch:

> Hey! Thanks for letting me know. It was great getting to know you and good luck with the move! xx

The way to be kind in the final text is to not put any unnecessary information that is hurtful. Put just enough information to make it clear that it is over – be firm. Understandably, there will be situations where the person does not take rejection well. Let them react however they want. Once you have communicated your message, you don't need to say anything further. This was a text I sent to a guy before a first date because, in between us planning the date and actually going on it, he kept making insensitive jokes about Covid. I realized we weren't going to get on and I communicated that in my response:

> Hey! How was yesterday? xx

> Heya! Yeah, yesterday was a busy one and in terms of going out, I don't think this is going to work and so I'm not going to take you up on that offer. Not sure our sense of humour is a great match. Take care xx

> Lol I mean surely you can tell that isn't a real pick-up line. Was just a joke because some people have it as their bio on their dating apps but yeah whatever xx

Nothing more needed to be said, so I left it at that. While on the tame side of bad responses, it still reiterated that I made the right decision, because I don't know any 30-year-old who says "whatever" like a petulant child. Do not measure the success of your text on the response you receive. It does not matter if they don't receive it well; you can rest easy in knowing you did the right thing. If they continue to text after, then I reply more firmly and make my intentions clear:

> Hey! Thanks for reaching out and as per my previous message, I am no longer interested so would appreciate if you would stop texting me xx

If they get abusive, I set my boundaries of how I deserve to be spoken to and treated:

> I understand you are upset and how you are speaking to me is unacceptable. This conversation is over and I will now be blocking you. Take care

Of course, there is a point in the dating timeline where texting is not appropriate and you need to either have that conversation over the phone or in person. That is down to your discretion. I personally never loved the idea of dragging someone across London to a location to end it because if I were them, I would feel resentful that I'd travelled all that way for nothing. My cut-off line therefore sits somewhere around the fifth date. When I would deem an in-person conversation necessary is when you've been dating long enough that the break-up is more of a discussion than a decision that has already been made.

In difficult conversations, I do not see texting as a lesser form of communication. I'm neither for nor against texting – it can give you more time to process and choose your words and it can also be a way to be misinterpreted, as you lose the tone of voice in written words. For me, I needed texting in my early stages of dating because I was still learning how to communicate. Texting allowed me to unlearn the need to interrupt and raise my voice, and made me realize I was only doing so when I felt attacked or was insecure that I wasn't eloquent enough. When I was given time and space to think, I was able to take space to be selective in my choice of words. Nowadays, I would always prefer a phone call because you are able to better gauge how the other person is feeling. Ultimately, your medium of communication is your choice. If you feel texting is not working for you, you can swap to another medium by saying "Can I call you?" or "Can we talk about it when I see you in person?"

Forget Me Nots

- Remove the idea that you doing anything differently would have resulted in a different outcome
- Ghosting indicates poor communication skills, and you don't want to be with someone who can't communicate their feelings
- You don't need to be mean to get your point across and most people appreciate you letting them know
- You don't have to end it perfectly, but you do have to end it

Take Action Toolkit

There have been a lot of text examples within this book, and now it's time to make your own text templates. Having them in an accessible location like the notes section of your phone means they are to hand when you need them. As much as I've used the term "hard conversations", they aren't difficult – you are just out of practice. Usually, I will alter each one slightly to make it personal, but if you have a structure for what you want to say, filling in the rest becomes easy.

How Do I Know if I Need to End It?

The first guy I dated after my dating detox was a drastic shift from the previous people. For the first time, I could say I had chosen a good person, but other than that, there was nothing much there. After the fifth date, I was talking to my best friend about it when she turned to me and asked, "Have you ever broken up with someone?" I stared at her, confused. Of course I had. She knew I had. She was there when I broke up with my first boyfriend. My friend explained what she meant: "Choosing to break up with someone is different to being treated so badly that you are forced to do the dirty work for them." She was right. I had technically done the breaking-up, but only when the relationship was as good as dead. He had checked out months before, but just never had the decency to let me know. In another relationship where I technically ended it, he hadn't seen me in six weeks. I might have had the final word in both situations, but I can't really claim those were my decisions. I always waited until I was backed into a corner because I hated the thought that I would ever hurt anyone. Being selfless, I was much more OK with being the person who was hurt.

This new empowered dating challenged that. I realized that this first guy post-detox didn't need to be the worst person ever in order for me to end it. He was kind and interesting – there was just no romantic connection. For the first time, I could see that that was enough of a reason. We both deserved a romantic connection, so I pulled on my big-girl pants and replied to his text.

> Hey! How was board game night?

> Hey! Board game night was fun! Want to be honest and I've been thinking over the weekend. Had a great time on Friday but I keep trying to convince myself I can do everything at the same time and that work is going to slow down but the reality is, it hasn't. I hate being the person who moans and complains about how tired and busy they always are and so I really need to be doing more to be changing that. It's been wonderful getting to know you and really enjoyed spending time with you but I think I need to focus on myself and my career for now. I don't think I have the time and energy you deserve to make this work and don't think it would be fair to you to pretend like I do. Hope you understand and take care xx

> That's totally fine. It's been great getting to know you too, your job is super interesting and inspiring and I wish you all the best and hope you do manage to get everything balanced one of these days xx

As it was the first time I'd ever ended something on my own terms, I over-justified my reasons and gave more of an explanation than was necessary. Also, I was so scared that I sent the text on the Tube when I had no signal (and when I was on the way to a meeting), so I wouldn't obsessively check my phone. He had responded by the time I even got off the Tube. The fact it was such a kind response spoke volumes. The dating detox had done me well, and that text gave me a little moment of pride.

His lovely reply was confirmation of something I had already known on some level: that I had upgraded the kind of people I was dating. His response was proof of the maturity and great communication that I now expected in my dating life.

From an early age, we are told not to quit, and to persevere until you improve. I wasted a lot of time attempting to improve at the piano when I neither enjoyed it nor was very good. Knowing when to quit is a skill. Within my career, quitting has been essential to my success. Every coach I knew had an online course when I started in the industry, yet every time I sat down to work on mine, I had to fight my own resistance to it. I only had 6,000 words left to finish, but something just felt wrong. I listened to my intuition and one day, impulsively, I put it in my trash folder and hit delete. I ended up putting all the time and energy I would've used on finishing the course into my first book, *Am I Ugly?*

Now, eight years on and writing my third book, having still not released an online course, I'm glad I made that shift early on. I could pound out the 100,000 words in that first book faster and with more enjoyment than 6,000 words of a course I didn't want to create; ever since, I have always listened to that instinct to quit. I quit my blog when I started finding it boring, I quit Snapchat when Instagram Stories were created, I quit Periscope when I found it was taking me away from living in the moment, I quit my first podcast when something felt off about it and for every published book of mine, there are many more half-written manuscripts and proposals that I pulled the plug on. When something in my business isn't working, I am very good at being flexible, pivoting when I need to, not wasting any more time on a venture that isn't playing to my skills and not viewing it as a failure but as feedback that informs my next decision.

I now see dating in the same way. The permission I give myself to quit means trying things becomes low-risk. Anytime I try anything new, I tell myself I can leave whenever I want to. When I go on a date, I tell myself the same. How I squash that fear of hurting their feelings is that I remind myself I am thinking too highly of my impact on others. I was acting as if me rejecting them would wound them for life and, as amazing as I am, I do not hold that much power – nor do you.

There are three main reasons why we are tempted to stay when we know we shouldn't. The first is the sunk-cost fallacy. This is our tendency to follow through with a situation if you have invested time and energy into it. The thinking is that you've already invested so much time that it would be a waste to start all over again, but just because a relationship ends doesn't mean it was a waste. And if you still believe it is, then five wasted months is better than six. It's never going to get easier. The longer you leave it, the greater the sunk cost. The second reason is the endowment effect, which refers to an emotional bias that causes individuals to more highly value an object they already own. This is why they let you test-drive a car, because while you are driving it, you pretend it's yours and the perceived worth of it goes up. But if you own the car, you need to decide when you have reached the point of spending more on the repairs than the vehicle itself is worth. The third reason is the status quo bias, the tendency to stick with how things are rather than the unknown. You have three well-documented emotional biases that want to keep you stuck and encourage the belief that you are never going to find anything better. The best way to combat these biases is a mantra I use in many areas of my life: this or something better!

Most people know the right time to quit, they are just too scared to have the conversation. Of course, there are times when you can pull the plug prematurely. But if you have set your boundaries, asked for your needs to be met and they aren't being met, then you know it's time. A good relationship is worth fighting for – but you can't be the only one fighting. Consider how hard it is to change yourself and you will know how foolish it is to try to change someone else. There is strength in knowing when you need to walk away from something that is no longer fulfilling you.

In one of my break-ups, the tipping point came when I had gone to visit him in Reading. I was catching the train back to London and I was quite drunk. He was worried that I wouldn't get back safely, so asked a guy on the platform if he would look after me and make sure I got into a cab on the other side. I insisted I was fine – because who said this guy was any safer than me on my own? – but, being tipsy, didn't put up a fight. This man and I ended up chatting and discovered we were both in the same situation. We both had boyfriends who couldn't have been less interested and rarely made an effort. We were lamenting it when an older woman overheard us.

"I have to interrupt. You both sound like you are in so much pain. These boys are not treating you how you deserve. I have been divorced twice and what I've learned is you need to ask yourself two questions: do they see the good in you before they see the bad? When you are around them, do you like yourself?"

This guy and I walked off the train speechless. My boyfriend was right; this guy was a good person to make sure I got home safe. What he didn't know was he would also be the person who would convince me to end it. As he put me in a cab, he turned to me and said, "I need to end it." My reply:

"So do I." This happened when I was 20 years old and I still remember it, because these two questions have stood the test of time. It sets the benchmark higher than merely asking if your partner is bad for you and instead asks if they are good for you.

Love is not a reason to stay in a relationship. It was only recently that love was even considered a factor when deciding on a long-term partner. In that short space of time, it's become the defining characteristic of relationships. Historically, other factors would have included wealth, social status and family name, but today we still need to have more than just love. Compatibility, communication and a match of values are much better determinants for the quality of your relationship. You will always find another to love. You have loved before and you will love again. Finding a match is rarer, and compatibility is more important than love. Whether it's how you want to spend your weekends or longer-term issues like whether you want kids, you cannot overlook this for the sake of love.

Love is a lofty concept and people have various definitions of it. They can truly believe they love you, but if your version of love makes you feel bad, it's not a version of love that you want. If you've been brought up in a household where you've been criticized or body shamed under the guise of love, then it's understandable that you believe that's love too. As bell hooks writes, "Learning faulty definitions of love when we are quite young makes it difficult to be loving as we grow older." If it doesn't look like love and it doesn't feel like love, it's not love. Criticism is not love. When I highlight bad treatment, my clients often retort, "But I love them!" and to that, I say, "So what?" You need to be able to separate how you feel about a person and how they treat you. Love is not enough. Love without respect is meaningless. Love without trust is pointless. Love without boundaries is co-dependency. As Don Miguel Ruiz says in *The Four Agreements* (1997), "If someone is not treating you with love and respect, it is a gift if they walk away from you." Behaviour matters, and asking yourself "Is this how I want to be treated?" will illuminate more than asking whether you love them.

Anything can be categorized as love, but it is clearer to determine if their behaviour is loving. Esther Perel says it best: when a client of hers says "I care about my partner", Perel's next question is "How do you show it?" Over the course of a lifetime, people change, and therefore your love can change too. There are no guarantees in life. In the beginning, it is easy to demonstrate love when it is new and fresh but over time, this might disappear. The way to notice is to focus on the way they speak to you, the effort they put in and the time they spend with you. Change "love" the noun into "loving" the verb. You shouldn't have to question if you are loved; it should be demonstrated so clearly that you know.

Forget Me Nots

- You need to decide when you are spending more on the repairs than the car is worth
- A good relationship is worth fighting for – but you can't be the only one fighting for it
- They can say they like you or love you, but if they aren't treating you in a way that you deserve, the words are empty
- Just because you love them doesn't mean they are good for you; what matters more than love is compatibility

Take Action Toolkit

One of the greatest tools that I have is a list of letters I have written to myself for all scenarios. This is a resource I have built over the years through key moments. It's like my personalized self-help book because we unconsciously write in the exact language and phrasing that will resonate with us the most. Find a notebook and start creating your own resource. For example, I have a letter written the evening I had delivered my TEDx Talk. I was so close to declining the talk because I didn't feel ready, so the letter is titled "For when you are scared and want to say no". There are countless times I've looked back at that letter when I've felt the same fear as I did before my TEDx Talk, but now I have the evidence of it going right. I personally like to write them when I am at my most emotionally charged. In a similar vein, I have a letter from the day I got my first book deal. It is titled "For when you want to give up". The ones from my dating life have been lifesavers. I have one from the first time I fell in love that is titled "When you are tempted to settle" and I have one from my first break-up called "Why you should trust your instinct". While I never wrote any of these with the intention to share, I will share one with you below from 2017, when I was in the middle of working on my first book and I'd let a guy consume my thoughts enough that it was distracting from my writing. It is titled "When you start to lose yourself".

Dear Michelle,

Please see the reality of the situation. If he is good enough, you don't need to live in fantasy. You are an incredible person with a full life, friends and family that care about you and a career you love. This book is so important to you and this guy is not worth the distraction.

You have been the kind of person who let a guy derail her life and you didn't like that version of yourself, so this is your opportunity to do it differently. This is not the kind of guy you want in your life. See it as useful practice and now let it go. You want to be proud of how you acted and how conscious you were through the experience.

You are loved by a lot of people and you don't need him to fill that space. You are busy and you have a book to write. You have more things to do in a day than to think about someone whose behaviour demonstrates they don't care about you. Time to let it go and embrace how wonderful your life already is!

How Do I Get Over a Relationship That Was Never a Relationship?

There is a quote that is floating around on social media that makes my eyes roll every time I see it: "Stop having relationship problems with someone who you aren't in a relationship with." I get that it is trying to send the message that if someone hasn't made enough room for you in their life, they shouldn't be causing this much stress. What I hate about it is that it puts the shame on the individual, and we don't need more shame. It also presupposes that everyone wants a relationship. It implies you need to reach a certain threshold in order to make your problems valid. While it sounds like a smart quote due to the play on words, it's a stupid message – because whenever two humans interact, there can be communication problems. And that's not even specific to dating.

These days, the chances of you getting your heart broken by someone you were never official with have never been higher, with a decreasing emphasis on labels and talking stages that now extend for months. It can hurt just as much, and sometimes more. A label is not a prerequisite for feeling heartbreak, loss or pain. Very early on in my dating life, I removed the hierarchy between official and non-official by describing every ex-type thing as an ex. I lost the categorization of who was serious enough for my hurt to be valid. I allowed it all to hurt. Denying the pain doesn't stop it from existing, and when you invalidate yourself because it "wasn't even a real relationship", you are just making it hurt worse.

We often measure the amount of heartbreak we are allowed to feel based on how long we were dating. But that is rarely the greatest indicator of the pain we feel. If anything, intensity is the best predictor – the steeper the incline, the more brutal the fallout. An intense, short-lived thing with an ambiguous ending can cause more destruction than a sustainable, long-term relationship that has run its course. Do not measure it in chronological time; measure it in intensity and it will make more sense. There are guys who I haven't even been on a first date with who have hurt me more than guys I have dated for months. There have been guys who I have casually dated who have hurt me more than ex-boyfriends have. When you are in the depths of heartbreak, it's easier to judge yourself for feeling more than you supposedly should. You are trying to use logic and rationale to explain emotions and it doesn't work that way. If you want to make sense of it, look at the context of the situation, how much they sold you on your future together, how much you believed it, how much understanding you were given around the end and extraneous factors like how you are feeling in your own life at that exact moment. For example, break-ups within the pandemic were more difficult than usual because the quality of life was lower in general. Previously, I personally would have jumped right back into my amazing, full life when a dating situation was over. But when you are in the midst of a lockdown, you can't. Lockdown meant I couldn't go on in-person dates and the rest of my life was a shell of what it used to be pre-pandemic. Both of these reasons meant I found myself needing weeks to recover before jumping back in. You don't need to understand why this one hurts more than the last; the only important thing here is that it hurts.

The first thing to do is validate everything you are feeling from the get-go. How you feel is valid and you are allowed to grieve the loss just like any other break-up. Break-ups can bring up conflicting emotions. Let all emotions exist. One emotion is not right or wrong and you don't need to get rid of one to give another validity. The ending of a relationship can stir up feelings around abandonment, loss and grief. Emotions are designed to be temporary; the only reason they stick around longer is because you aren't processing them. Remove the idea that you are "losing" the break-up if you let yourself feel what you need to feel. The "don't let them see you cry" mentality hurts you more than it hurts them, and there is no shame in letting something hurt. When you give yourself permission to feel the full extent of your pain, it can be healed and you won't carry it into your next relationship.

Missing them is not confirmation that you made the wrong decision. You don't want them – you want the feeling they gave you. The next time you are tempted to go down the rabbit hole of "what if?", ask yourself what a person who loves themselves would do. Someone who loves themselves would not entertain that thought. People who love themselves don't send drunk texts to people who don't want them. People who love themselves don't reread messages from people who don't matter anymore.

The best way you can protect yourself in this fragile time is to close the door on it completely. Delete their number, delete their messages, block them on social media and set whatever boundaries you need, whether that's directly telling them to not contact you or informing them that if they don't stop calling, you will block their number. Make the decision from the strongest part of you, and protect the part of yourself that will be tempted when you feel lonely, sad, horny or drunk. You can't text a number you don't have. You don't need to have a number you won't use. It's about increasing the activation energy. If we rewind to physics classes at school, activation energy is the energy required for the transition to even start.

We can apply this to habits. When I want to focus on writing, I put my phone in another room, increasing the activation energy required to go on social media. If I want to go to the gym more, I lower the activation energy by putting my gym clothes by my bed so the amount of energy required to get ready is reduced. The same works with break-ups. Increase the amount of activation energy required to stalk your ex. By blocking them, you will have to unblock them to see their account, increasing the difficulty (and reducing the temptation) of peeking at their page. By increasing the length of time required to do something, you make it a conscious action if you do it. As Carl Jung said, "Until you make the unconscious conscious, it will direct your life and you will call it fate."

Stalking your ex is a form of self-abuse. When you linger on their social media pages, you prevent yourself from healing. In the past, you could break up and never have to encounter them again. Nowadays, you can still see what they had for breakfast or, more importantly, how happy or sad they are without you. It is the equivalent of picking a scab that is trying to heal. What are you looking for specifically? Whether it's confirmation that they are missing you, regret around the break-up or whether they are dating someone new, you take the risk that you won't find what you are looking for. In fact, you might find the exact opposite, which will deepen the shit feeling you already have and make you feel worse about yourself. If they are out having fun, you tell yourself that you meant nothing. If they smile in an Instagram picture, you tell yourself they have already moved on.

All of these are stories. It's like reading one word and deciding you know how the book ends. You are filling in the gaps and, when you are in a bad headspace, you are going to be filling in the gaps with things that can hurt you the most.

When you cut all contact, you are protecting yourself from the future you. I'm not asking you to delete their number for the empowered person reading this book, I'm asking you to delete it for 2 a.m. you, who is alone and not surrounded by people who will tell you to make the right decision, the you most in need of protection and at your most vulnerable. There is a reason you only think of them when you are sad.

When a relationship ends, I make a list of reasons why I made the decision and everything I learned from it. We tend to have a selective memory when recalling past relationships, and this list prevents me from romanticizing the past. I keep this list in the notes section of my phone so that when I get the urge to check their social media, I can go there instead. Learn from every relationship and it won't be a loss. These lists have become the cornerstone for improving my love life. You can't know what you don't know, and sometimes we have to learn lessons the hard way. Sometimes we need to fuck up to do better. Being able to gain the lessons from each experience means I left many break-ups actually feeling grateful for what they taught me in the time we had together.

Forget Me Nots

- Denying the pain doesn't stop it from existing, and when you invalidate yourself because "it wasn't even a real relationship", you are just making it hurt more
- Do not measure hurt in dating by the relationship's chronological time – measure it in intensity
- You can't text a number you don't have, and you don't need to have a number you won't use
- Missing them is not confirmation that you made the wrong decision

Take Action Toolkit

When I grow from a situation, it becomes really hard for me to frame it as a "waste of time", regret it or see it as a mistake. The lists I mention above have become my best resources to improve my love life because they are written in the exact words I need to hear. The advice in those lists will always be better than any advice in a love-life book because it's customized to me and built from my own experience. Here are the lists I want you to create:

- "Lessons I want to take away from this situation"
- "Red flags I noticed and did nothing about"
- "What specifically I would have done differently if I had the lessons I have now"

How Do I Move On?

The way we speak about the ending of a relationship is flawed. We are told blanket statements like, "It takes half the length of time you were in a relationship to get over it", as if the road map to recovery is the same for everyone. We are told that "time heals all wounds", as if time itself does the healing. It's not the time, but what you do with the time. That's why there are 80-year-olds still waxing lyrical about their first girlfriend decades later. Ultimately, the definition of "moving on" is blurry. Some people start new relationships without getting over the last, and others even move on before they have broken up.

There is no time frame for how long it takes to heal and there are so many factors other than time that dictate your ability to move on. As a culture, we hyper-focus on closure and forgiveness when neither are essential for healing. We tell ourselves that we need to understand why, but in reality, there is no reason that will ever feel satisfying enough. Closure is a mindset that you can achieve yourself, but if you give that power to someone else, you will continue to feel powerless. We use closure as a way to hold on to a relationship or as an excuse to reach out again. Not hearing from them is closure, being ignored is closure, sometimes the disrespect is closure. Decide that for yourself. When it comes to forgiveness, this is letting go of the "what if?" and the past that could have been. It's letting go of the possibility that things could have been different.

Because closure and forgiveness are such enigmatic terms, they are hard to achieve. How do we know we have reached that point if we can't even define it? Healing looks different to each person, but when I know I have moved on, I can specifically measure it by a reduction in how often I think about them. In order to do this, I need to process the grief that arises and give those feelings the time they deserve.

There is a misconception around the emotion of grief: that it only arises in the context of death. Of course, that is when grief is the most intense, but it is associated with any loss. As a result, you can grieve the end of a job, the loss of a family home and, indeed, the end of a relationship. As a culture, we don't have a very broad emotional vocabulary, and sadness and grief are often confused. They are different emotions and they manifest differently in the body. Grief often brings up a sense of helplessness, powerlessness and apathy. It feels heavy, like it's consuming your whole body, and tends to bring up a sense that it will last forever in a way that sadness doesn't. All of this is part of the grieving process. When we prevent ourselves from going through that process, we become tarred by our past.

I once dated a guy whose motto in life was "screw them over before they screw you". When I ended things, he called me gullible and naive. His parting words were: "One day, someone is going to screw you over so badly and you will become sceptical like the rest of us." God knows he tried, but that statement made me even more determined to never treat future partners badly because I had been mistreated by a handful. There is a certain satisfaction knowing that he couldn't take my trusting and loving nature away from me unless I decided to give him that power. This is what happens when you let one bad experience tar all future encounters. If you never heal from what hurt you, you bleed on people who didn't cut you. We all know people who talk about the past as if the best years are behind them, whether it's that person who still goes on about how they would have made the national football team if they hadn't torn their ACL or someone reminiscing about how it will never get as good as their university days. Those people have not mourned the loss in that stage of life and it keeps resurfacing in their mind in an attempt to try to heal that wound.

The way to notice the distinction between sadness and grief in your own body is to recall a time you have experienced either of them. Starting with sadness, go back into your body at the time and recall how you were breathing, sitting and feeling. Notice the sensations and locate them within your body. Are they in your stomach, your heart, your throat? What do they feel like? Are they heavy or do they feel foggy and indistinct? Are they warm? Do you feel them pushing down or are they a light feeling? Once you are able to pinpoint these sensations, open your eyes and come back into the room. Shake it off, play a song or simply ask yourself what you had for breakfast that morning. This is called "changing states" so that the previous feelings of sadness don't linger. Then repeat the process for grief by recalling a time in life when you were going through a loss. Examples could include the loss of a friendship, the feelings of loss when everything got cancelled during the pandemic or the loss of the relationship you wish you had with your parents. You now have two physical experiences in your body to compare. When grief or sadness arises, you will be able to distinguish them.

Now that you know how to detect grief, you have to learn how to feel it. You need to stop pretending you weren't hurt. Healing happens the moment you acknowledge that pain. When I talk about empowered dating, this does not mean an absence of painful emotions. Instead, the empowerment comes from knowing I am strong enough to feel my feelings and I will be OK no matter what. I grieve every relationship, no matter how long or short. The problem is that while it's common to hear people say "feel your feelings", very rarely do they teach you how. I'm going to teach you how to do it with grief, but you can apply this to any emotion.

How to feel your feelings

First, do a mental scan of your body and notice any area of discomfort. Locate one specific sensation and place your attention on it. It may help to place your hand on top of that location and then breathe in deeply through your nose and out of your mouth. Imagine the pain and energy releasing with every out breath. The pain may intensify or the sensation may move. Observe it with curiosity and follow it around the body as your breathing deepens. When people avoid their feelings, this is the pain they are avoiding – so embrace it and let it hurt. You might find it comforting to have a conversation with that sensation. These are some questions you can ask:

- What do you want to tell me?
- What do you need from me right now?
- What are you here to teach me?
- What do you want to hear from me?

Listen to the answers with compassion. If you don't know what an empathetic voice sounds like because you were never around one growing up, here are ways you can validate your grief:

- You are allowed to feel this way.
- This is so shit.

- I'm sorry you are in so much pain.
- You are OK. You are safe. I am here.
- I know, darling. I know it hurts.
- You are not alone. I am going to sit here with you until this feeling passes.

If you get too caught up in your thoughts or go off into a story about the relationship, then simply return your focus to the sensation in your body and go back to breathing into it. You might get the urge to cry, shake your body, scream or rub the physical location in your body in circular motions. Allow yourself to do that and learn what works best for you. The first time you do this, you might only be able to sit still for five minutes, but over time, your tolerance will build up. Sometimes your brain will pop in to tell you that you are bored. That is your ego trying to protect you from the pain. In these instances, I pop on a healing playlist and commit to sitting there until the playlist ends. If you want examples of healing songs, I have a number of playlists on my Spotify.

Remember, this is a new skill you are learning and it will take time. Once you are more practiced at it, it is worth going and revisiting past relationships from a time when you didn't know how to grieve. Sometimes it's hard to turn the page when you know these relationships won't be in the next chapter. Change is hard, and we scare ourselves by thinking that going through a break-up is the same as being single. It's not. Take this example: when you move to a new country, you might be experiencing sadness, grief around missing your old home and the loss of your friends being nearby. At that moment, it's easy to assume this new country is horrible – but it's not the country, it's the change. Once you are adjusted, you realize that the new country has a lot to offer, but you were just confusing it with the discomfort around the shift. Returning to being single and dating is the same. People will return to dating apps thinking being single is awful when actually, it's the break-up that is awful. Going back on dating apps symbolizes a death to any potential reality where you both had a future together, and that can be incredibly painful. The fact that you are taking time to grieve is brave. It means you will be able to meet the next person with a fresh start.

Treat your broken heart like a broken arm. Just because the cast is removed doesn't mean you can go back to lifting weights in the gym. It takes time to be fully recovered and there will be days where it will feel like you never broke it, and days when that familiar pain returns. It doesn't mean you are going backwards; it is part of your healing process. It might take you more or less time to feel ready to get back in the dating pool, depending on the circumstances. If it feels intimidating, just dip a toe in. Sometimes you will go on a date, only to realize that you spent the entire evening comparing them to your ex and that you might need more time. You can only know if you try. Any time you jump into a pool, it always feels freezing. Stay in there long enough, though, and it warms up.

The final part of my grieving process is cemented when I ask myself one question: "If you knew it was going to end, would you still have replied to that first message?" For me, the answer will always be yes, because trading in the experience would also mean forgoing all I learned from it. This holds true for me, even for an emotionally abusive situation I was in. I would go through it again because it taught me so many lessons to make sure that was my one and only situation like that. It made me say "never again". It gave me a determination to want better for myself and to work on myself so that I was never in that position again. Everything I learned is what makes the person sitting here today.

Forget Me Nots

- Closure is an illusion that we hold on to so we can hold on to the relationship, but it can be a mindset that you achieve yourself
- The end goal is to allow them to take up less space in your brain
- Grief is an emotion associated with any loss – you can feel grief at the end of any relationship, no matter how long it lasted
- Healing happens the moment you acknowledge that pain

Take Action Toolkit

We have been taught to muffle our cries and hide our tears. In order to process grief, you need to actually do the opposite. Find yourself some privacy and allow yourself to cry audibly. If you struggle to find privacy, go out in nature or sit in your car or stand under the shower. Find somewhere you won't be disturbed. Allowing yourself to make a sound releases the physical emotion from your body. If you need something to help provoke the tears, find a sad video on YouTube, your favourite sad movie or a playlist that allows you to tap into your emotions.

I DON'T DESERVE THIS

Chapter 11
If It Doesn't End . . .

A Good Relationship Is Worth Waiting for

When I first wrote the proposal for this book, I was sitting on a guy's couch. It was our fourth date, although according to him, it was our seventh (he counts meals as separate dates) and I was spending a few days at his because he had an empty house. He was meant to be just another guy on a long list of people I've dated – I never imagined I would be sitting here over a year into a relationship with the same guy. I guess that a hazard of being on dating apps for a while is that you might eventually find yourself in a relationship.

I wanted to write a book from the perspective of a single woman who loves dating and has no goal of a relationship. Oh, the irony! The reason I wanted to write the book as a single woman is because I was sick of being told how to date by people who hadn't been on a first date in over a decade and had no clue about the realities of being on dating apps. I wanted to unpick this idea that the only way to deem your dating life a success is if it comes to an end. I didn't need a relationship to confirm that my advice works. My advice does work – but my relationship is not proof of that, my incredible years of dating are. I didn't want to perpetuate the idea that ending up coupled equals a happy ending, or that the only happy ending can occur if you follow the relationship escalator laid out for all of us that takes us from moving in, to getting engaged, to getting married and having kids. I wanted to be the example that being single is a valid life choice, and it was for eight years of my life. He was just the first person who came along who was worth giving up being single for.

Being in a relationship now, I am grateful more than ever for that single period because all the advice that fills the pages of this book was gleaned in that time. That time taught me everything I needed to know to have the relationship I have now. We met on a dating app because "how you meet doesn't matter". We dated without a label for four months because "there is no rush" and we communicated directly from the start because "asking is always better than assuming". That single period made me who I am today, and it made this book what it is too. Just like being single taught me a lot, being in a relationship has taught me a lot as well. Being in the healthiest relationship I have ever been in has left me with a few lessons and this book felt incomplete without sharing those with you.

Let go of the fairy tale

Movies and social media have sold us one version of romantic. According to TikTok, my relationship is rubbish if he doesn't plaster me all over his social media, wouldn't love me if I was a worm and doesn't share his location with me. Wait till they find out his lock screen isn't a picture of us. People show their love in different ways and we need to be able to acknowledge that. Otherwise, we will believe others are living the fairy tale that we aren't. Being in a healthy relationship for the first time meant I had to release a lot of my romanticized notions about what a relationship should be. Much like how, when you start writing a book, you have to destroy the perfect concept in your head to make it a reality, I had to let go of what I thought a relationship should be to actually be in one.

My relationship wouldn't be as healthy as it is if it was burdened by the weight of my expectation. You have to remember that the movies cut out the boring bits. As my life coach Michelle

Zelli says, "You have to be OK living in the mundane." Healthy relationships are calm and safe, and if you are used to chaos and intensity, that can be boring. In my childhood, quiet and peaceful felt like the calm before the storm and it can be tempting to pre-empt the chaos. Sinking into it instead has allowed me to unlearn these unhealthy patterns and realize that being in love also means spending evenings watching three episodes of *Better Call Saul* cuddled next to each other in silence.

Everyone is difficult to date

I spent so many years believing I was difficult to date because I have big emotions and feel things deeply. In the past, people have made me feel like that was a reason I was hard to love. As a result, I am quite sensitive to them calling me "emotional". Everyone has a sore spot – you just need to find someone who won't poke that spot. Everyone has a past, their own insecurities and something you will have to "deal with". It's not just about compatibility, it's about the incompatibility you can handle. It occurred to me one evening when I was watching a TV show where the main character's husband was really stingy and they were having an argument about what she was spending. I realized I couldn't live with that. Of course, my boyfriend and I have incompatibilities, but they are ones that annoy me, not ones that would make me end it. It's very easy to notice the things you do disagree on; it's harder to notice the ones that have never been an issue.

You will change each other

I believe that you become the five people that you spend the most time with and that includes the person you're in a romantic relationship with. You will rub off on each other. When I was co-dependent, I would change for a man and when I started to learn to do better, I vowed it would never happen again. But in a relationship, you don't change *for* each other, you change *because* of each other. Psychotherapist Philippa Perry distinguishes this as the difference between "adaptation" and "mutual impact". My boyfriend even changed what I was looking for. The first word I would use to describe him is "kind", and it both shocks and saddens me that if I go back through the list of criteria I was looking for in people, kind was never on there. Sometimes you get what you need, not what you want.

It will bring up all your childhood wounds

Every romantic relationship, even the healthy ones, will trigger you and put a mirror to your deepest wounds. The difference is that in a healthy one, you will feel safe enough to tell them. I always thought that no matter how much you love someone, there will be a part of you that will remain secret – the messiest, most chaotic and most unlovable part. For me, it's always been my medical trauma and the emotional side that comes along with that. But when I needed a brain scan for the first time in a decade and he came home to find me bawling in the shower, I realized how life-changing it is to let someone see the part of you that you are most ashamed of. Despite the fact I was soaking wet, he held me as I continued to wail in a way that I'd never let anyone see.

In that moment, I learned to trust that I'm not the burden that society told me I was. Growing up in hospital, I never realized how much I had learned to hide my illness, pretend I was fine when I wasn't and apologize whenever I felt ill – until I was with a person who made me feel heard and understood. There is so much beauty in letting another person truly see every part of you and for them to continue to love you and not be scared off by it.

You will behave badly

I once asked a married friend what love was and she said, "It's the moment you want to get really angry and be mean to each other, and instead, you remind yourself that you love this person and choose to say it kindly." I thought it was unromantic and practical, but what I didn't understand at the time was that it's crucial. Everyone is human and everyone has a childish part of them. I might be a life coach who teaches communication, but there will be times when I forget everything I have unlearned and default to the teenager in me that only knew how to shut down and run away. It very rarely happens any more, but a year into our relationship, it did and I ended up sleeping in another room. The next morning, he asked that I not do that. I apologized and promised it would never happen again. The next time we had a conflict, and I found myself turning to leave the bedroom, I turned back. "I really want to leave right now, but I promised you I wouldn't sleep in another room, so I'm standing here instead, but I want you to know I'm very angry." We ended up laughing and I've kept my promise ever since. We've both been childish at times, but we don't define each other by our worst moments. Learn from it, grow from it, keep your promises and don't do it again.

You can't pick and choose which parts of them you love

My boyfriend is the kind of guy who wants to get to the airport three hours early. On our first holiday together, he insisted we go to the gate the moment it was announced, despite the fact we were in a tiny airport. I said we were too early, and I was right. As a result, we ended up standing in line at the gate 90 minutes before they had even announced they were boarding. Needless to say, I was annoyed. After expressing my annoyance, I asked for space and stood in the queue next to him reading a book. Five minutes later, I put my book down and told him that I wasn't annoyed anymore. He was shocked: "That was quick." I explained that I realized I couldn't be annoyed at the airport version of him when it was the same part of him that had organized every part of this trip, and planned every aspect so I didn't have to do a thing. They were the same part of him and I can't pick and choose when his organization is convenient for me and when it's annoying. Your partner will not be perfectly designed for you.

Maintenance is better than repairs

If you have ever played *The Sims*, you will know that if you spend time on upgrading the objects, the objects will break down less often. Relationships work the same way. Why wait until it's broken to invest in maintenance? You can get so used to the good that you never stop to notice it and over time, it becomes easier to comment on the bad. It's easy to notice the one time they are late, and not every time before that when they were on time. Dr John Gottman found that in couples who stay together, the ratio of appreciation to complaint is 5:1. Even more than a year in, my boyfriend still thanks me for letting him stay over and, when he leaves, he will send a detailed text acknowledging every part of our date together. When you expect things, you stop appreciating them, and as William James said, "The deepest craving of human nature is the need to be appreciated."

We have become awful at dismissing the basic things as the bare minimum. But when you have gratitude for small but sweet things, that gratitude amounts to a great relationship. The first time we went on a double date, my friend's partner stood her up. Understandably, she was embarrassed. In addition to feeling empathy for her, I felt an appreciation for my boyfriend, so as we turned to leave, I thanked him for always showing up. Did I need to thank him for not being a dick? No. But it's not about needing to – it's about wanting to. It might be the bare minimum to some people, but if it wasn't there, you would notice it. Make an effort to say more appreciative things than critical ones.

* * *

Our relationship trajectory was slow. It took us four months to become official, five months to say "I love you" to each other and six months to meet each other's families. There wasn't one singular moment that made me decide to be in a relationship. I had outgrown doing that. It's more that over a number of months there were many moments where he displayed characteristics that made me curious to get to know him more, and small moments where he set himself apart from the rest in ways he probably didn't even realize because it was so natural to him. Things like: he will never make a cup of tea without going around the entire household and asking every single person if they would like one and will make it to their specific requirements because he knows how everyone takes their tea. And it's not just cute things like that. It's a small moment when we were having a conflict and, because I'm so headstrong and opinionated, I'd been used to people conceding my talking points to get a conversation over with.

He doesn't concede. There was a moment he had been in the wrong, and he was able to say "I am sorry, I'm in the wrong, and also you are taking this too far." Sometimes, when you are in the wrong, you become apologetic for everything. It was impressive to me that he still held his boundaries and kept me accountable for my side of the street. Moments like that let me see that he made me better, and remind me of that woman on the train, who said it boils down to whether you like who you are around them and if they see the good in you before the bad. He did both.

My sister is 12 years older than me and, in many ways, has been my second mum. Prior to her marriage, she was in a seven-year relationship. When I got into my relationship, I became curious about hers. I asked her what the difference was between the guy she ended up marrying and the one she didn't. She said that people often like to think the one they stay with is drastically different from the last, but it's not true. There are just a few small but crucial differences. She said that for her, it always came down to respect and whether she was proud to introduce them as her partner. I knew what she meant. When I introduced my partner to my friends, it was the first time I was able to say, "I know you'll like him." It was also the first time that I didn't care whether they did. I already knew how special what we had was and I didn't need external validation to confirm it.

My small and crucial differences have been that he's attentive in a way I have never experienced. As I write this, I'm sitting by the pool in Italy with him next to me. I am typing this into the notes section of my phone and tearing up just thinking about how much I love this person. Just as I start to well up, he asks me if I am OK. He said my breathing changed. This is what I mean, and he's been this way from the very start. Shortly after our third date, I had to go to a funeral in Bristol. As bad timing goes, I matched with him a few days after I had found out a friend had died by suicide, and so was in the midst of grief when we first started dating. He had texted me to ask how the funeral went. I was so used to being single that I told him a standard line that would keep most people out. I said that it was shit but I was just going to cry and get an early night. She had left a letter and I wanted to read it; I would speak to him tomorrow. He was going out for drinks with his friends so I told him to have a great night and ended the conversation there. A few hours later, I got a text.

> I thought it would be romantic to surprise you but I realized I'm going to be way later than I planned. Please don't go to sleep! xx

"I thought you might want a hug," he said as he turned up at my door. He was right, I did. In my last book, I had spoken about asking for what you need and, in that moment, he taught me that you can also just ask for what you want. I didn't need a hug, but I did want one. When he arrived, I told him that I would have been fine. "I know you will be fine. I know you can do this alone, but you don't have to." His response meant more to me than all the empty words I had been told in the past. The crucial difference was his actions have always spoken louder than his words. He has never been scared off by my big emotions. Being around him brings me a sense of safety that I've not felt before.

We became official two weeks before I got the deal for this book, and then came the dilemma of whether to actually include it. You see, this isn't the first time I have been in this situation. My first book was a memoir. When I was finishing it, I was dating someone and wanted to include that relationship for the most up-to-date version of my life. At the last moment, a friend who was an author said to me, "Don't include it unless you are prepared to be asked about him for the rest of your life." To this day, I am thankful I decided against that and removed all mention of that guy. Five years on, I was now in the same predicament with the added difficulty that this is a dating book. Writing honestly, I can't say that I am ready to be asked about him forever. What I can say is I am willing to take that risk. Dating is all about risk and, if I've learned anything from my years of dating, the risk is always worth it, even if it brings pain and heartbreak with it. I ultimately decided to include our relationship because whether we stay together or not truly does not matter in the context of this book.

My friend reminded me recently that right before our first date, I actually made a quip: "If this was my last first date, I'd be fine with that." I won't lie, writing this does make it feel like a full-circle moment, and it isn't because I am ending the book in a relationship. It's because I am ending this book in a healthy relationship. It's a full-circle moment for the 15-year-old who was bullied for being a "late bloomer" and sat out of school dances because she was so convinced no boy would like her. It's a full-circle moment for the 18-year-old who laughed along with her friends as they joked about how her love life was such a mess. It's a full-circle moment for the 20-year-old who was so desperate to be loved that she ended up in a relationship that did more harm than good. And it's a full-circle moment for that 24-year-old who decided to take a small risk and DM that guy, "Hey stranger! How's things? xx" and, in so doing, kick-start her dating life. For every time I stressed over how to word a text to end it, for every time I worried if I would hurt their feelings if I ended a date after one drink, for every time I got ghosted and moved on to the next one and even that one time I was stood up and then made a plan to go on three more dates the next week, it was all worth it. That little girl deserved to be loved, and she finally is. Not just by him, but by me.

Whether this relationship ends or not, it has changed my definition of love. I grew up in a world where the phrase "I'm only telling you because I love you" was used a lot. He showed me what love actually looks like, and how it can be kind and supportive. I never understood romantic songs when they spoke of loving someone the next day more than the last, or about how someone could be both your partner and best friend, but I get them now. I can't say my current relationship is my forever relationship, (mainly because I don't think anyone can!) but what I can say is that it is healthier than any I could have imagined for myself. I had never had an example of a healthy relationship growing up and for that first example to be my own has changed me fundamentally as a person. So my final message to you is to stay single . . . until you find someone worth giving it up for.

Acknowledgements

Throughout writing this book, I was battling some of my worst health in a decade, and a bout of Covid that left me with brain fog I couldn't shift for months. I'm beyond grateful for all the people in my life who kept the faith while I had none. Most days, what got me through was a quote by Jordan Peele – "When I'm writing the first draft I'm constantly reminding myself that I'm simply shovelling sand into a box so that later I can build castles" – but even when I was covered in sand and couldn't find the shovel, there were many people who just calmly observed with a quiet trust in me that I knew what I was doing. This book wouldn't be what it is without their confidence in me.

Thank you to Michelle Zelli. Without you, there would be no book to write. For every time I came into your office ranting about the chef or the golfer, thank you for your patience with me and only rolling your eyes some of the time. When I didn't trust my own instincts, I knew I could always trust yours. Most of all, thanks for reminding me not to run when I'd found a good thing.

Thank you to Honey Ross. I am so grateful you knew we would be friends before I did. You are my secret weapon, the colleague I never knew I needed. Learning about love together has been such a joy and it's been so comforting to have someone on the same journey. Knowing you are always on the other end of the phone has saved me from getting lost in my own web of thoughts more times than I can count, and you have truly made my writing better for it.

Thank you to Hayley Steed, my wonderful literary agent and, more importantly, a brilliant wingwoman. I can't believe this book originated from a text I sent you after a one-night stand – thank you for always obliging my silly ideas! Your continued support has made me brave enough to keep writing. Thank you for always saying yes to a night out. Our single period will never be forgotten and we will always have *Magic Mike*.

Thank you to everyone at Madeleine Milburn agency. It has been amazing to grow with you and it brings me so much joy to have been with you from the early days and have had the privilege to watch you flourish over the years. Thank you for always being champions of my writing and turning the cogs in the background so I can focus on getting the words on the page.

Thank you to Issy Wilkinson and the whole Welbeck team. Thank you for always giving me the freedom to write in my authentic voice, no matter how controversial I get. Thank you for believing in this book, even when I was completely lost in the process. It has been wonderful being able to do this all again with you, and especially in person this time!

Thank you to everyone at Belle PR. Thank you for always being my cheerleaders and it's such a joy to have you in my corner for everything that I do. You really are a dream team!

Thank you to my inner circle. Terri, Megan, Helen, Jordann, Grace and Helena, you all taught me love first. Thank you for listening to every voice note, guiding me through every date, fling and chaotic life phase and, most of all, for never saying "I told you so" when it all went tits up. You loved me before I knew how to love myself and taught me that I was worth loving.

And thank you to Ben. It isn't easy dating an author, let alone one writing a dating book. Thank you for never getting sick of hearing about the latest piece of dating research I found and holding my hand through the rollercoaster of emotions that is being an author. It means the world that you trusted me to write whatever I wanted about us. Our love story will always be my favourite. Thank you for always giving me a safe space to land. I love you so much and this is just the beginning for us!

Further Reading

All About Love (1999) – bell hooks
Come as You Are (2015) – Emily Nagoski
Conversations on Love (2021) – Natasha Lunn
Eight Dates (2019) – John Gottman, Julie Schwartz Gottman, Doug Abrams and Rachel Carlton Abrams
Mating in Captivity (2006) – Esther Perel
Pretending (2020) – Holly Bourne
The Couple (2021) – Helly Acton

Notes

....
....
....
....
....
....
....
....
....
....
....
....
....
....
....
....
....
....
....
....
....
....
....
....
....
....
....

Notes

Notes

....
....
....
....
....
....
....
....
....
....
....
....
....
....
....
....
....
....
....
....
....
....
....
....
....
....
....
....

Notes

....
....
....
....
....
....
....
....
....
....
....
....
....
....
....
....
....
....
....
....
....
....
....
....
....
....
....
....